Excel® 2007
Top 100

Simplified®

TIPS & TRICKS

by Denise Etheridge

Visual

Wiley Publishing, Inc.

Excel® 2007: Top 100 Simplified® Tips & Tricks

Published by

Wiley Publishing, Inc.
111 River Street
Hoboken, NJ 07030-5774

Published simultaneously in Canada

Copyright © 2007 by Wiley Publishing, Inc., Indianapolis, Indiana

Library of Congress Control Number: 2007926010

ISBN: 978-0-470-12674-5

Manufactured in the United States of America

10 9 8 7 6 5 4 3 2 1

Trademark Acknowledgments

Contact Us

For general information on our other products and services contact our Customer Care Department within the U.S. at 800-762-2974, outside the U.S. at 317-572-3993, or fax 317-572-4002.

For technical support please visit www.wiley.com/techsupport.

WILEY

Wiley Publishing, Inc.

U.S. Sales

Contact Wiley at
(800) 762-2974 or
fax (317) 572-4002.

PRAISE FOR VISUAL BOOKS

"I have to praise you and your company on the fine products you turn out. I have twelve Visual books in my house. They were instrumental in helping me pass a difficult computer course. Thank you for creating books that are easy to follow. Keep turning out those quality books."
Gordon Justin (Brielle, NJ)

"What fantastic teaching books you have produced! Congratulations to you and your staff. You deserve the Nobel prize in Education. Thanks for helping me understand computers."
Bruno Tonon (Melbourne, Australia)

"A Picture Is Worth A Thousand Words! If your learning method is by observing or hands-on training, this is the book for you!"
Lorri Pegan-Durastante (Wickliffe, OH)

"Over time, I have bought a number of your 'Read Less - Learn More' books. For me, they are THE way to learn anything easily. I learn easiest using your method of teaching."
José A. Mazón (Cuba, NY)

"You've got a fan for life!! Thanks so much!!"
Kevin P. Quinn (Oakland, CA)

"I have several books from the Visual series and have always found them to be valuable resources."
Stephen P. Miller (Ballston Spa, NY)

"I have several of your Visual books and they are the best I have ever used."
Stanley Clark (Crawfordville, FL)

"Like a lot of other people, I understand things best when I see them visually. Your books really make learning easy and life more fun."
John T. Frey (Cadillac, MI)

"I have quite a few of your Visual books and have been very pleased with all of them. I love the way the lessons are presented!"
Mary Jane Newman (Yorba Linda, CA)

"Thank you, thank you, thank you...for making it so easy for me to break into this high-tech world."
Gay O'Donnell (Calgary, Alberta,Canada)

"I write to extend my thanks and appreciation for your books. They are clear, easy to follow, and straight to the point. Keep up the good work! I bought several of your books and they are just right! No regrets! I will always buy your books because they are the best."
Seward Kollie (Dakar, Senegal)

"I would like to take this time to thank you and your company for producing great and easy-to-learn products. I bought two of your books from a local bookstore, and it was the best investment I've ever made! Thank you for thinking of us ordinary people."
Jeff Eastman (West Des Moines, IA)

"Compliments to the chef!! Your books are extraordinary! Or, simply put, extra-ordinary, meaning way above the rest! THANKYOU THANKYOU THANKYOU! I buy them for friends, family, and colleagues."
Christine J. Manfrin (Castle Rock, CO)

CREDITS

Project Editor
Sarah Hellert

Acquisitions Editor
Jody Lefevere

Copy Editor
Kim Heusel

Technical Editor
Suzanne Borys, PhD
James Floyd Kelly

Editorial Manager
Robyn Siesky

Business Manager
Amy Knies

Editorial Assistant
Laura Sinise

Manufacturing
Allan Conley
Linda Cook
Paul Gilchrist
Jennifer Guynn

Book Design
Kathie Rickard

Production Coordinator
Erin Smith

Layout
Carrie A. Foster
Jennifer Mayberry
Heather Pope
Amanda Spagnuolo

Screen Artist
Jill A. Proll

Proofreader
Broccoli Information Management

Quality Control
Cynthia Fields
Jessica Kramer
Charles Spencer

Indexer
Infodex Indexing Services, Inc.

Wiley Bicentennial Logo
Richard J. Pacifico

Special Help
Malinda McCain
Barbara Moore
Christine Williams

**Vice President and Executive
Group Publisher**
Richard Swadley

Vice President and Publisher
Barry Pruett

Composition Director
Debbie Stailey

ABOUT THE AUTHOR

Denise Etheridge is a certified public accountant as well as the president and founder of Baycon Group, Inc. She publishes Web sites, provides consulting services on accounting-related software, and authors computer-related books. You can visit www.baycongroup.com to view her online tutorials.

This book is dedicated to my mother, Catherine Austin Etheridge

How To Use This Book

Excel 2007: Top 100 Simplified® Tips & Tricks includes 100 tasks that reveal cool secrets, teach timesaving tricks, and explain great tips guaranteed to make you more productive with Excel. The easy-to-use layout lets you work through all the tasks from beginning to end or jump in at random.

Who is this book for?

You already know Excel basics. Now you'd like to go beyond, with shortcuts, tricks, and tips that let you work smarter and faster. And because you learn more easily when someone *shows* you how, this is the book for you.

Conventions Used In This Book

❶ Steps

This book uses step-by-step instructions to guide you easily through each task. Numbered callouts on every screen shot show you exactly how to perform each task, step by step.

❷ Tips

Practical tips provide insights to save you time and trouble, caution you about hazards to avoid, and reveal how to do things in Excel 2007 that you never thought possible!

❸ Task Numbers

Task numbers from 1 to 100 indicate which lesson you are working on.

❹ Difficulty Levels

For quick reference, the symbols below mark the difficulty level of each task.

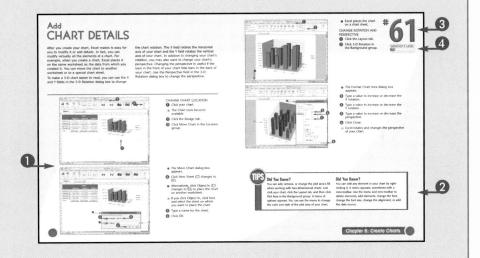

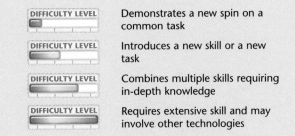

DIFFICULTY LEVEL	Demonstrates a new spin on a common task
DIFFICULTY LEVEL	Introduces a new skill or a new task
DIFFICULTY LEVEL	Combines multiple skills requiring in-depth knowledge
DIFFICULTY LEVEL	Requires extensive skill and may involve other technologies

Table of Contents

3 Copy, Format, and More

4 Manipulate Records

Table of Contents

Table of Contents

Boost Your Efficiency

You can use Microsoft Excel 2007 to work with numbers. In fact, wherever you use numbers — doing taxes, running a small business, maintaining a budget, or anything else — Excel can help make your work easier, quicker, and more accurate.

Excel 2007 provides you with many ways to enter, present, explore, and analyze data. This chapter focuses on ways in which you can boost your efficiency when using Excel. You learn how to use the Excel AutoFill feature, to group and outline, to check the accuracy of your data and more.

The AutoFill feature enables you to fill a row or column quickly with a series of values, numbers, dates, or times generated from one or more values you have entered. This chapter will show you how to use the AutoFills that come standard with Excel and how to create your own AutoFills.

You can use grouping and outlining to hide parts of your worksheet, enabling you to focus in on the data in which you are interested, thereby making data analysis easier. This chapter steps you through the process of grouping and outlining.

Sometimes you may want to double-check the accuracy of your data. One of the final tasks in this chapter teaches you how you can increase the accuracy of your data entry by letting Excel read back your data to you.

Validate with a
VALIDATION LIST

Excel enables you to restrict the values a user can enter in a cell. By restricting values, you ensure that your worksheet entries are valid and that calculations based on them thereby are valid as well. During data entry, a validation list forces anyone using your worksheet to select a value from a drop-down menu rather than typing it and potentially typing the wrong information. In this way, validation lists save time and reduce errors.

To create a validation list, type the values you want to include into adjacent cells in a column or row. You may want to name the range. See Task #11 to learn how to name ranges. After you type your values, use the Data Validation dialog box to assign values to your validation list. Then copy and paste your validation list into the appropriate cells by using the Paste Special Validation option.

You may want to place your validation list in an out-of-the-way place on your worksheet or on a separate worksheet.

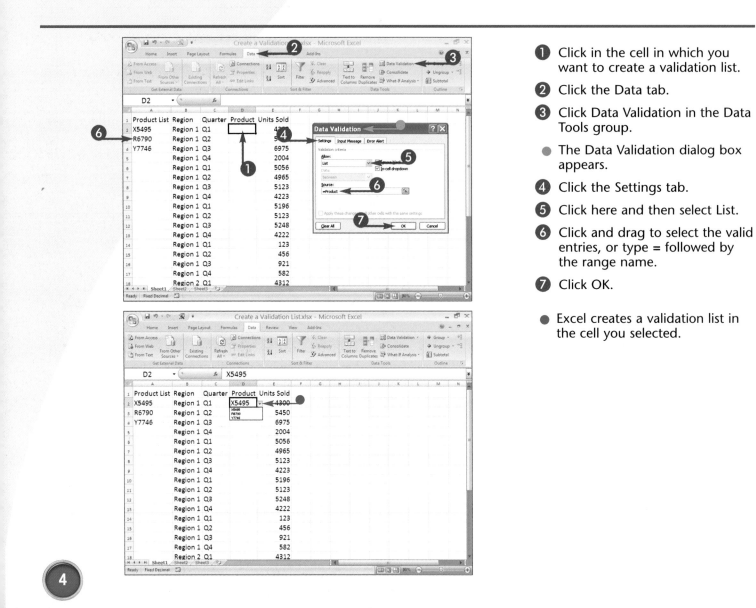

1 Click in the cell in which you want to create a validation list.

2 Click the Data tab.

3 Click Data Validation in the Data Tools group.

● The Data Validation dialog box appears.

4 Click the Settings tab.

5 Click here and then select List.

6 Click and drag to select the valid entries, or type = followed by the range name.

7 Click OK.

● Excel creates a validation list in the cell you selected.

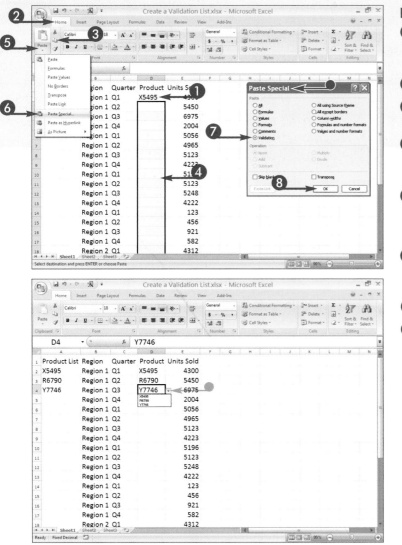

#1

DIFFICULTY LEVEL

PASTE YOUR VALIDATION LIST

1. Click in the cell that contains your validation list.

2. Click the Home tab.

3. Click the Copy button in the Clipboard group.

4. Select the cells in which you want to place the validation list.

5. Click Paste in the Clipboard group.

   A menu appears.

6. Click Paste Special.

● The Paste Special dialog box appears.

7. Click Validation (○ changes to ◉).

8. Click OK.

   Excel places the validation list in the cells you selected.

● When users make an entry into the cell, they must pick from the list.

TIPS

Did You Know?

Validation lists can consist of numbers, names of regions, employees, products, and so on.

Remove It!

To remove a validation list, click in any cell that contains the validation list you want to remove, click the Home tab, and then click Find and Select in the Editing group. A menu appears. Click Go To Special. The Go To Special dialog box appears. Click Data validation, click Same, and then click OK. The Go To Special dialog box closes. Click the Data tab and then click Data Validation in the Data Tools group. A menu appears. Click Data Validation. The Data Validation dialog box appears. Click Clear All and then click OK.

Validate with
DATA ENTRY RULES

You can use data entry rules to ensure that data entered has the correct format, and you can restrict the data entered to whole numbers, decimals, dates, times, or a specific text length. You can also specify whether the values need to be between, not between, equal to, not equal to, greater than, less than, greater than or equal to, or less than or equal to the values you specify.

As with all data validation, you can create an input message that appears when the user enters the cell,

as well as an error alert that displays if the user makes an incorrect entry. Error alerts can stop the user, provide a warning, or just provide information.

After you create your data entry rule, copy and paste it into the appropriate cells by using the Paste Special Validation option. See Task #1 under Paste Your Validation List to learn how to copy and paste your data entry rule.

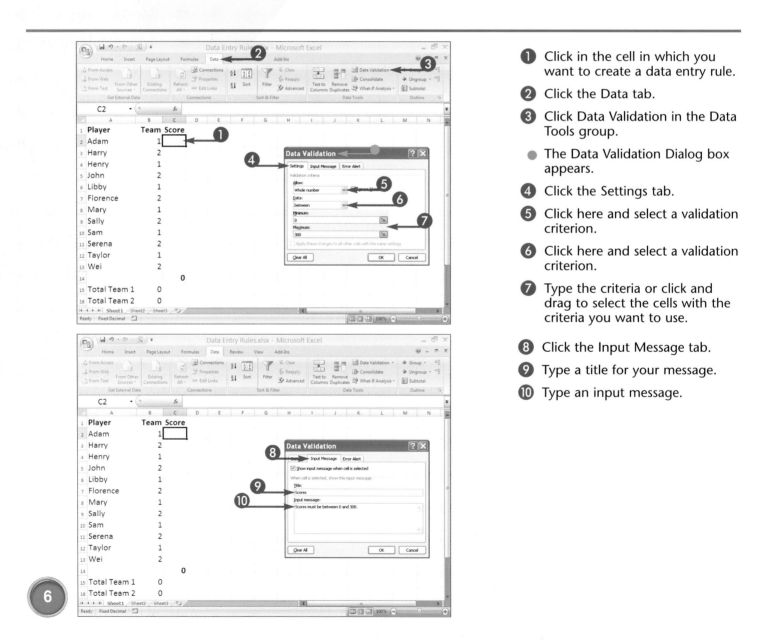

❶ Click in the cell in which you want to create a data entry rule.

❷ Click the Data tab.

❸ Click Data Validation in the Data Tools group.

● The Data Validation Dialog box appears.

❹ Click the Settings tab.

❺ Click here and select a validation criterion.

❻ Click here and select a validation criterion.

❼ Type the criteria or click and drag to select the cells with the criteria you want to use.

❽ Click the Input Message tab.

❾ Type a title for your message.

❿ Type an input message.

#2

DIFFICULTY LEVEL

⑪ Click the Error Alert tab.

⑫ Click here and select a style.

Choose Stop if you want to stop the entry of invalid data.

Choose Warning if you want to display a warning to the user, but not prevent entry.

Choose Information to provide information to the user.

⑬ Type a title.

⑭ Type an error message.

⑮ Click OK.

Excel creates the data entry rule.

● When you click in the cell, Excel displays your input message.

● When you enter invalid data, Excel displays your error alert.

TIPS

Important!

After you create your data entry rules, use the steps outlined in Task #1 under Paste Your Validation List to place your data entry rules in the cells in which you want them.

Did You Know?

If you use cells to specify your validation criteria in Step 7, you can change the criteria as needed without changing the validation rule.

Did You Know?

When you make an incorrect entry, the Stop Error Alert style displays the error message you entered and prevents you from making an entry that does not meet your criteria. The Warning Alert style and the Information Alert style allow you to enter data that does not meet your criteria.

Extend a series with
AUTOFILL

AutoFill gives you a way to ensure accurate data entry when a particular data series has an intrinsic order: days of the week, months of the year, numeric increments of two, and so on.

To use AutoFill, start by typing one or more values from which you will generate other values. Select the cell or cells you want to extend. Selecting two or more cells determines the step size, or increment, by which you want to jump in each cell. With the cells

selected, click the Fill handle in the lower-right corner and drag. When you release the mouse button, Excel fills the cells with values.

After filling the cells, Excel provides a menu button. Click the button to open a menu that enables you to change the fill. You can copy the initial value; fill the series one day at a time; or extend it by weekdays, months, or years, depending on the type of fill you create.

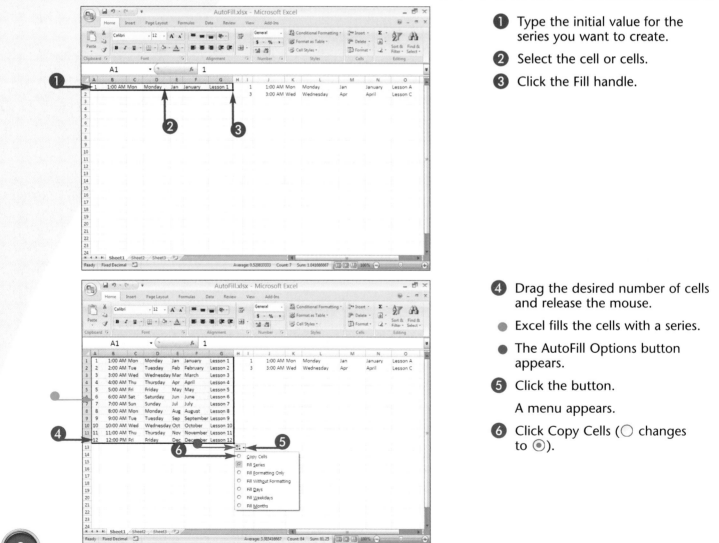

❶ Type the initial value for the series you want to create.

❷ Select the cell or cells.

❸ Click the Fill handle.

❹ Drag the desired number of cells and release the mouse.

● Excel fills the cells with a series.

● The AutoFill Options button appears.

❺ Click the button.

A menu appears.

❻ Click Copy Cells (○ changes to ◉).

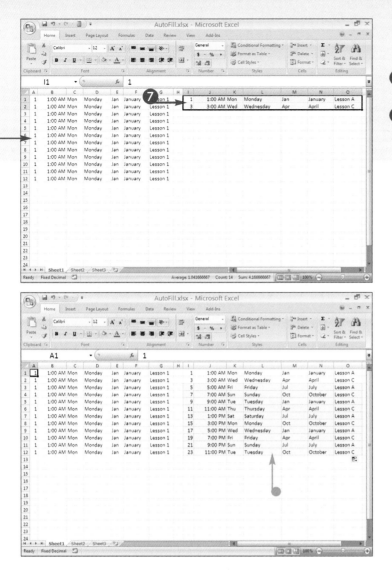

- Excel changes the series to a copy of the original cell.

7 Type a pattern of entries.

8 Repeat Steps 2 to 4.

- Excel fills the cell with the pattern.

TIP

Did You Know?

When you release the mouse button after creating a series, the AutoFill Options button (▦▾) appears. Click the button to view a menu of options. If you want to fill with the days of the week, you can click Fill Days or Fill Weekdays to fill with Monday through Friday (○ changes to ◉). You can also click the Fill Formatting Only option (○ changes to ◉) to change the formatting of the cell without changing the contents. Click the Fill Without Formatting option (○ changes to ◉) to change the contents of the filled cells without changing the formatting. You can extend a series in any direction: up, down, left, or right.

Insert
SYMBOLS OR SPECIAL CHARACTERS

In Excel, you are not restricted to the standard numerals, letters, and punctuation marks on your keyboard. You can also select from hundreds of special characters, such as foreign letters and currency characters such as the Euro (€). Each font has a different set of special characters. A smaller set of standard characters, called symbols, is always available as well; they include dashes, hyphens, and quotation marks.

Symbols and special characters serve many uses in Excel. Many financial applications, for example, call

for currency symbols. Symbols and special characters are useful in column and row heads as part of the text describing column and row content, for example, Net sales in €.

Using symbols and special characters in the same cell with a value such as a number, date, or time usually prevents the value from being used in a formula. If you need to use a symbol in a cell used in a formula, use a number format. If you need to create a custom number format, see Task #98.

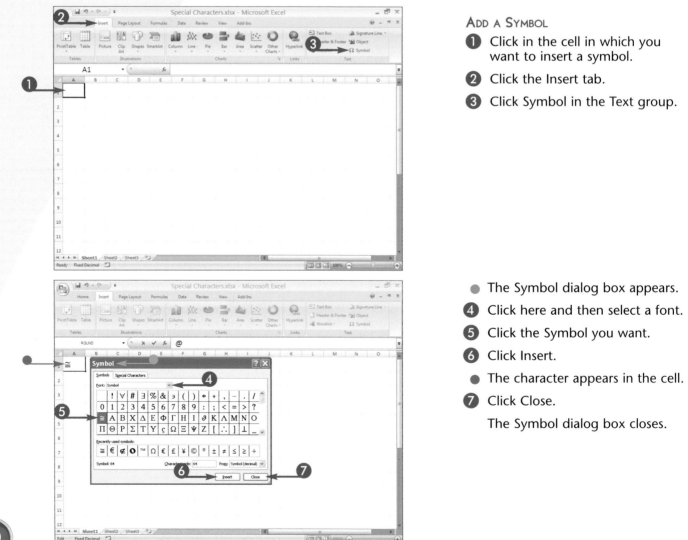

ADD A SYMBOL

① Click in the cell in which you want to insert a symbol.

② Click the Insert tab.

③ Click Symbol in the Text group.

● The Symbol dialog box appears.

④ Click here and then select a font.

⑤ Click the Symbol you want.

⑥ Click Insert.

● The character appears in the cell.

⑦ Click Close.

The Symbol dialog box closes.

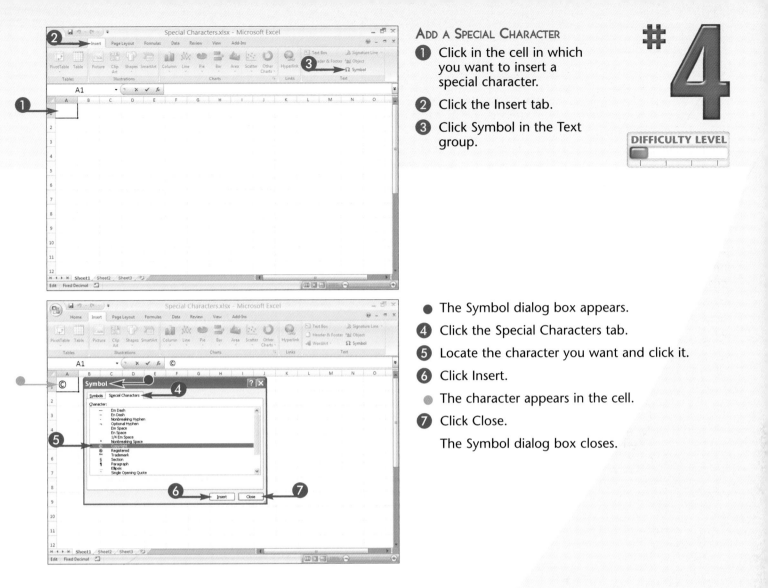

ADD A SPECIAL CHARACTER

1 Click in the cell in which you want to insert a special character.

2 Click the Insert tab.

3 Click Symbol in the Text group.

● The Symbol dialog box appears.

4 Click the Special Characters tab.

5 Locate the character you want and click it.

6 Click Insert.

● The character appears in the cell.

7 Click Close.

The Symbol dialog box closes.

TIPS

Did You Know?

In Excel, entries are numbers, dates, times, letters, or special characters. You can only use numbers, dates, and times in numeric calculations. Excel treats letters and special characters as blanks or zeroes in calculations. To have a currency symbol appear with a value, as in $400, and use the cell value in a calculation, you must apply a currency, accounting, or custom format.

Did You Know?

Excel fonts are based on Unicode, a set of 40,000 characters enabling the display of characters from approximately 80 languages, including right-to-left alphabets such as Hebrew. To use a language other than English, attach an appropriate keyboard and use the Control Panel to set the Regional and Language options.

Hide rows by
GROUPING AND OUTLINING

You can use the Excel grouping and outlining feature to hide sets of columns and/or rows. For example, you can hide the details relating to weekly sales so you can compare monthly sales. Your outlines can include up to eight levels of detail.

Outlining a set of rows or columns creates a clickable button on the far left or top of your worksheet. The button displays either a minus sign or a plus sign, depending on what is displayed in the worksheet. Click the minus sign to hide rows or columns, and

the plus sign to display them again. Adjacent to the button is a solid line that indicates, by its length, the approximate number of rows or columns Excel has hidden.

Outlining was designed for use with structured information such as lists but can be used with any worksheet. When you outline a PivotTable, outlining has the same effect as it does in any other worksheet.

ADD A GROUP

① Click and drag to select the rows or columns to hide.

② Click the Data tab.

③ Click Group in the Outline group.

You can also select the rows or columns and then press Shift+Alt+Right Arrow.

● The Group dialog box appears.

④ Click to select either the Rows or the Columns option (○ changes to ◉).

Click Rows if you want to group rows.

Click Columns if you want to group columns.

⑤ Click OK.

- Excel creates a new left or top margin with a minus sign.

6 To hide the rows, click the minus sign.

The rows disappear, and a plus sign replaces the minus sign.

- To display the rows again, click the plus sign.

REMOVE A GROUP

1 Click the Data tab.

2 Click Ungroup.

- The Ungroup dialog box appears.

3 Click to select either the Rows or the Columns option (○ changes to ◉).

Click Rows if you want to ungroup rows.

Click Columns if you want to ungroup columns.

4 Click OK.

Excel removes the group.

TIPS

Did You Know?

You can nest outlines; that is, you can place one group of outlined rows or columns inside another. For example, within each year, you can group each month, and within each month, you can group each week.

Did You Know?

You can also hide rows and columns by clicking and dragging the lines that separate the column letters or the row numbers. Also, if you click and drag over column letters or row numbers and then right-click, a menu appears. Click Hide to hide the column or row or Unhide to display hidden columns or rows.

FIND AND REPLACE
formats

Cells can contain numbers, text, comments, formats, and formulas. With Excel, you can search for any of these elements to view them, replace them, or perform some other action. You may, for example, find and replace values to correct mistakes, or perhaps you need to return to a value to add a comment or apply formatting.

The Excel Find and Replace dialog box is available on the Home tab in the Editing group or by pressing Ctrl+H. The Find feature is part of Find and Replace and is available on the Home tab in the Editing group or by pressing Ctrl+F.

To find and replace formats, specify what you are seeking and with what you want to replace the item you are seeking. Click the Options button in the Find and Replace dialog box to specify additional details. Use the Within drop-down menu to indicate whether to search the current worksheet or the current workbook. Click the Formatting button to restrict your search to characters formatted in a certain way, such as bold or percentages.

① Click the Home tab.

② Click Find & Select in the Editing group.

A menu appears.

③ Click Replace.

Alternatively, you can press Ctrl+H to open the Find and Replace dialog box.

● The Find and Replace dialog box appears.

④ Click Options if your dialog box does not look like the one shown here.

Note: The Options button allows you to toggle between the short and long form of the dialog box.

⑤ Click here and select Choose Format from Cell.

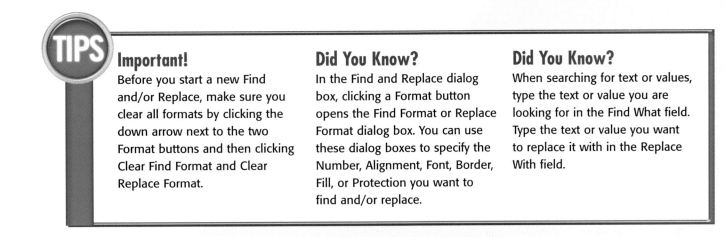

The Find and Replace dialog box disappears.

⑥ Click in a cell that has the format you want to replace.

This example selects green fills.

● The Find and Replace dialog box reappears.

● A preview of the format you selected appears.

⑦ Click here and select Choose Format from cell.

The Find and Replace dialog box disappears.

⑧ Click in a cell that has the format you want to use as a replacement.

This example selects a cell with no fill.

The Find and Replace dialog box reappears.

● A preview of the format you selected appears.

⑨ Click Replace All.

● Excel replaces the formats.

Excel replaces all of the green fills with plain fills.

⑩ Click OK.

⑪ Click Close.

● You can click Replace to make one change at a time.

● If you want to find instead of replace formats, click Find All or Find Next to highlight cells in the worksheet but not replace formats.

TIPS

Important!
Before you start a new Find and/or Replace, make sure you clear all formats by clicking the down arrow next to the two Format buttons and then clicking Clear Find Format and Clear Replace Format.

Did You Know?
In the Find and Replace dialog box, clicking a Format button opens the Find Format or Replace Format dialog box. You can use these dialog boxes to specify the Number, Alignment, Font, Border, Fill, or Protection you want to find and/or replace.

Did You Know?
When searching for text or values, type the text or value you are looking for in the Find What field. Type the text or value you want to replace it with in the Replace With field.

ADD COMMENTS
to your worksheet

A comment is a bit of descriptive text that enables you to document your work when you add text or create a formula. If someone else maintains your worksheet, or others use it in a workgroup, your comments can provide useful information. You can enter comments in any cell you want to document or otherwise annotate.

Comments in Excel do not appear until you choose to view them. Excel associates comments with individual cells and indicates their presence with a tiny red triangle in the cell's upper-right corner. View

an individual comment by clicking in the cell or passing your cursor over it. View all comments in a worksheet by clicking the Review tab and then clicking Show All Comments.

When you track your changes, Excel automatically generates a comment every time you copy or change a cell. The comment records what changes in the cell, who makes the change, and the time and date of the change. To learn more about tracking changes, see Task #34.

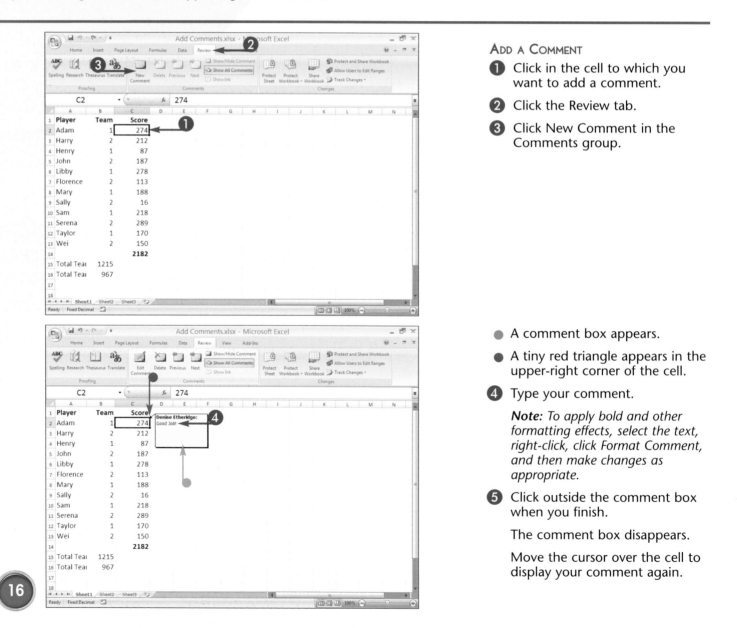

see Task #34.

ADD A COMMENT

1. Click in the cell to which you want to add a comment.

2. Click the Review tab.

3. Click New Comment in the Comments group.

● A comment box appears.

● A tiny red triangle appears in the upper-right corner of the cell.

4. Type your comment.

   Note: To apply bold and other formatting effects, select the text, right-click, click Format Comment, and then make changes as appropriate.

5. Click outside the comment box when you finish.

   The comment box disappears.

   Move the cursor over the cell to display your comment again.

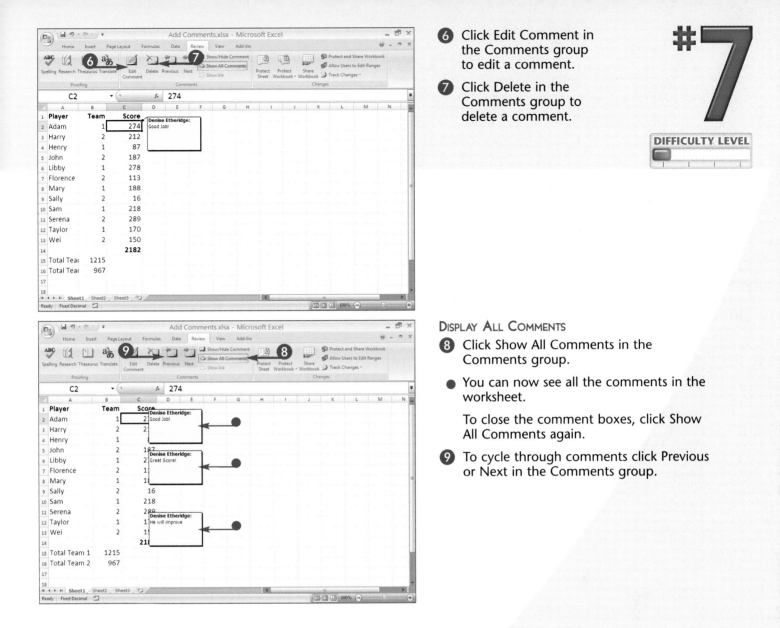

6 Click Edit Comment in the Comments group to edit a comment.

7 Click Delete in the Comments group to delete a comment.

DISPLAY ALL COMMENTS

8 Click Show All Comments in the Comments group.

● You can now see all the comments in the worksheet.

To close the comment boxes, click Show All Comments again.

9 To cycle through comments click Previous or Next in the Comments group.

TIPS

Did You Know?

To set the name that displays when you enter a comment, click the Office button, and then click Excel Options. The Excel Options dialog box appears. Click Popular and then type the name you want to appear in the comment box in the User Name field.

Did You Know?

When a comment gets in the way of another comment or blocks data, you can move it. Position your cursor over the comment box border until the arrow turns into a four-sided arrow. Click and drag the comment to a better location and then release the mouse button. Your comment remains in this position until you display all comments again.

Let Excel
READ BACK YOUR DATA

If you have a large amount of data to enter, especially numbers, you may want to check the accuracy of your data entry by having the data read back to you while you match it against a printed list. Excel can read back your data. All you have to do is specify the data you want to read, click a button, and Excel begins reading. You can choose to have Excel read across the first row and then move to the next row, or down the first column and then move to the next column. You can also have Excel read data as you enter it.

However, before Excel can read your data, you must add the following buttons to the Quick Access toolbar: Speak Cells, Speak Cells — Stop Speaking Cells, Speak Cells by Columns, Speak Cells by Rows, and Speak Cells on Enter. To learn how to add buttons to the Quick Access toolbar, see Task #95. You can find the buttons needed for this task in the Commands Not in the Ribbon section.

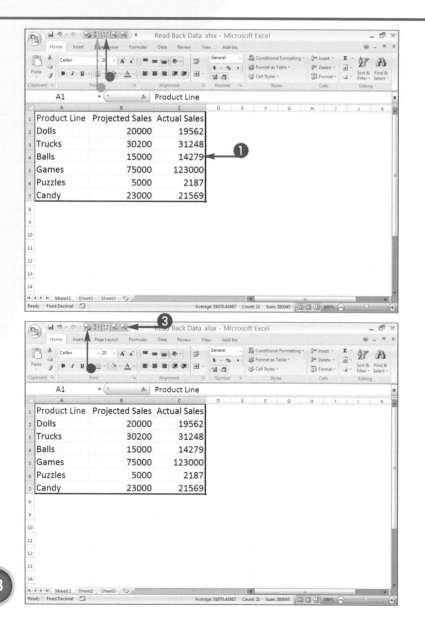

READ CELLS

❶ Click and drag to select the cells you want Excel to read.

❷ Click either the Speak by Columns or the Speak by Rows button.

● Click Speak by Columns if you want Excel to read down the columns.

● Click Speak by Rows if you want Excel to read across the rows.

❸ Click the Speak Cells button.

Excel reads the cells.

● To stop the reading of cells, click the Speak Cells — Stop Speaking Cells button.

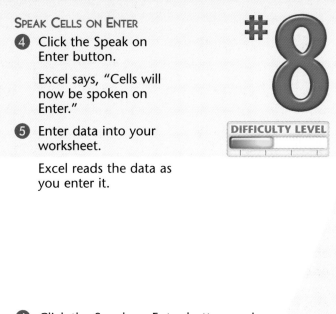

SPEAK CELLS ON ENTER

④ Click the Speak on Enter button.

Excel says, "Cells will now be spoken on Enter."

⑤ Enter data into your worksheet.

Excel reads the data as you enter it.

DIFFICULTY LEVEL

⑥ Click the Speak on Enter button again.

Excel says, "Turn off Speak on Enter."

Excel stops reading the data as you enter it.

TIPS

Important!

To have Excel read your worksheet, you must have speakers attached to your computer and you must set the Speech, Sound, and Audio Devices option in the Control Panel properly. Click the Start button, Settings, and then Control Panel to check these device settings.

Did You Know?

You can also check the accuracy of your data entry by performing a spell check. Just click the Review tab, Proofing, and then Spelling. If your worksheet has errors, the Spelling dialog box appears and offers suggestions for the correct spelling. You can accept one of the suggestions or click one of the other dialog box options.

Create your own
SORT OR AUTOFILL

In Excel, you can sort your data alphabetically, by days of the week, or by months of the year. See Chapter 4 to learn more about sorting your data. You can also automatically fill cells with the days of the week or months of the year by using Excel's AutoFill feature. See Task # 3 to learn more about AutoFill.

If you have a data series you use often, you can create your own custom list and use it to fill cells automatically or to sort a list. For example, you collect data by region and you always list the data

in the following order: North East, South East, North Central, South Central, North West, and South West. You can create a custom list that enables you to AutoFill and sort based on your list.

Use the Custom List dialog box to create your custom list. You can type your list into the Custom List dialog box or import your list from cells in your worksheet. You access your custom list the same way you would any other custom list or AutoFill.

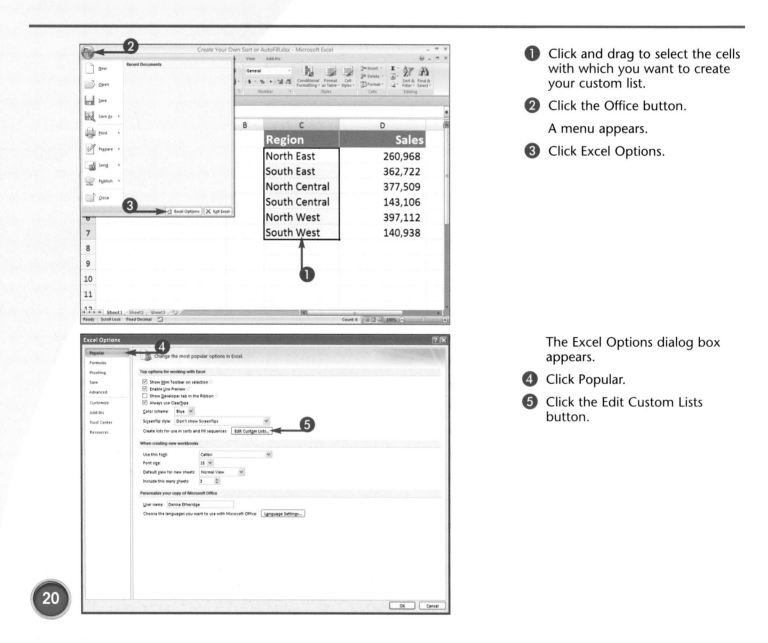

① Click and drag to select the cells with which you want to create your custom list.

② Click the Office button.

A menu appears.

③ Click Excel Options.

The Excel Options dialog box appears.

④ Click Popular.

⑤ Click the Edit Custom Lists button.

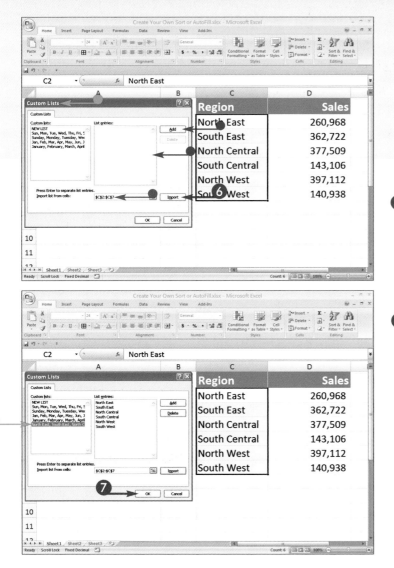

- The Custom Lists dialog box appears.

- The range you selected in Step 1 appears here.

  You can click and drag or type the range in the Import list from cells field.

- Alternatively, you can type your list here and then click Add.

6 Click Import.

- Your list appears as a custom list.

7 Click OK.

  Your list is ready to use.

TIPS

Did You Know?

To create an AutoFill using your custom list, type the first item in your list. Click and drag the fill handle located in the lower-right corner of the cell. Excel fills the cells with your custom list. If Excel does not fill the cells with your custom list, click the AutoFill Options button (⊞▾) that appears and then click Fill Series (○ changes to ◉).

Did You Know?

To sort using the custom list you created, click and drag to select the items you want to sort. Click the Data tab and then click Sort in the Sort & Filter Group. The Sort dialog box appears. In the Order field, click Custom List. The Custom List dialog box appears. Click your list and then click OK. For detailed instructions, see Chapter 4.

Chapter 2

Work with Formulas and Functions

Excel provides you with tools for storing numbers and other kinds of information. However, the real power of Excel comes from manipulating all this information. You can use formulas and functions to calculate in Excel.

The more than 300 functions built into Excel enable you to perform tasks of every kind, from adding numbers to calculating the internal rate of return for an investment. You can think of a function as a black box. You put your information into the box, and out come the results you want. You do not need to know any obscure algorithms to use functions.

Each bit of information you provide is called an argument. Excel's Function Wizard provides guidance for every argument for every function. A formula consists of an equal sign, one or more functions, their arguments, operators such as the division and multiplication symbols,

and any other values required to get your results.

Many Excel functions do special-purpose financial, statistical, engineering, and mathematical calculations. The Function Wizard arranges functions in categories for easy access. The Payment (PMT) function in the Financial category, for example, enables you to determine an optimal loan payment for a given principal, interest rate, and length of loan.

This chapter introduces useful techniques for making formulas and functions even easier, including the Function Wizard and the Excel calculator. You can also find tips for working more efficiently with functions by naming cells, creating constants, and documenting your work. Finally, you can find tips for functions such as IF and special-purpose functions such as PMT and Internal Rate of Return (IRR).

Top 100

ENTER FORMULAS
using a variety of methods

In Excel, you can carry out calculations such as simple arithmetic in three ways. One method is to use the plus (+), minus (−), multiplication (*), and division (/) signs. Start by typing an equal sign and the values to be added, subtracted, multiplied, or divided, each separated by an operator; for example, =25 + 31. Press Enter, and Excel does the math and displays the answer in the same cell. You can also type an equal sign, click in a cell that contains the value you want to perform an operation on, and then type the operator.

A second method involves functions. Functions perform calculations on your information and make the results available to you. To use a function, type an equal sign followed by the function; for example, =SUM(). Place the numbers you want to add inside the parentheses, separating them with commas. If the numbers are on the worksheet, click the cells.

A third method is to use Excel's AutoSum feature, which offers a point-and-click interface for several functions, including SUM, AVERAGE, and COUNT.

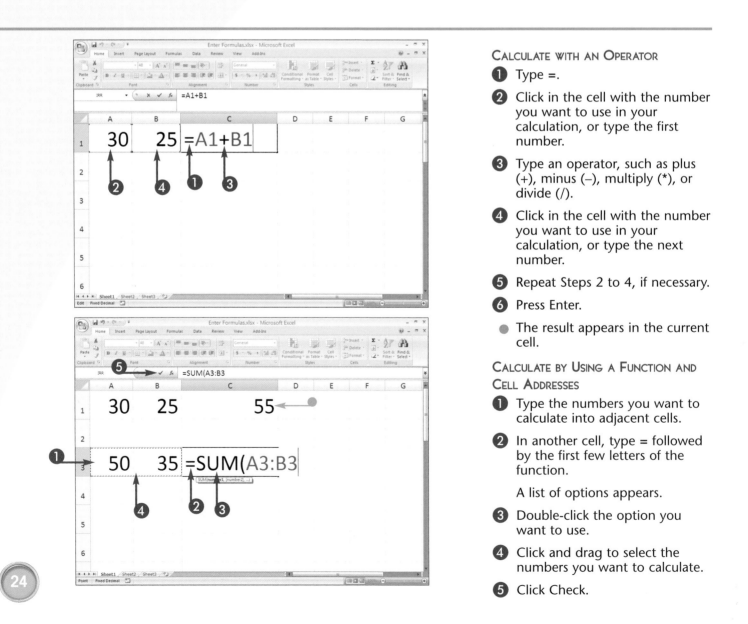

CALCULATE WITH AN OPERATOR

1. Type =.

2. Click in the cell with the number you want to use in your calculation, or type the first number.

3. Type an operator, such as plus (+), minus (−), multiply (*), or divide (/).

4. Click in the cell with the number you want to use in your calculation, or type the next number.

5. Repeat Steps 2 to 4, if necessary.

6. Press Enter.

● The result appears in the current cell.

CALCULATE BY USING A FUNCTION AND CELL ADDRESSES

1. Type the numbers you want to calculate into adjacent cells.

2. In another cell, type = followed by the first few letters of the function.

   A list of options appears.

3. Double-click the option you want to use.

4. Click and drag to select the numbers you want to calculate.

5. Click Check.

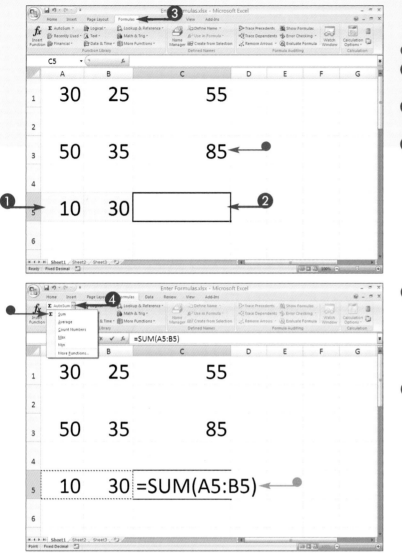

- The result appears in the cell.

CALCULATE BY USING AUTOSUM

1. In adjacent cells, type numbers.
2. Click the cell in which you want the result.
3. Click the Formulas tab.

4. Click here and select an option.

- This example uses SUM.
- Excel places =sum() in the cell, with the cell address for numbers you may want to add.

5. To accept the cell addresses chosen by Excel, press Enter.

To select other addresses, click and drag them and then press Enter.

The result appears in the cell selected in Step 2.

TIPS

Did You Know?
You can click the chevron (⌄) at the end of the formula bar to expand and collapse the bar. Expanding the formula bar lets you enter longer formulas.

Did You Know?
When you click and drag over multiple cells, Excel automatically places the average, a number count, and the sum of the values on the status bar, at the bottom of the screen.

Did You Know?
You can add buttons for equal, plus, minus, divide, and multiply to the Quick Access toolbar. You can use these buttons to enter formulas quickly. To learn how to add buttons to the Quick Access toolbar, see Task #95.

Name
CELLS AND RANGES

In Excel, you can name individual cells and groups of cells, called ranges. A cell named Tax or a range named Northern_Region is easier to remember than the corresponding cell address. You can use named cells and ranges directly in formulas to refer to the values contained in them. When you move a named range to a new location, Excel automatically updates any formulas that refer to the named range.

When you name a range, you determine the scope of the name by telling Excel whether it applies to the

current worksheet or the entire workbook. You can name several ranges at once by using Excel's Create from Selection option. You can use the Name Manager to delete named ranges.

Excel range names must be fewer than 255 characters. The first character must be a letter. You cannot use spaces or symbols except for the period and underscore. It is best to create short, memorable names. To learn how to use a named range, see Task #13.

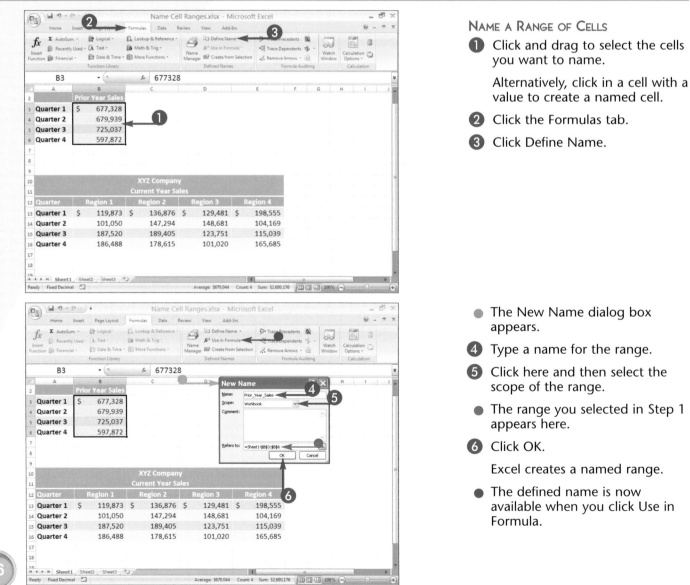

NAME A RANGE OF CELLS

1. Click and drag to select the cells you want to name.

   Alternatively, click in a cell with a value to create a named cell.

2. Click the Formulas tab.

3. Click Define Name.

- The New Name dialog box appears.

4. Type a name for the range.

5. Click here and then select the scope of the range.

- The range you selected in Step 1 appears here.

6. Click OK.

   Excel creates a named range.

- The defined name is now available when you click Use in Formula.

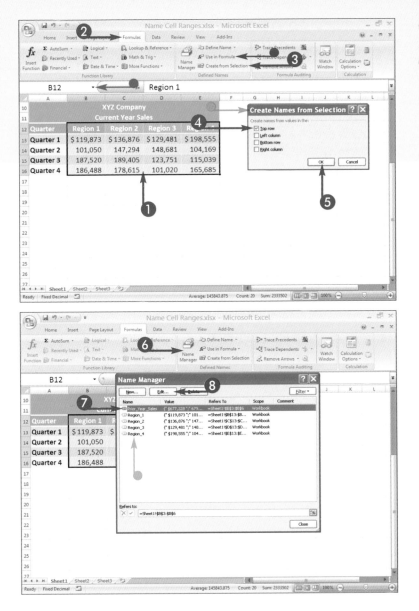

11

① Click and drag to select the cells you want to include in the named range.

Include the headings; they become the range names.

② Click the Formulas tab.

③ Click Create from Selection.

● The Create Names from Selection dialog box appears.

④ Click the location of the range names (☐ changes to ☑).

⑤ Click OK.

● The defined names are now available when you click Use in Formula.

● You click here to move to a named range.

⑥ Click Name Manager.

● All the range names appear in the Name Manager.

⑦ Click a name.

⑧ Click Delete.

Excel deletes the named range.

![TIPS]

Did You Know?

If you click the Edit button in the Name Manager dialog box, you can change the range name or the cell address to which a named range refers.

Did You Know?

When you click the down arrow on the left side of the formula bar, a list of named ranges appears. Refer to Step 5 under Create Named Ranges from a Selection. If you click one of the named ranges, you move to the cells it defines.

Did You Know?

When creating a formula, if you click and drag to select a group of cells that have a range name, Excel automatically uses the range name instead of the cell address.

Define a
CONSTANT

Use a constant whenever you want to use the same value in different cells and/or formulas. With constants, you can refer to a value, whether it is simple or consists of many digits, by simply using the constant's name.

You can use constants in many applications. For example, sales tax rate is a familiar constant that, when multiplied by the subtotal on an invoice, results in the tax owed. Likewise, income tax rates are the constants used to calculate tax liabilities. Although

tax rates change from time to time, they tend to remain constant within a tax period.

To create a constant in Excel, you need to type its value in the New Name dialog box, the same dialog box you use to name ranges as shown in Task #11. When you define a constant, you determine the scope of the constant by telling Excel whether it applies to the current worksheet or the entire workbook. To use the constant in any formula in the same workbook, simply use the name you defined.

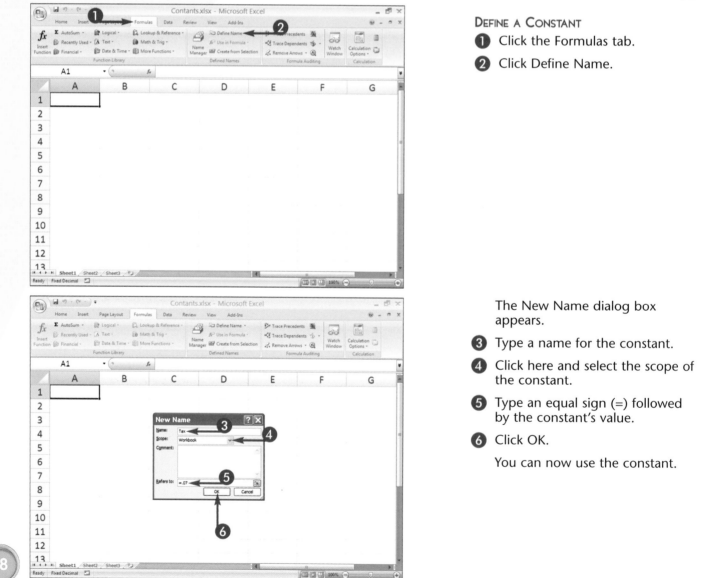

DEFINE A CONSTANT

① Click the Formulas tab.

② Click Define Name.

The New Name dialog box appears.

③ Type a name for the constant.

④ Click here and select the scope of the constant.

⑤ Type an equal sign (=) followed by the constant's value.

⑥ Click OK.

You can now use the constant.

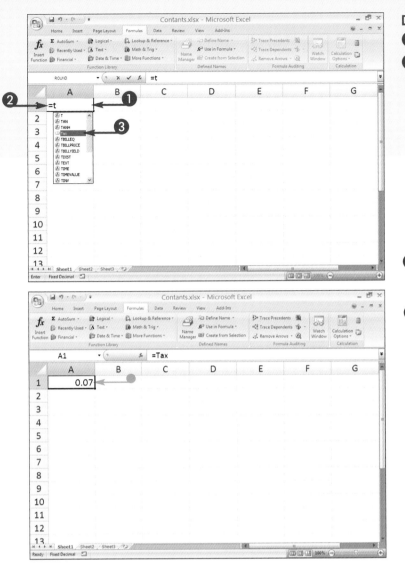

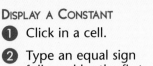

DISPLAY A CONSTANT

1 Click in a cell.

2 Type an equal sign followed by the first letter or letters of the constant's name.

A menu appears.

Note: *If you do not know the constant's name, click the Formulas tab and then Use in Formula. When the menu appears, click the name and then press Enter.*

3 Double-click the name of the constant.

4 Press Enter.

● The constant's value appears in the cell.

Note: *To use named constants and ranges in formulas, see Task #13.*

TIP

Did You Know?

You can use Excel's name manager to rename, edit, or delete named ranges and constant values. On the Formulas tab, click Name Manager. The Name Manager dialog box appears. Double-click the name you want to edit. The Edit Name dialog box appears. Make the changes you want and then click OK. To delete a constant, click the name in the Name Manager dialog box and then click Delete. If you want to create a new constant, click New in the Name Manager dialog box. The New Name dialog box appears; you can make your entries. In addition to formulas, you can also enter text as a constant value. Simply type the text into the Refers To field.

CREATE FORMULAS
that include names

Constructing formulas can be complicated, especially when you use several functions in the same formula or when multiple arguments are required in a single function. Using named constants and named ranges can make creating formulas and using functions easier by enabling you to use terms you have created that clearly identify a value or range of values. An argument is information you provide to the function

so the function can do its work. A named constant is a name you create that refers to a single, frequently used value; see Task #12. A named range is a name you assign to a group of related cells; see Task #11.

To insert a name into a function or use it in a formula or as a function's argument, you must type it, access it by using Use in Formula on the Formulas tab, or select it from the Function Auto-complete list.

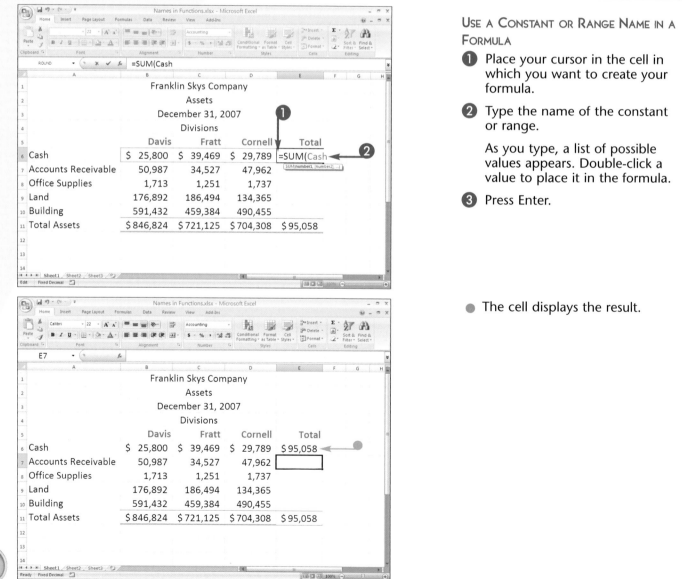

see Task #12. ... see Task #11.

USE A CONSTANT OR RANGE NAME IN A FORMULA

1 Place your cursor in the cell in which you want to create your formula.

2 Type the name of the constant or range.

As you type, a list of possible values appears. Double-click a value to place it in the formula.

3 Press Enter.

● The cell displays the result.

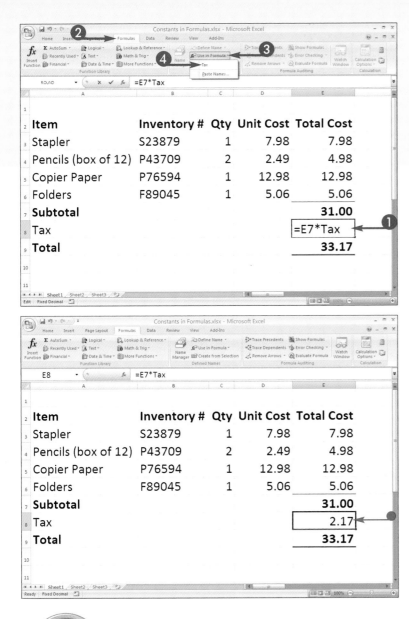

Note: Use this technique if you forget the name of a constant or range.

1 Begin typing your formula.

2 Click the Formulas tab.

3 Click Use in Formula.

A menu appears.

4 Click the constant or range name you want to use.

If necessary, continue typing your formula and press Enter when you finish.

5 Press Enter.

● Excel feeds the selected constant or range name into the formula, which then displays a result based on it.

TIPS

Did You Know?

To create several named constants at the same time, create two adjacent columns, one listing names and the other listing the values — for example, state names and state sales tax rates. Select both columns. Click the Formulas tab and then click Create from Selection. The Create Names from Selection dialog box appears. Click a check box to indicate which column or row to use for the name. Click OK. Click Name Manager to see the constants listed in the Name Manager dialog box. Use the same procedure to create named ranges.

Did You Know?

Naming a formula enables you to reuse it by merely typing its name. To create a named formula, click in the cell that contains the formula, click Formulas, and then click Define Name. The New Name dialog box appears. Type a name for the formula in the Names field, define its scope, and then click OK.

Calculate with
THE FUNCTION WIZARD

Excel's Function Wizard simplifies the use of functions. You can take advantage of the wizard for every one of Excel's functions, from the sum (SUM) function to the most complex statistical, mathematical, financial, and engineering function. One simple but useful function, ROUND, rounds off values to the number of places you choose.

You can access the Function Wizard in two ways. One way involves selecting a cell where the result is to appear and then clicking the Insert Function button and using the Insert Function dialog box to select a function. Another way, which is a bit quicker, makes sense when you know the name of your function. Start by selecting a cell for the result. Type an equal sign (=) and the beginning of the function name. In the list of functions that appears, double-click the function you want and then click the Insert Function button.

Both methods bring up the Function Arguments box, where you type the values you want in your calculation or click in the cells containing the values.

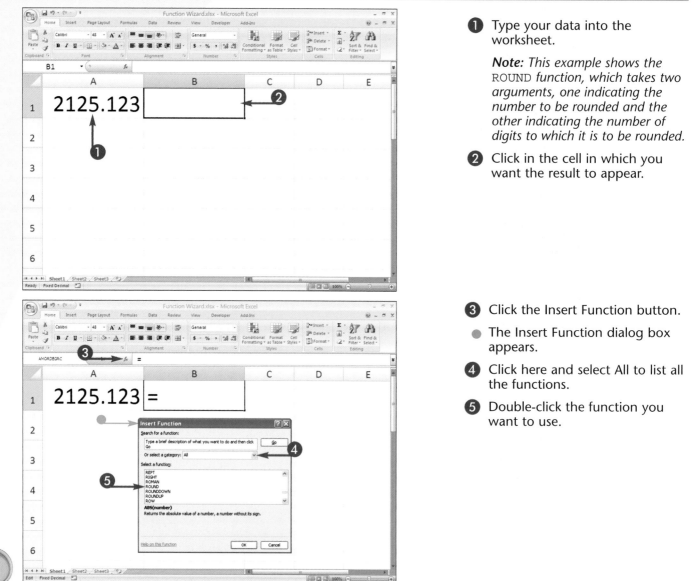

① Type your data into the worksheet.

Note: This example shows the ROUND *function, which takes two arguments, one indicating the number to be rounded and the other indicating the number of digits to which it is to be rounded.*

② Click in the cell in which you want the result to appear.

③ Click the Insert Function button.

● The Insert Function dialog box appears.

④ Click here and select All to list all the functions.

⑤ Double-click the function you want to use.

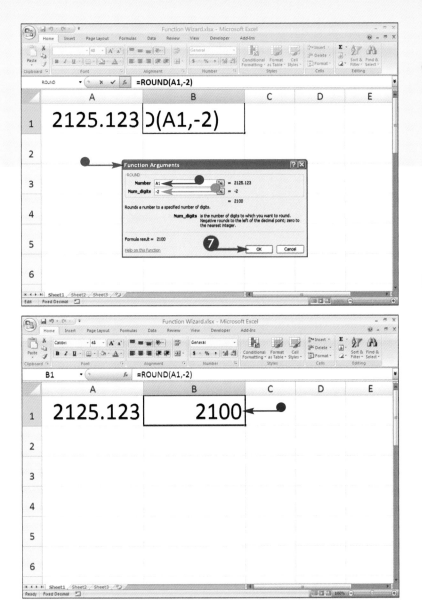

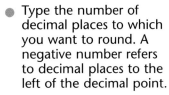

- The Function Arguments dialog box appears.

⑥ Click in the cell(s) or type the values requested in each field.

- For this example, click in the cell containing the value you entered in Step 1.

- Type the number of decimal places to which you want to round. A negative number refers to decimal places to the left of the decimal point.

⑦ Click OK.

- The result appears in the cell.

TIPS

Did You Know?

If you do not know which function you want to use, type a question in the Search for a Function field in the Insert Function dialog box. For help with the function itself, click Help on This Function in the Function Arguments dialog box.

Caution!

Do not confuse the ROUND function with number formatting. ROUND works by evaluating a number in an argument and rounding it to the number of digits you specify in the second field of the Function Arguments dialog box. When you format numbers, you simplify the appearance of the number in the worksheet, making the number easier to read. The underlying number is not changed.

Figure out
LOAN TERMS

You can use Excel's Payment (PMT) function when buying a house or car. This function enables you to compare loan terms and make an objective decision based on factors such as the amount of the monthly payment.

You can calculate loan payments in many ways when using Excel, but using the PMT function may be the simplest because you merely enter the arguments into the Function Wizard. To make your job even easier, enter your argument values into your worksheet before launching the wizard. Then by

clicking in a cell, you can enter the value of the cell into the wizard.

The PMT function takes three required arguments. For RATE, enter an annual interest rate such as 5 percent and then type .05 divided by 12 to calculate the monthly rate. For NPER, number of periods, enter the number of loan periods for the loan you are seeking. For PV, present value, enter the amount of the loan. The monthly payment appears surrounded by parentheses, signifying that the number is negative, or a cash outflow.

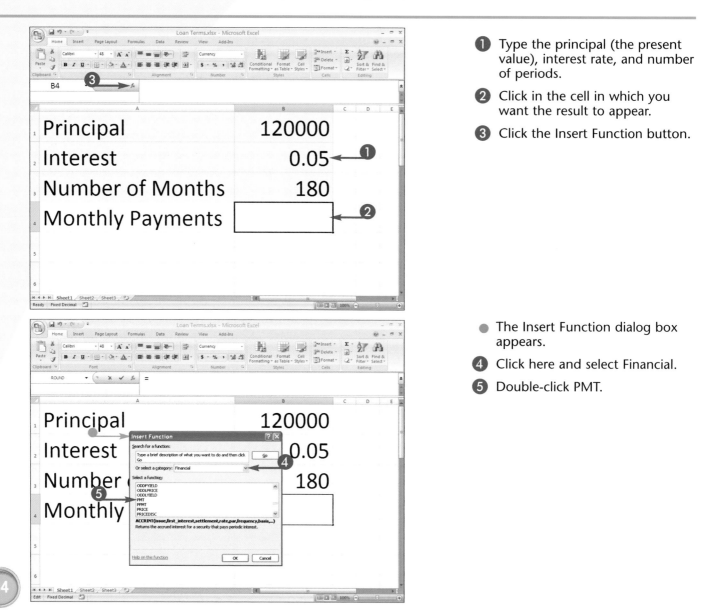

① Type the principal (the present value), interest rate, and number of periods.

② Click in the cell in which you want the result to appear.

③ Click the Insert Function button.

● The Insert Function dialog box appears.

④ Click here and select Financial.

⑤ Double-click PMT.

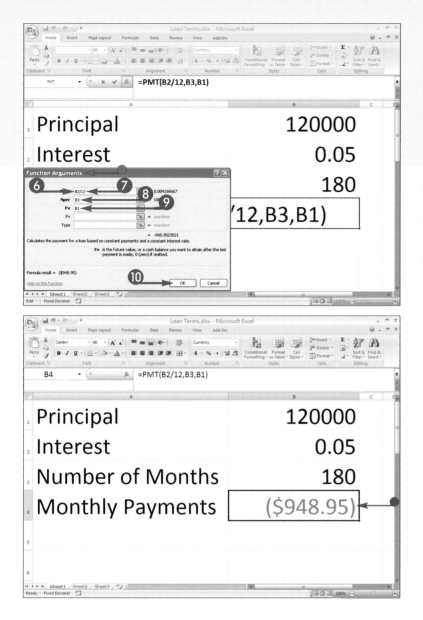

- The PMT Function Arguments dialog box appears.

6 Click in the cell with the interest rate.

7 Divide the interest rate by the number of periods per year; for example, type **12**.

8 Click in the cell with the number of periods.

9 Click in the cell with the principal.

10 Click OK.

- The result appears in the cell.

Note: *The result shows the amount of a single loan payment.*

Note: *You can repeat Steps 1 to 10 for other combinations of the three variables.*

TIPS

Did You Know?

In a worksheet, you can create a loan calculator showing all the values at once. Place the labels Principal, Interest, and Number of Months of a loan period in a column. Type their respective values into adjacent cells to the right. Use references to those cells in the Function Arguments dialog box for PMT.

Did You Know?

Excel's Goal Seeking feature enables you to calculate payments. With Goal Seeking, you can set up a problem so you specify a goal, such as payments less than $1,100 per month, and have Excel vary a single value to reach the goal. The limitation is that you can vary only one value at a time. See Task #59 for more information.

Determine the
INTERNAL RATE OF RETURN

You can use Excel's Internal Rate of Return (IRR) function to calculate the rate of return on an investment. When using the IRR function, the cash flows do not have to be equal, but they must occur at regular intervals. As an example, you make a loan of $6,607 on January 1, year 1. You receive payments every January 1 for four succeeding years. You can use the IRR function to determine the interest rate you receive on the loan.

Your loan of $6,607 is a cash outflow, so you enter it as a negative number. Each payment is a cash inflow,

so you enter them as positive numbers. When using the Internal Rate of Return function, you must enter at least one positive and one negative number.

Optionally, you can provide, as the second argument, your best-guess estimate as to the rate of return. The default value, if you do not provide an estimate, is .10, representing a 10 percent rate of return. Your estimate merely gives Excel a starting point at which to calculate the IRR.

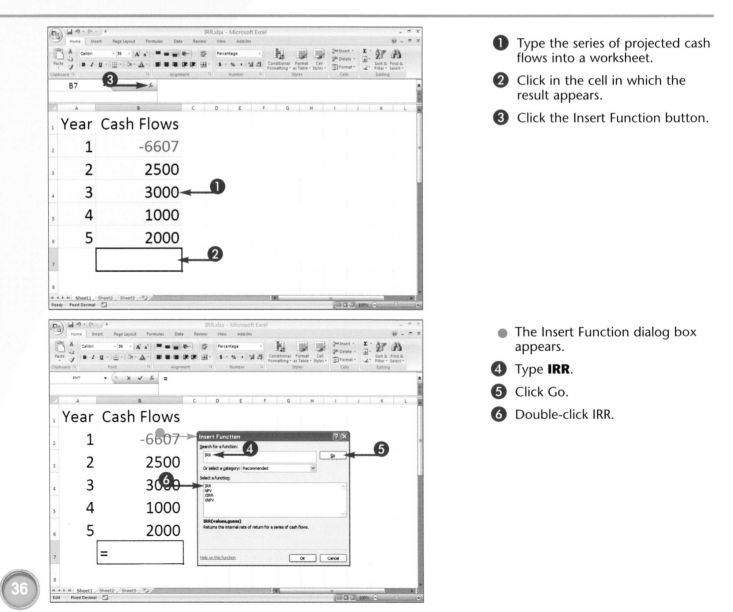

① Type the series of projected cash flows into a worksheet.

② Click in the cell in which the result appears.

③ Click the Insert Function button.

● The Insert Function dialog box appears.

④ Type **IRR**.

⑤ Click Go.

⑥ Double-click IRR.

● The IRR Function Arguments dialog box appears.

⑦ Click and drag the cash-flow values entered in Step 1 or type the range.

● Optionally, you can provide an estimated rate of return just to get Excel started.

⑧ Click OK.

Year	Cash Flows
1	-6607
2	2500
3	3000
4	1000
5	2000
	R(B2:B6)

Function Arguments

IRR

Values   B2:B6   = {-6607;2500;3000;1000;2000}

Guess   = number

= 0.11996388

Returns the internal rate of return for a series of cash flows.

Guess   is a number that you guess is close to the result of IRR; 0.1 (10 percent) if omitted.

Formula result = 12%

Help on this function   OK   Cancel

● The cell with the formula displays the results of the calculations as a percent with no decimal places.

Repeat Steps 1 to 8 for each set of anticipated future cash flows.

Year	Cash Flows
1	-6607
2	2500
3	3000
4	1000
5	2000
	12%

=IRR(B2:B6)

TIPS

Did You Know?

The IRR function is related to the Net Present Value (NPV) function, which calculates the net present value of future cash flows. Whereas IRR returns a percentage — the rate of return on the initial investment — NPV returns the amount that must be invested to achieve the specified interest rate.

Caution!

Excel's IRR function has strict assumptions. Cash flows must be regularly timed and take place at the same point within the payment period. IRR may perform less reliably for inconsistent payments, a mix of positive and negative flows, and variable interest rates.

Determine the
NTH LARGEST VALUE

Sometimes you want to identify and characterize the top values in a series, such as the RBIs of the top three hitters in Major League Baseball or the purchases, in a given period, for your five largest purchasers.

The LARGE function evaluates a series of numbers and determines the highest value, second highest, or Nth highest in the series, with N being a value's rank order. LARGE takes two arguments: the range of cells you want to evaluate and the rank order of the value

you are seeking, with 1 being the highest, 2 the next highest, and so on. The result of LARGE is the value you requested.

Another way to determine the first, second, or Nth number in a series is to sort the numbers from biggest to smallest and then simply read the results, as shown in Chapter 4. Sorting is less useful when you have a long list or when you want to use the result in another function, such as summing the top five values.

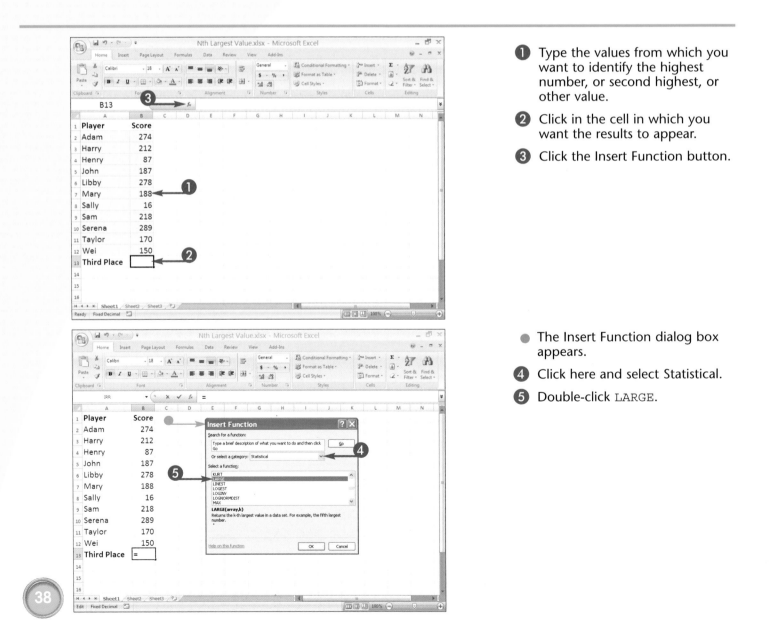

① Type the values from which you want to identify the highest number, or second highest, or other value.

② Click in the cell in which you want the results to appear.

③ Click the Insert Function button.

● The Insert Function dialog box appears.

④ Click here and select Statistical.

⑤ Double-click LARGE.

- The Function Arguments dialog box appears for the LARGE function.

6 Click and drag to select the cells you want to evaluate, or type the range.

7 Type a number indicating what you are seeking: 1 for highest, 2 for second highest, 3 for third highest, and so on.

8 Click OK.

- The cell displays the value you requested.

  If K in Step 7 is greater than the number of cells, a #NUM error appears in the cell instead.

TIPS

Apply It!

To add the top three or other highest values in a series, you can use LARGE three times in a formula: =LARGE(Sales,3) + LARGE(Sales,2) + LARGE(Sales,1), with Sales being the named range of sales values.

Did You Know?

Other useful functions work in a similar manner to the LARGE function. SMALL evaluates a range of values and returns a number. For example, if you enter 1 as the K value, it returns the lowest number, 2 for next lowest, and so on. The MIN and MAX functions return the lowest and highest values in a series, respectively. They take one argument: a range of cell values.

Create a
CONDITIONAL FORMULA

With a conditional formula, you can perform calculations on numbers that meet a certain condition. For example, you can find the highest score for a particular team from a list that consists of several teams. The Team number is the condition and you can set the formula so only the values for players on a particular team are evaluated.

A conditional formula uses at least two functions. The first function, IF, defines the condition, or test, such as players on Team 1. To create the condition, you

use comparison operators, such as greater than (>), greater than or equal to (>=), less than (<), less than or equal to (<=), or equal to (=).

The second function in a conditional formula performs a calculation on numbers that meet the condition. Excel carries out the IF function first and then calculates the values that meet the condition defined in the IF function. Because two functions are involved, when you use the Function Wizard, one function, IF, is an argument of another function.

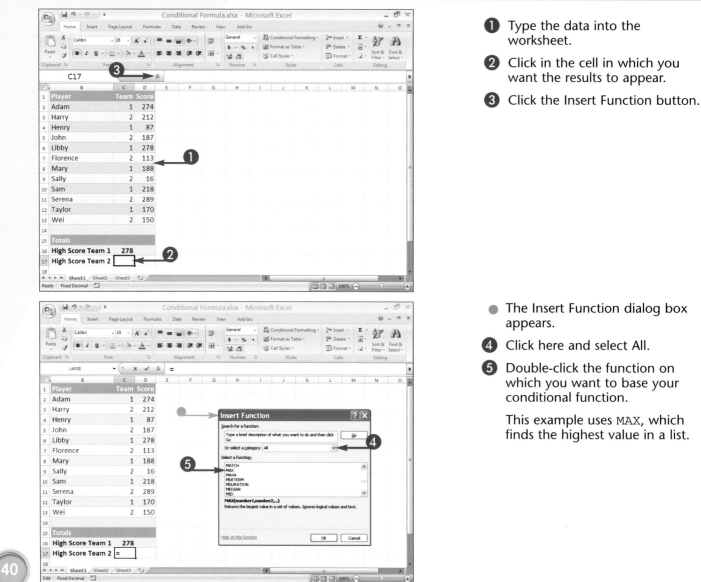

① Type the data into the worksheet.

② Click in the cell in which you want the results to appear.

③ Click the Insert Function button.

● The Insert Function dialog box appears.

④ Click here and select All.

⑤ Double-click the function on which you want to base your conditional function.

This example uses MAX, which finds the highest value in a list.

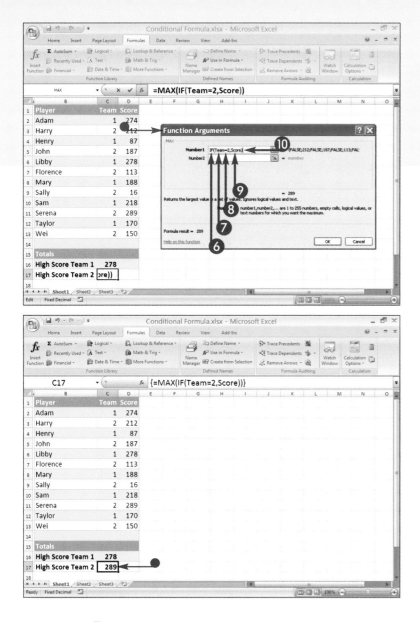

- The Function Arguments dialog box appears.

6 Type **If(**.

7 Type the range or range name for the series you want to evaluate.

8 Type a comparison operator, the condition, and then a comma.

9 Type the range or range name for the series that you want to calculate.

10 Type **)**.

11 Press Ctrl+Shift+Enter.

- The result appears in the cell with the formula.

TIPS

Important!

IF is an array function. It compares every number in a series to a condition and keeps track of the numbers meeting the condition. To create an array function, press Ctrl+Shift+Enter instead of pressing Enter or clicking OK to complete your function. You must surround arrays with curly braces ({ }). The braces are entered automatically when you press Ctrl+Shift+Enter but not when you press Enter or click OK when using the Function Arguments dialog box.

Did You Know?

IF has an optional third argument. Use the third argument if you want to specify what happens when the condition is not met. For example, you can use IF to test whether any sales values exceed 9,000, and then display True if such values exist and False if they do not.

Calculate a
CONDITIONAL SUM

You can use conditional sums to identify and sum investments whose growth exceeds a certain rate. The SUMIF function combines the SUM and IF functions into one easy-to-use function.

SUMIF() is simple, relative to a formula that uses both SUM() and IF(). SUMIF() enables you to avoid complicated nesting and to use the Function Wizard without making one function an argument of the other. However, using two functions — SUM and IF — gives you more flexibility. For example, you can use IF to create multiple complex conditions.

SUMIF takes three arguments: a range of numbers, the condition being applied to the numbers, and the range to which the condition applies. Values that meet the condition are added together. For example, you can create a function that evaluates a list to determine the team a person is on and for all persons on Team 1 it can add the scores. The third argument, the range to which the condition applies, is optional. If you exclude it, Excel sums the range you specify in the first argument.

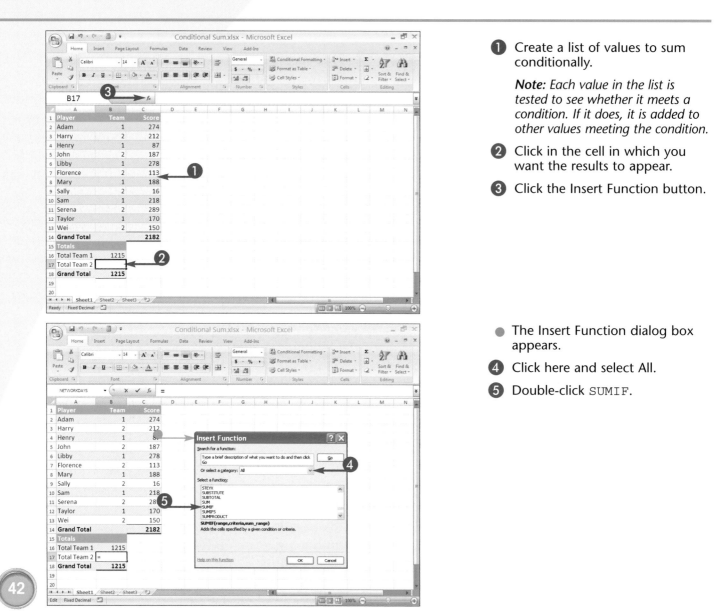

① Create a list of values to sum conditionally.

Note: Each value in the list is tested to see whether it meets a condition. If it does, it is added to other values meeting the condition.

② Click in the cell in which you want the results to appear.

③ Click the Insert Function button.

● The Insert Function dialog box appears.

④ Click here and select All.

⑤ Double-click SUMIF.

● The Function Arguments dialog box for SUMIF appears.

⑥ Type the range or range name for the series you want to evaluate.

⑦ Type a comparison operator and a condition.

⑧ Type the range or range name for the series to be summed if the condition is met.

⑨ Click OK.

DIFFICULTY LEVEL

● The result appears in the cell with the formula.

TIPS

Did You Know?
The COUNTIF function works like SUMIF. It combines two functions, COUNT and IF, and takes two arguments: a series of values and the condition by which the values are tested. Whereas SUMIF sums the values, COUNTIF returns the number of items that passed the test.

Did You Know?
You can use the Conditional Sum Wizard, an Excel add-in. The Conditional Sum Wizard has four self-explanatory steps. The last step diverges from the SUMIF Function Wizard in that both the condition and the result can appear on your worksheet. You can thus display conditions and results side by side to compare them. To learn how to install this add-in, see Task #94.

Add a
CALCULATOR

Often you may want to do quick calculations without using a formula or function. In Excel, you can place a calculator on the Quick Access toolbar so it is always available. The Excel calculator is one of many commands you can add to the Quick Access toolbar.

You can use the calculator as you would any electronic calculator. Click a number, choose an operator — such as the plus key (+) to do addition — and then click another number. Press the equal sign key (=) to get a

result. Use MS to remember a value, MR to recall it, and MC to clear memory.

Statistical and mathematical functions are available in the calculator's scientific view by clicking View and then Scientific. In this view, you can cube a number, find its square root, compute its log, and more. In both standard and scientific views, you can transfer a value from the calculator to Excel by displaying it, copying it, and pasting it into a cell.

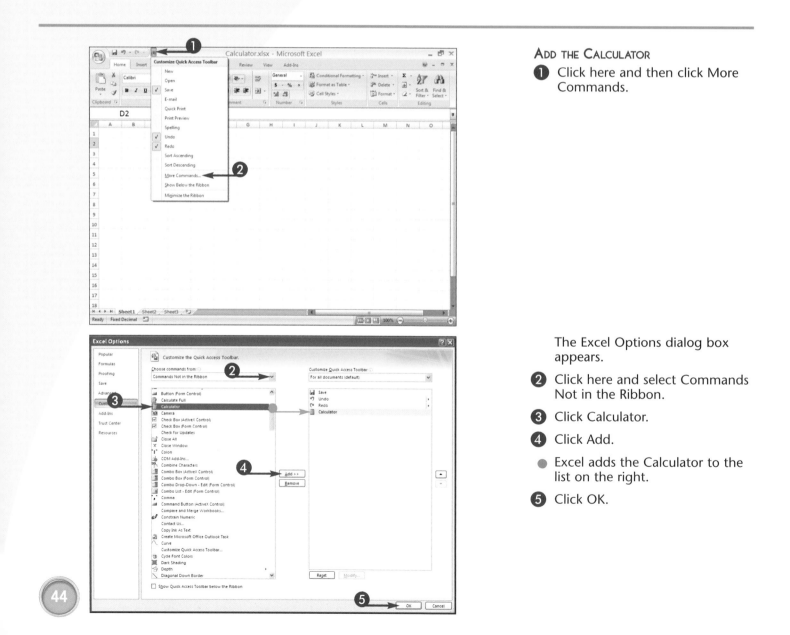

ADD THE CALCULATOR

① Click here and then click More Commands.

The Excel Options dialog box appears.

② Click here and select Commands Not in the Ribbon.

③ Click Calculator.

④ Click Add.

● Excel adds the Calculator to the list on the right.

⑤ Click OK.

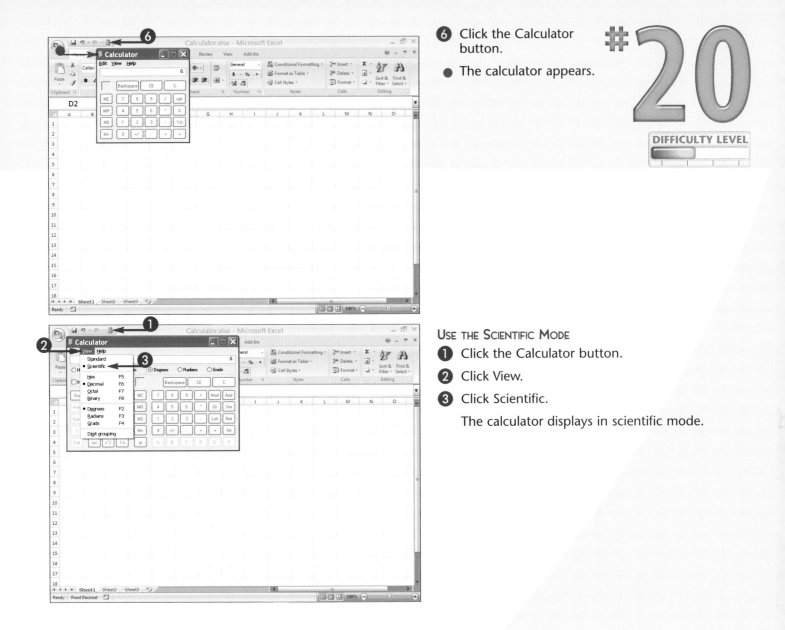

6 Click the Calculator button.

● The calculator appears.

USE THE SCIENTIFIC MODE

1 Click the Calculator button.

2 Click View.

3 Click Scientific.

The calculator displays in scientific mode.

TIPS

Apply It!

To calculate an average, switch to the scientific view and enter the first number to be averaged. Click the Sta button to display the Statistics box. Click Dat. Back in the calculator, click another value to average and click Dat. Keep entering data and clicking Dat until you have entered all the values. Click Ave to find the average.

Did You Know?

For complete instructions on using the Excel calculator, open the calculator. On the calculator's menu, click Help and then Help Topics. The Calculator dialog box appears. Click the Contents tab and then Calculator. A list of topics appears. Click any topic to learn more about the calculator.

Find
PRODUCTS AND SQUARE ROOTS

Many Excel users are familiar with the basic operations available by clicking the AutoSum button: addition, subtraction, minimum, maximum, and count. Fewer are familiar with two other basic operations available by using a mathematical function. Using the PRODUCT function, you can multiply two or more numbers, and using the SQRT function, you can find the square root of a number.

Excel can calculate the square roots of positive numbers only. If a negative number is the argument, as in SQRT(-1), Excel returns #NUM in the cell.

You can compute a PRODUCT or SQRT by entering the values to be used in the function into the worksheet. If you do not want the values to appear in the worksheet, start by clicking in the cell where the result is to appear and pressing an equal sign (=), typing the function name — PRODUCT or SQRT — and parentheses. Click the Insert Function button (fx) to enter your values for the formula.

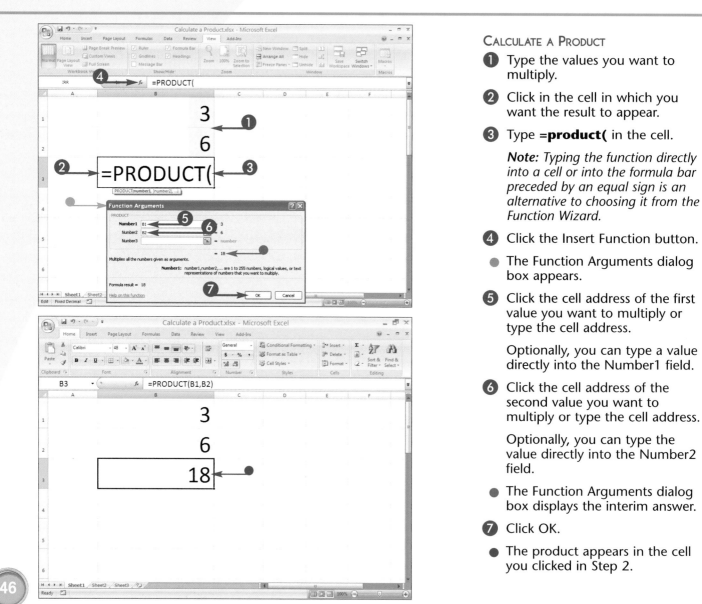

CALCULATE A PRODUCT

① Type the values you want to multiply.

② Click in the cell in which you want the result to appear.

③ Type **=product(** in the cell.

Note: Typing the function directly into a cell or into the formula bar preceded by an equal sign is an alternative to choosing it from the Function Wizard.

④ Click the Insert Function button.

● The Function Arguments dialog box appears.

⑤ Click the cell address of the first value you want to multiply or type the cell address.

Optionally, you can type a value directly into the Number1 field.

⑥ Click the cell address of the second value you want to multiply or type the cell address.

Optionally, you can type the value directly into the Number2 field.

● The Function Arguments dialog box displays the interim answer.

⑦ Click OK.

● The product appears in the cell you clicked in Step 2.

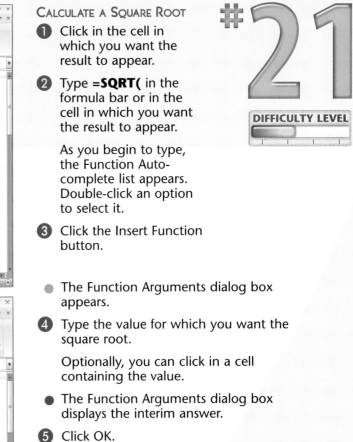

① Click in the cell in which you want the result to appear.

② Type **=SQRT(** in the formula bar or in the cell in which you want the result to appear.

As you begin to type, the Function Auto-complete list appears. Double-click an option to select it.

③ Click the Insert Function button.

● The Function Arguments dialog box appears.

④ Type the value for which you want the square root.

Optionally, you can click in a cell containing the value.

● The Function Arguments dialog box displays the interim answer.

⑤ Click OK.

● The square root appears in the cell.

TIPS

Apply It!
Related to PRODUCT and SQRT is POWER. To find the power of any number, such as 3 to the 9th power, use the Power function.

Did You Know?
Each argument in PRODUCT can have more than one value, for example, 2, 3, and 4. These values can be represented as an array, a series of numbers enclosed in curly braces: {2,3,4}. Each value in the array is multiplied, so the product of {2,3,4} is 24. Arrays can be multiplied by each other. Each value in the array has to be a number.

Perform
TIME CALCULATIONS

Using Excel formulas and functions, you can perform calculations with dates and times. You can find, for example, the number of hours worked between two times or the number of days between two dates. Date and time functions convert every date and time into a serial value that can be added and subtracted and then converted back into a recognizable date or time.

Excel calculates a date's serial value as the number of days after January 1, 1900, so each date can be represented by a whole number. Excel calculates a time's serial value in units of 1/60th of a second.

Every time can be represented as a serial value between 0 and 1.

A date and time, such as January 1, 2000, at noon, consists of the date to the left of the decimal and a time to the right. Take the example August 25, 2005, at 5:46 PM. The date and time serial value is 38589.74028.

Subtracting one date from another involves subtracting one serial value from another and then converting the result back into a date or time.

FIND THE DIFFERENCE BETWEEN TWO TIMES

1. Type the first time in a cell.

   Note: If you do not include AM or PM, Excel defaults to a.m. If you want p.m., you must type PM.

2. Type the second time in a cell.

3. Click in the cell in which you want the results to appear.

4. Type an equal sign (=).

5. Click in the cell with the later time.

6. Type a minus sign (–).

7. Click in the cell with the earlier time.

8. Press Enter.

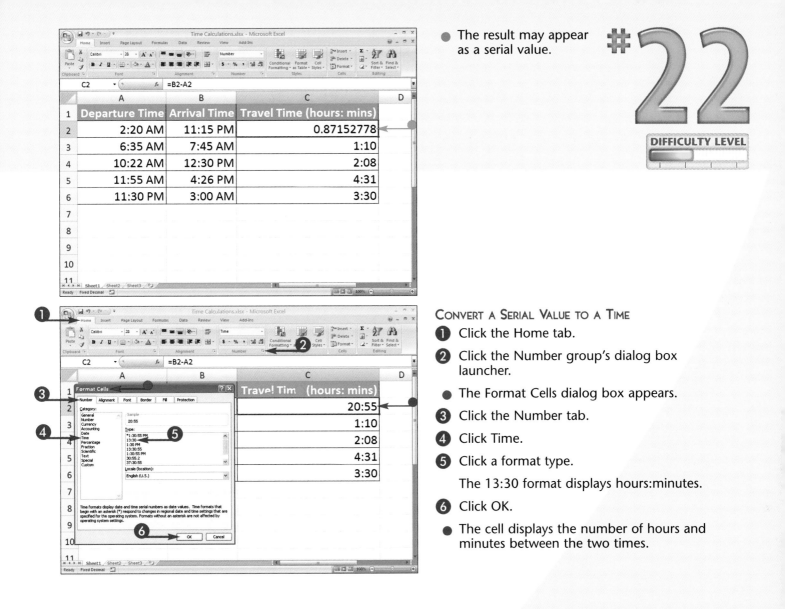

● The result may appear as a serial value.

DIFFICULTY LEVEL

CONVERT A SERIAL VALUE TO A TIME

① Click the Home tab.

② Click the Number group's dialog box launcher.

● The Format Cells dialog box appears.

③ Click the Number tab.

④ Click Time.

⑤ Click a format type.

The 13:30 format displays hours:minutes.

⑥ Click OK.

● The cell displays the number of hours and minutes between the two times.

TIPS

Did You Know?

In subtracting times that cross midnight, such as 11 p.m. to 2 a.m., you need a programming function called modulus, or MOD. The formula is =MOD(later time – earlier time, 1). Thanks to John Walkenbach's *Excel 2003 Bible* (Wiley Publishing, 2003) for this tip.

Did You Know?

If subtracting times or dates yields a negative time or date, this error is reflected by a series of pound signs (######).

Did You Know?

Showing a time or date in the General format displays its serial value. Use a Time or Date format to display a recognizable date or time. To display a time in hour:minute format, right-click it, click Format Cell, click Time, and click the 13:30 format.

Perform
DATE CALCULATIONS

One special-purpose Date and Time function enables you to find the number of workdays between two dates. Like other Excel functions, Date and Time functions make use of the Function Wizard. As with all functions, the wizard works with data you type into the wizard, such as a specific date, and with data you have typed into cells in your worksheet.

To calculate the number of workdays between two dates, you use the NETWORKDAY function. The function's arguments include a start date, an end

date, and optionally, any intervening holidays that automatically reduce the number of workdays between the two dates. Excel automatically deducts the number of weekend dates.

Excel can perform date arithmetic on any date after January 1, 1900. If you use dates before then, Excel treats them as text and does not perform a calculation on them. Instead, it gives you a #VALUE! error.

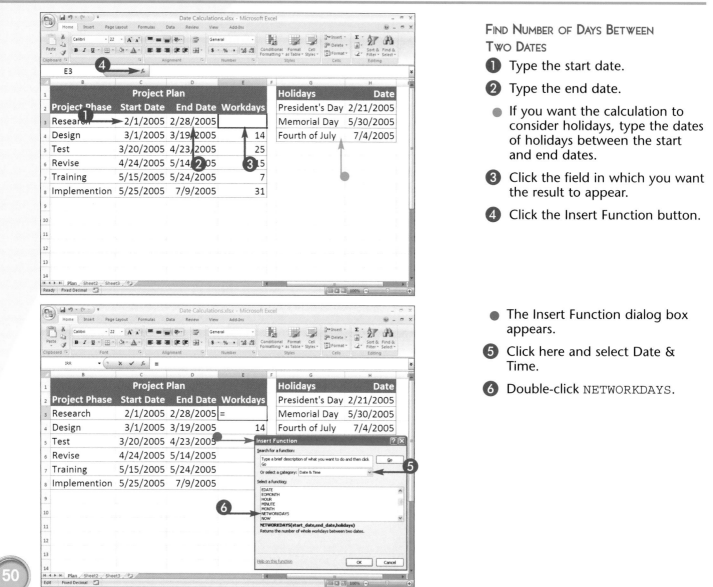

FIND NUMBER OF DAYS BETWEEN TWO DATES

1 Type the start date.

2 Type the end date.

● If you want the calculation to consider holidays, type the dates of holidays between the start and end dates.

3 Click the field in which you want the result to appear.

4 Click the Insert Function button.

● The Insert Function dialog box appears.

5 Click here and select Date & Time.

6 Double-click NETWORKDAYS.

- The Function Arguments dialog box appears.

7 Click in the cell containing the start date or type the cell address.

8 Click in the cell containing the end date or type the cell address.

- Optionally, click and drag the range of holidays or type the range.

9 Click OK.

- The cell with the formula displays the net workdays between the two dates.

TIPS

Did You Know?

In Excel you can enter the current date simply by clicking in the cell in which you want the date to appear and pressing the Ctrl and semicolon keys at the same time.

Did You Know?

There are more than 15 ways you can format a date, including August 1, 1956; Aug 1, 1956; 01-Aug-56, Wednesday, August, 1956, 8/1; and 8/1/56.

Did You Know?

When calculating NETWORKDAYS, if your start date is later than your end date, Excel returns a negative number.

Copy, Format, and More

If you have used Word, you know that copying text for use in another document or application enables you to reuse material and minimize retyping and errors. Basic copying in Excel is similar: Select the value and then click the Copy button in the Ribbon. In the new location, click in the cell where you want to place the value and then click Paste. But copying can be both more involved and more powerful in Excel because so many elements can occupy a cell: values, functions, formulas, formats, styles, and more. You can copy any of these elements between cells, worksheets, workbooks, and even applications. You can copy one value at a time, such as a specific number or specific bit of text, or many consecutively arranged values at the same time, such as a range.

Excel makes use of the copy features built into Windows as well as those built into Office 2007. You can store as many as 24 different items on the Office Clipboard for pasting into Excel and other Office applications.

In this chapter, you learn to use the Office Clipboard. You also learn to transpose a row into a column, to copy styles from one worksheet to another, to copy formulas from one cell to another, to change text to numbers, and much more. If you share your workbooks with others, you may want to use the tip on keeping track of the changes.

Top 100

CHECK YOUR FORMULAS
for errors

When you create formulas, you can nest a formula within another formula. Because there are so many intermediate steps when you nest formulas, determining the accuracy of your results may be difficult. You can use the Evaluate Formula dialog box to check the result of intermediate calculations to determine if your result is correct.

When you open the Evaluate Formula dialog box, you see your formula. The Evaluate Formula dialog box steps you through the calculation one expression at a time so you can see how Excel evaluates each

argument. Click the Evaluate button to begin the process. Excel underlines individual expressions. You can click the Evaluate button again to see the results of an expression. The results of expressions appear in italics.

If you base the reference on another formula, you can click the Step In button to display the formula. Click the Step Out button to return to the reference. After you step through the entire formula, Excel displays the result and a Restart button. Click the Restart button to evaluate your expression again.

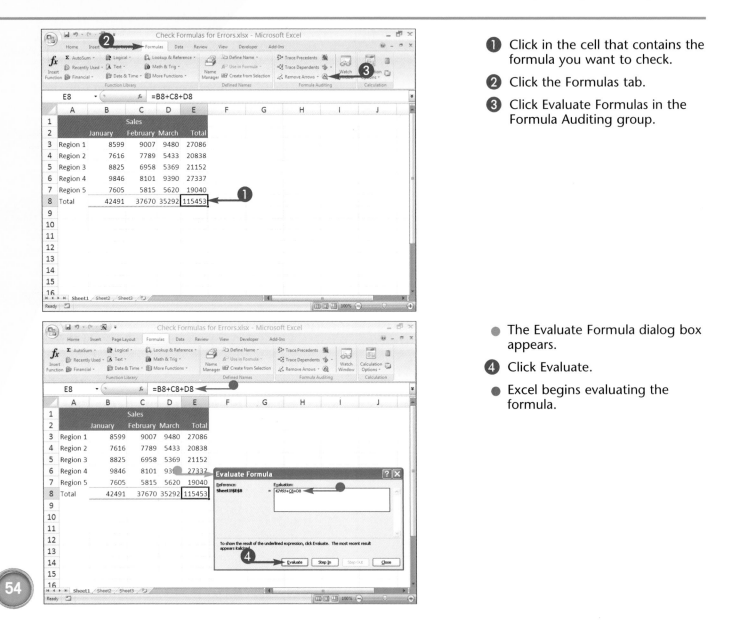

① Click in the cell that contains the formula you want to check.

② Click the Formulas tab.

③ Click Evaluate Formulas in the Formula Auditing group.

● The Evaluate Formula dialog box appears.

④ Click Evaluate.

● Excel begins evaluating the formula.

⑤ Continue clicking Evaluate to review each expression.

● Click Step In to review the results of an expression.

● Click Step Out to return to the expression.

● When Excel reaches the end of the formula, it displays the results.

● Click Restart to evaluate the formula again.

⑥ Click Close to close the dialog box.

TIPS

Did You Know?

The maximum number of functions you can nest within a function is 64.

Did You Know?

The #### error occurs when a cell is not wide enough or when you use a negative date or time. The #DIV/0 error occurs when you try to divide by zero. The #N/A error occurs when a value is not available to your function. The #VALUE error occurs when you use the wrong type of argument or operand.

TRACE
precedents and dependents

When you create a formula, Excel evaluates all the values in the formula and returns the result. If Excel cannot calculate the formula, it displays an error in the formula's cell. You can use the Excel trace features to help you locate your error.

You can view a graphical representation of the cells a formula refers to by clicking in the cell and then clicking Trace Precedents in the Formula Auditing group on the Formulas tab. This option draws blue arrows to each cell referenced by your formula. By selecting this option, you can identify the exact cells used by your formula.

If you want to find out which formulas use a specific cell, you can view a graphical representation by clicking in the cell and then clicking Trace Dependents in the Formula Auditing group on the Formulas tab. This option draws blue arrows to each cell that contains a formula that uses the active cell as an argument. If you perform this function before deleting a value, you can determine if your deletion affects a formula in your worksheet.

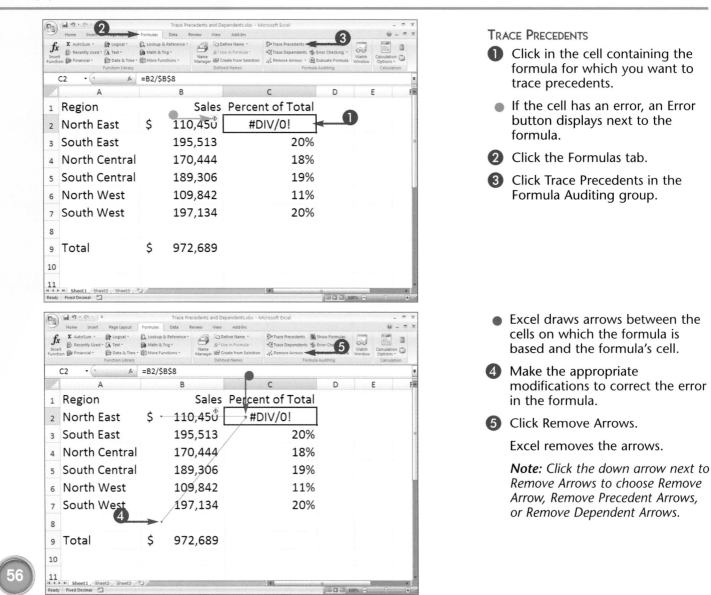

TRACE PRECEDENTS

① Click in the cell containing the formula for which you want to trace precedents.

● If the cell has an error, an Error button displays next to the formula.

② Click the Formulas tab.

③ Click Trace Precedents in the Formula Auditing group.

● Excel draws arrows between the cells on which the formula is based and the formula's cell.

④ Make the appropriate modifications to correct the error in the formula.

⑤ Click Remove Arrows.

Excel removes the arrows.

Note: *Click the down arrow next to Remove Arrows to choose Remove Arrow, Remove Precedent Arrows, or Remove Dependent Arrows.*

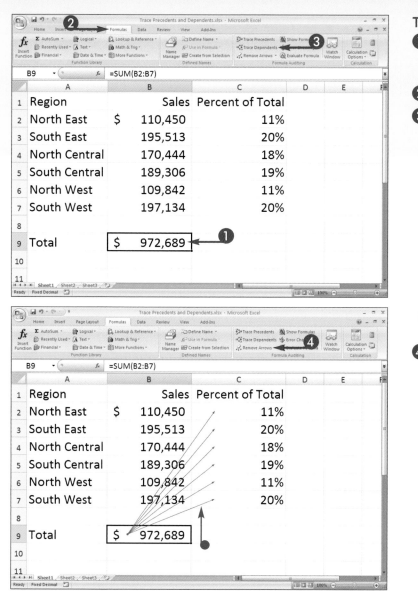

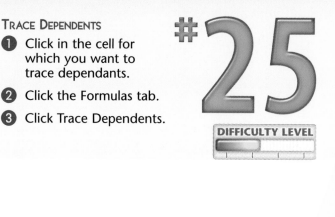

TRACE DEPENDENTS

1 Click in the cell for which you want to trace dependants.

2 Click the Formulas tab.

3 Click Trace Dependents.

● Excel draws arrows between the formula's cell and the dependent cells.

4 Click Remove Arrows.

Excel removes the arrows.

Note: *Click the down arrow next to Remove Arrows to choose Remove Arrow, Remove Precedent Arrows, or Remove Dependent Arrows.*

TIP

Did You Know?

When working with large or complicated worksheets, where the result of the formula is dependent on the results of another formula in another cell, you may want to monitor cell values. To do so, you can use the Watch Window. To add a cell to the Watch Window, click Watch Window on the Formulas tab in the Formula Auditing group. The Watch Window appears at the bottom of your screen. Click the Add Watch button. The Add Watch dialog box appears. Click and drag to select the cells you want to watch and then click Add. You can now monitor the cells you have added to the Watch Window.

Change
TEXT TO NUMBERS

You can use formulas to perform complex calculations quickly and accurately on numbers, dates, or times. Sometimes, however, your numbers look like numbers but are, in fact, text — mere characters. If a number is left-aligned in a cell, it is probably text; true numbers, by default, are right-aligned.

In Excel, text and numbers are different data types. You should use numbers, but not text, in mathematical formulas and functions. Trying to include text in a mathematical calculation results in an error.

You can address the problem in several ways. You can use the Format Cells dialog box to reformat the text cells to numbers, but this method does not always work. A more reliable technique is to multiply each numeral by 1 to convert the data type from text to a number.

The numbers-as-text problem often occurs when you import data from another application — for example, an external database such as Access. Chapter 9 covers importing data in detail.

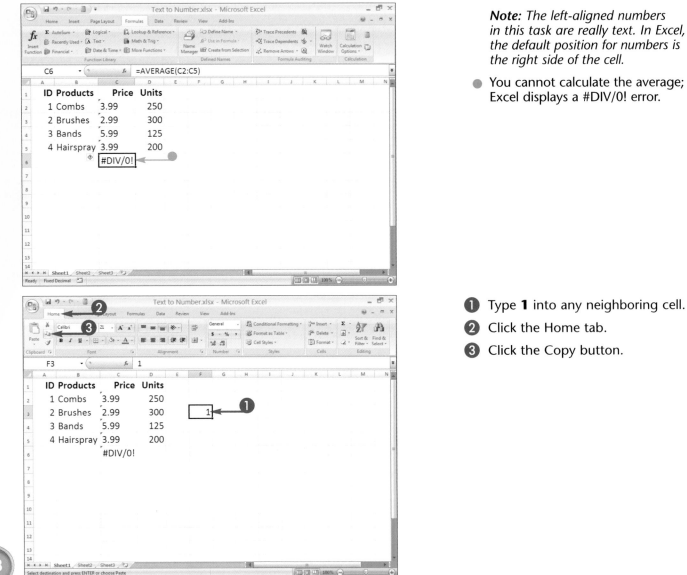

Note: The left-aligned numbers in this task are really text. In Excel, the default position for numbers is the right side of the cell.

● You cannot calculate the average; Excel displays a #DIV/0! error.

① Type **1** into any neighboring cell.
② Click the Home tab.
③ Click the Copy button.

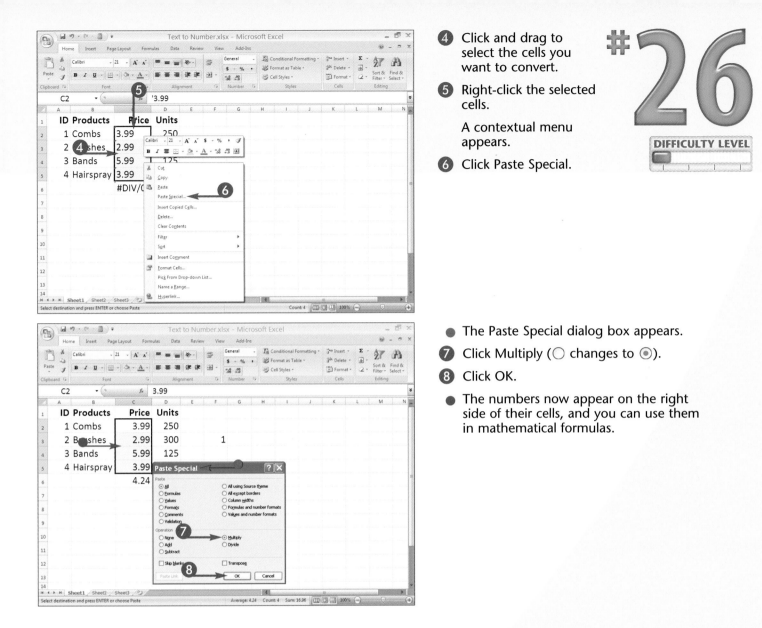

④ Click and drag to select the cells you want to convert.

⑤ Right-click the selected cells.

A contextual menu appears.

⑥ Click Paste Special.

● The Paste Special dialog box appears.

⑦ Click Multiply (○ changes to ⊙).

⑧ Click OK.

● The numbers now appear on the right side of their cells, and you can use them in mathematical formulas.

TIP

Did You Know?

Excel can convert text-based numbers to actual numbers. Click the Office button and then click Excel Options. The Excel Options dialog box appears. Click Formulas. In the Error Checking Rules section, select Numbers Formatted as Text or Preceded by an Apostrophe (☐ changes to ☑). Excel flags cells containing text by placing a green flag in the upper-left corner. Click the menu button appearing alongside any cells with this error. Click Convert to Number. If Excel is able to convert the text to a number, the numbers will right-align. This method does not always work.

CONVERT A ROW
to a column

When you create a worksheet, Excel gives you flexibility when working with rows and columns. At any time, you can insert new rows or columns, delete rows or columns, and move entire rows or columns while retaining most of their properties. Sometimes, however, you may want to transpose a row into a column — or vice versa.

Transposing comes in handy when you need to create a table, a special kind of worksheet discussed in Chapter 4. A table might consist of rows describing

products, with each column describing a feature of the product: its ID, its price, the quantity in inventory, and so on. Tables typically have many rows and fewer columns.

With Excel, you can copy, or transpose, a row into a column and vice versa by using the Paste Special dialog box. To ensure you have room for new worksheet data, you can place the transposed columns or rows on a different worksheet or in a new workbook.

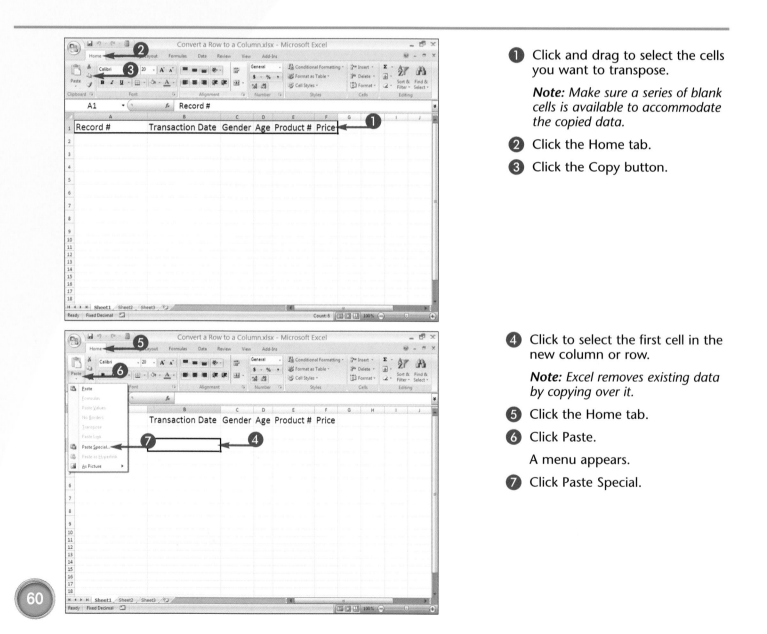

① Click and drag to select the cells you want to transpose.

Note: Make sure a series of blank cells is available to accommodate the copied data.

② Click the Home tab.

③ Click the Copy button.

④ Click to select the first cell in the new column or row.

Note: Excel removes existing data by copying over it.

⑤ Click the Home tab.

⑥ Click Paste.

A menu appears.

⑦ Click Paste Special.

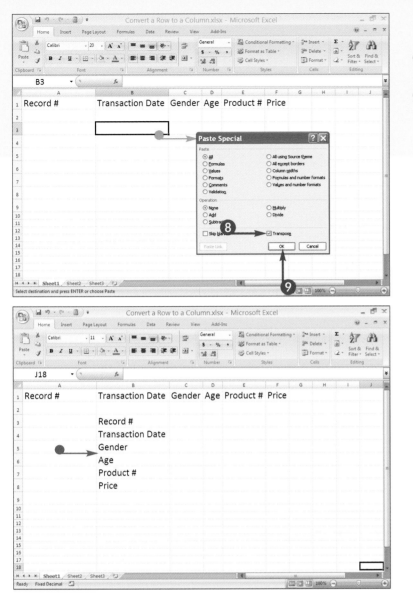

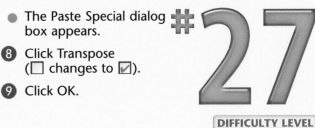
- The Paste Special dialog box appears.

8 Click Transpose
(☐ changes to ☑).

9 Click OK.

- The data appears in its new position.

Did You Know?

With the TRANSPOSE function, you can transpose a grid of cells. Start by selecting an area large enough to hold the new grid. In the Formula bar, type =TRANSPOSE (and then click the Insert Function button. The Function Arguments dialog box appears. Select the cells you want to transpose and then press Ctrl+Shift+Enter. Excel transposes the grid.

Did You Know?

You can avoid rearranging worksheets by designing them carefully. For long lists of people, things, transactions, and so on, arrange them in columns with descriptive column heads. Excel calls this type of layout a table. For more about tables, see Chapter 4.

Copy with the
OFFICE CLIPBOARD

With Office 2007, you can place content into a storage area called the Clipboard and paste the content into Excel or another Office application. Cut and copied content stays on the Clipboard until you close all Office applications. The Office clipboard can store up to 24 cut or copied items. All the items on the Clipboard are available for you to paste to a new location in Excel or in another Office document.

The Clipboard is not visible until you access it. In Excel, access the Clipboard by clicking the launcher

in the Clipboard group of the Home tab. You can use the Clipboard to store a range of cells. The Office Clipboard pastes the entire range, including all the values, but any formulas in the cells are not included when you paste.

After you paste an item from the Clipboard, Excel provides the Paste Options icon menu. You can use the menu to choose whether you want to use the source formatting or the destination formatting on the pasted data.

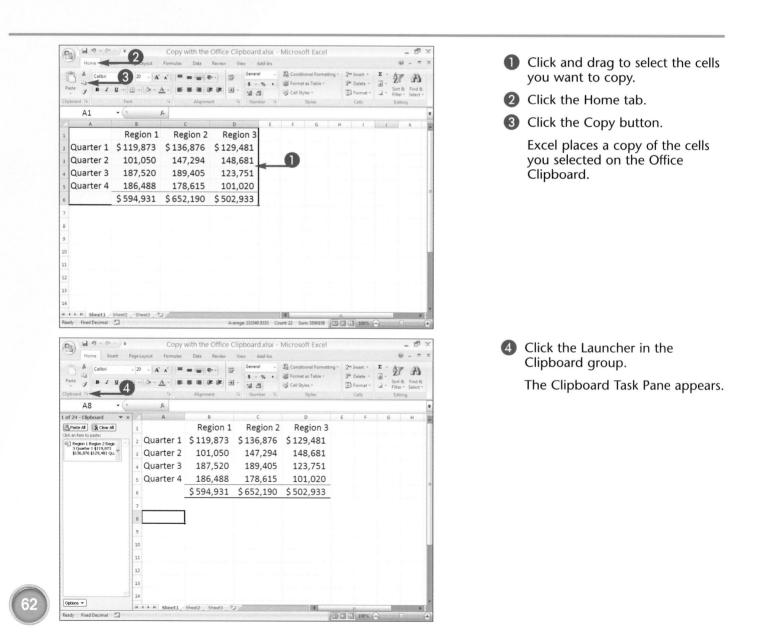

1 Click and drag to select the cells you want to copy.

2 Click the Home tab.

3 Click the Copy button.

Excel places a copy of the cells you selected on the Office Clipboard.

4 Click the Launcher in the Clipboard group.

The Clipboard Task Pane appears.

⑤ Click the destination cell.

⑥ Click the item you want to paste.

● The content is pasted into the new location.

● In the Paste Options icon menu, choose whether to keep the formatting of the copied item or change it to match the formatting of the new location. The default is to match the formatting of the new location. Press Esc to accept the default and remove the menu.

TIPS

Did You Know?

To copy a cell range within or between worksheets, click and drag to select a series of cells and then click the Copy button on the Home tab in the Clipboard group. To paste the range, navigate to the worksheet to which you want to copy the range, click in the cell where you want the range to start, and click Paste on the Home tab in the Clipboard group.

Did You Know?

To keep the Clipboard Task Pane from unexpectedly appearing while you are copying, open the pane, click the Options button on the lower left, and select Collect Without Showing Office Clipboard.

Adjust column widths with
PASTE SPECIAL

By clicking the Copy button on the Home tab, pressing Ctrl+C, or clicking Copy on a contextual menu, you can easily copy the contents of a range of cells so you can paste the contents somewhere else in your worksheet. Cells can contain a lot of information. When you paste with Paste Special, you decide exactly what information you want to paste.

You can choose to paste everything or you can choose to paste just one element of the cell's contents, such as the formula, value, format, comment, validation, or column width.

You can paste more than once. For example, when you paste by clicking Paste, Excel pastes the values, formulas, and formats but does not adjust the column widths. You can remedy this problem by pasting in two steps. In the first step, paste column widths. Excel adjusts the column widths. In the second step, paste your values, formulas, and formats.

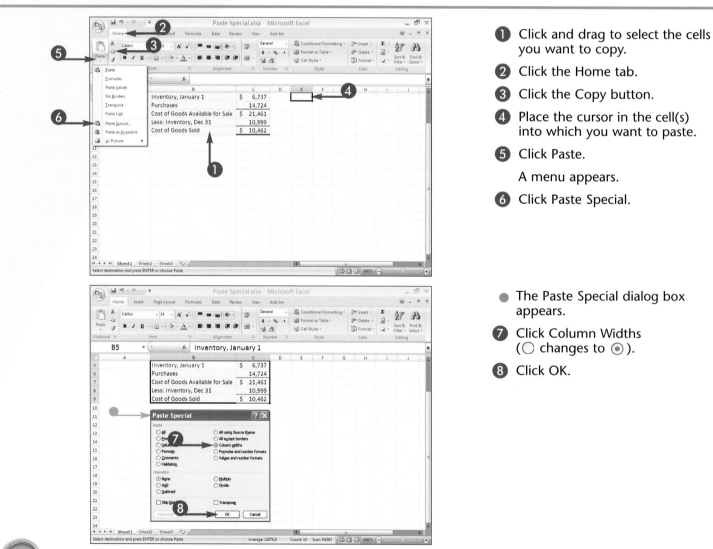

① Click and drag to select the cells you want to copy.

② Click the Home tab.

③ Click the Copy button.

④ Place the cursor in the cell(s) into which you want to paste.

⑤ Click Paste.

A menu appears.

⑥ Click Paste Special.

● The Paste Special dialog box appears.

⑦ Click Column Widths (○ changes to ◉).

⑧ Click OK.

● Excel copies the column widths from the source to the destination.

⑨ Click Paste.

● Excel pastes the contents of the cell.

You can press Esc to end the copy session.

TIPS

Did You Know?

You can choose the Skip Blanks option (☐ changes to ☑) in the Paste Special dialog box if your source includes any blanks. If you do, Excel will not overwrite a destination cell with a blank if the destination cell has data in it.

Did You Know?

You can press Ctrl+C to copy. You can press Ctrl+V to paste. You can press Ctrl+X to cut. Cutting moves data from its current location to the location where you paste it.

Did You Know?

The Office Clipboard holds graphical objects, so you can use it to bring digital pictures, WordArt, and clip art from other programs into Excel.

Specify how to paste with
PASTE SPECIAL

You can use the Format Painter to copy formats from one cell to another. You can also use Paste Special. Simply copy a cell with the format you want, and then use Paste Special to paste the format into other cells. See Chapter 7 to learn more about the Format Painter.

You can use the same steps to copy formulas or values from one location in your worksheet to another. When you want to use a cell's formula in other cells in your worksheet, paste the formula.

When you want the results of a formula but not the formula itself, paste the value.

You can also use Paste Special to perform simple arithmetic operations on each cell in a range. For example, in a list of prices, you may want to increase every price by 10 percent. You can use Paste Special to make the change quickly. Just type **1.10** in a cell and then select Multiply in the Paste Special dialog box.

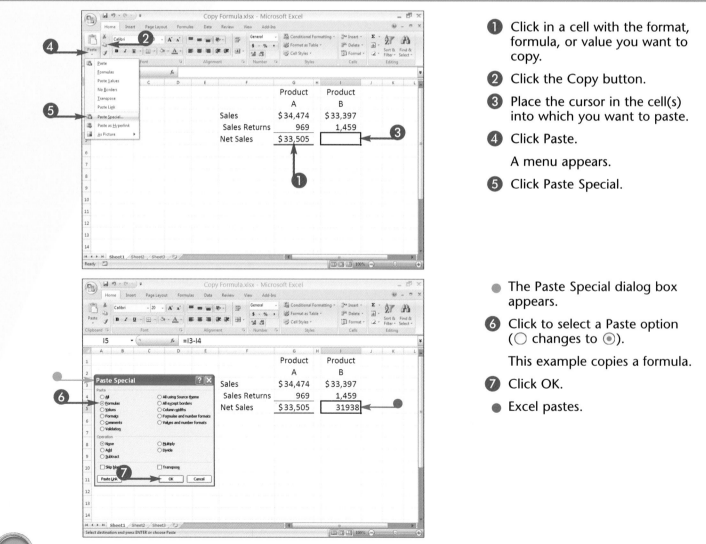

① Click in a cell with the format, formula, or value you want to copy.

② Click the Copy button.

③ Place the cursor in the cell(s) into which you want to paste.

④ Click Paste.

A menu appears.

⑤ Click Paste Special.

● The Paste Special dialog box appears.

⑥ Click to select a Paste option (○ changes to ⊙).

This example copies a formula.

⑦ Click OK.

● Excel pastes.

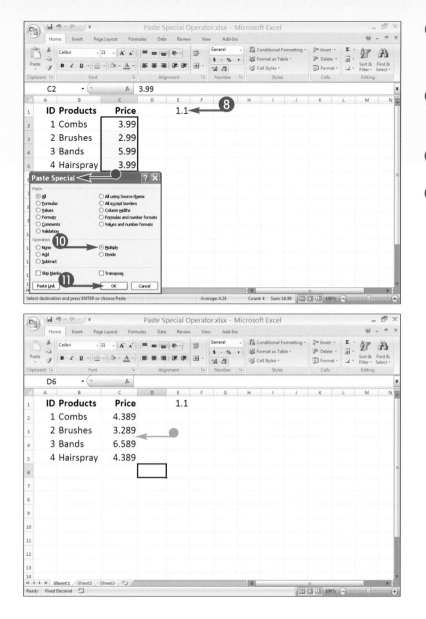

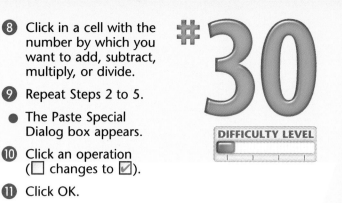

8 Click in a cell with the number by which you want to add, subtract, multiply, or divide.

9 Repeat Steps 2 to 5.

● The Paste Special Dialog box appears.

10 Click an operation (□ changes to ☑).

11 Click OK.

● Excel performs the operation you selected.

TIPS

Did You Know?
You can use the Paste Link option in the Paste Special dialog box to keep your source and destination data synchronized. If you click the Paste Link button when pasting, when you make changes to the source data, Excel automatically updates the destination data.

Did You Know?
You do not have to open the Paste Special dialog box to paste formulas and values. You can select these options directly from the Paste menu on the Home tab.

Create your own
STYLE

By using Excel's many format options, you can easily format numbers, text, and cells. A style is a named collection of formats you can share among users and apply across workbooks. Styles streamline the work of formatting so you and others can apply a consistent set of formats to worksheet elements such as row heads, column heads, and data values. Excel comes with many styles, which you can view in the Style gallery. To apply one of Excel's styles, select the cells you want to apply it to and then click the style.

You can create your own styles. To create a new style based on the current one, right-click the style in the Cell Styles gallery and then click Modify. The Style dialog box appears. Click Format. The Cells dialog box appears. Use the dialog box to select one or more formats. Click OK when you finish. Back in the Style box, give your new style a name, and then click OK.

GROUP FORMATS AS A STYLE

1 Click in a cell with formats you want to use as the basis for a style.

2 Click the Home tab.

3 Click Cell Styles.

The Styles gallery appears.

4 Click New Cell Style.

● The Style dialog box appears.

● This area describes the formats of the cell selected in Step 1.

5 Type a name for your style.

6 Click OK.

You can now apply the style throughout the current workbook.

APPLY A FORMAT STYLE

1 Click and drag to select the cells to which you want to apply the style.

2 Click the Home tab.

3 Click Cell Styles.

The Style gallery appears.

4 Click the style you created.

● Excel applies the style.

DIFFICULTY LEVEL

Did You Know?

You can use the Format Painter to apply styles, and you can copy, and paste formats from one cell to another. However, if you use a format often, consider creating a style. See Task # 71 to learn more about Format Painter.

Apply It!

You can build a style from the ground up rather than basing it on a formatted cell. Click the Home tab and then click Cell Styles. The Style gallery appears. Click New Cell Style and then in the Style dialog box click Format. The Format cells dialog box appears. You can use it to design your style.

COPY STYLES
to another workbook

A style is a collection of formats you use within a workbook. With styles, you maintain consistency in the way numbers, dates, times, borders, and text appear in cells. You can create a style based on any combination of formats available in the Format Cells dialog box, which you access by clicking the Format button in the Styles dialog box. One workbook can contain many styles.

Styles simplify your work and reduce the time required to format worksheets. With styles, you can change many cells at once by creating a style and applying the style to other cells. To use a style in another workbook, copy the style from one workbook to the other. When you copy a style into another workbook, Excel calls that merging.

To copy styles, you need to open both the workbook from which you want to copy the style and the workbook to which you want to apply it.

① Open the file with your custom style.

② Open the workbook into which you want to merge styles.

③ Click the Home tab.

④ Click Cell Styles.

The Styles gallery appears.

⑤ Click Merge Styles.

32

DIFFICULTY LEVEL

● The Merge Styles dialog box appears.

6 Click the workbook whose styles you want to use.

7 Click OK.

● The copied styles are now available in the new workbook.

Conditionally
FORMAT YOUR WORKSHEET

If you want to monitor your data by highlighting certain conditions, Excel's conditional formatting feature can aid you. For example, if your company offers a bonus whenever sales exceed 150,000 dollars, you can have Excel highlight cells containing sales figures whenever the value is more than 150,000 dollars. You can also have Excel highlight a cell when the entry is less than, between, or equal to a specified value. Use Excel's conditional formatting feature to monitor text, dates, duplicate values, the top N, the top N percent, the bottom N,

the bottom N percent, above average values, or below average values.

Changes affect conditionally-formatted data. If, after a change, a cell no longer meets the condition, Excel removes the highlighting. If, after a change, a cell meets the condition, Excel adds highlighting. You determine exactly what the condition is and what should happen if a cell meets the condition. Excel provides you with a list of formats from which to choose, and you can also create a custom format.

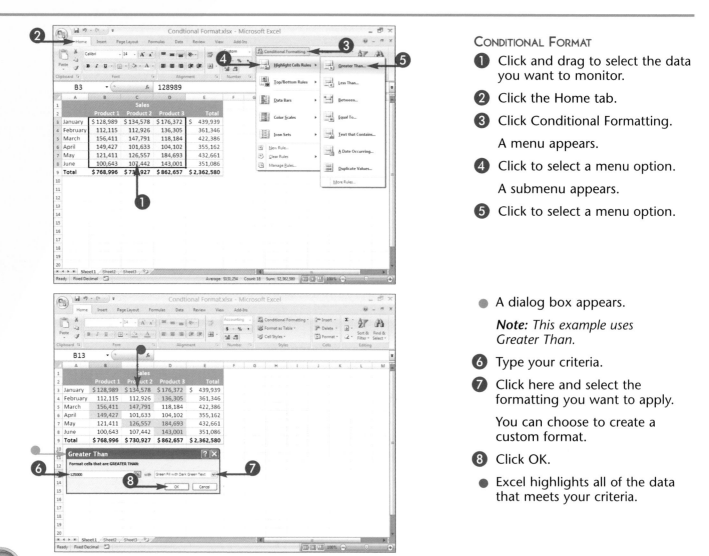

CONDITIONAL FORMAT

① Click and drag to select the data you want to monitor.

② Click the Home tab.

③ Click Conditional Formatting.

   A menu appears.

④ Click to select a menu option.

   A submenu appears.

⑤ Click to select a menu option.

● A dialog box appears.

   Note: This example uses Greater Than.

⑥ Type your criteria.

⑦ Click here and select the formatting you want to apply.

   You can choose to create a custom format.

⑧ Click OK.

● Excel highlights all of the data that meets your criteria.

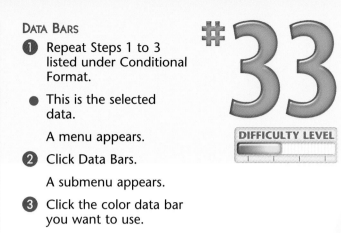

DATA BARS

1 Repeat Steps 1 to 3 listed under Conditional Format.

● This is the selected data.

A menu appears.

2 Click Data Bars.

A submenu appears.

3 Click the color data bar you want to use.

● Excel applies the data bars to the cells you selected.

TIPS

Did You Know?

Excel provides you with several colors to choose from when you add data bars to your worksheet. You can select another color. Click the Home tab and then click Conditional Formatting in the Styles group. A menu appears. Click Data Bars and then click More Rules. The New Formatting Rule dialog box appears. Use the Bar Color field to select a new color. Click OK.

Did You Know?

You can use color scales to conditionally format data. Color scales use gradations of color. For example, if you use Excel's yellow and green color scale, yellow represents lower values and green, higher values. To apply a color scale, select the cells to which you want to apply the scale, click the Home tab, click Conditional Formatting, click Color Scales, and then click the color scale you want to apply.

Conditionally
FORMAT YOUR WORKSHEET

Data bars enable you to discern at a glance how large a value in one cell is relative to the values in other cells. A data bar is a colored bar you place in a cell. The length of the bar represents the value of the cell relative to other cells — the longer the bar, the higher the value. Excel provides you with several bars from which to choose and you can design your own.

Color scales and icon sets are similar to data bars, except color scales use gradients of color to

represent the relative size of the cell value, and icon sets use icons to represent the relative size of the value.

Data bars, color scales, and icon sets all use rules to determine when to display what. You can use the rules defined by Excel or you can create your own rules. At the bottom of the data bar, color scale, or icon set menu, click More Rules to adjust rules.

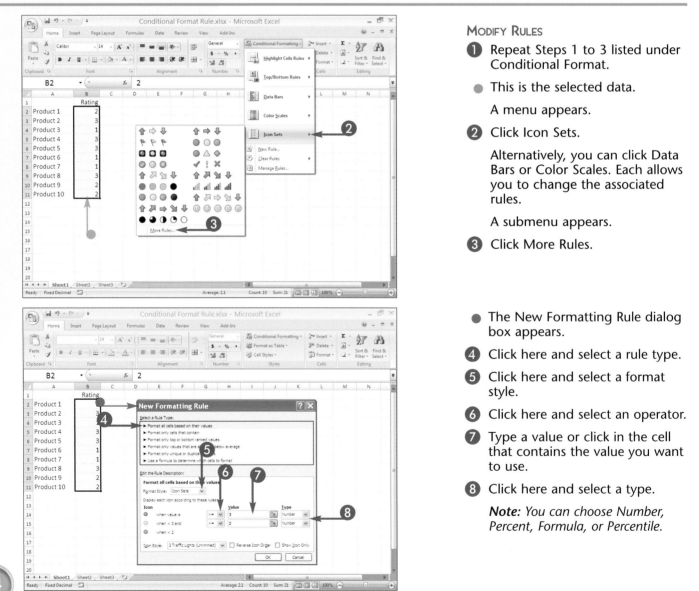

MODIFY RULES

1. Repeat Steps 1 to 3 listed under Conditional Format.

● This is the selected data.

   A menu appears.

2. Click Icon Sets.

   Alternatively, you can click Data Bars or Color Scales. Each allows you to change the associated rules.

   A submenu appears.

3. Click More Rules.

● The New Formatting Rule dialog box appears.

4. Click here and select a rule type.

5. Click here and select a format style.

6. Click here and select an operator.

7. Type a value or click in the cell that contains the value you want to use.

8. Click here and select a type.

   Note: You can choose Number, Percent, Formula, or Percentile.

9 Click here and select an icon style.

10 Click OK.

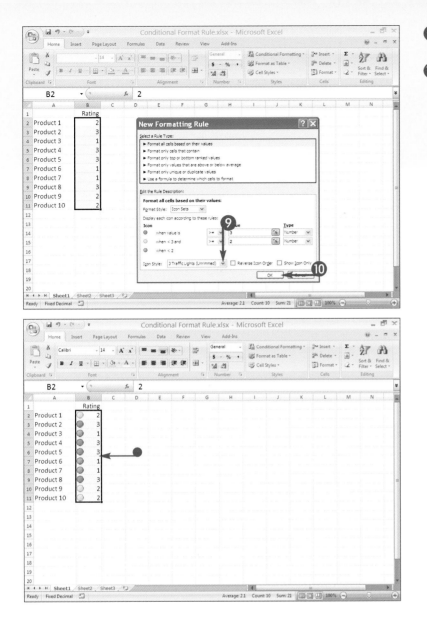

● Excel displays the results of your rule.

Did You Know?
You can Sort by Cell Color, Font Color, or Icon. Right-click in any cell that has conditional formatting applied to it. A context menu appears. Click Sort and then select the appropriate sort option. To learn more see Task #40.

Did You Know?
If you click Show Icon Only, Show Bar Only, or Show Color Only in the New Formatting Rule dialog box (☐ changes to ☑), Excel displays icons, bars, or color, but not the values in each cell.

TRACK CHANGES
while editing

If you work in a networked environment and several people work on the same worksheet, you may need to account for who makes what change, in which cells, and when. To do so, you can use the Track Changes feature.

In the Highlight Changes dialog box, use the When, Who, and Where options. Use When to define the time after which edits are tracked — for example, after a specific date or since you last saved. Use Who to identify the group whose edits you want to

track — for example, everyone in the workgroup, everyone but you, or a named individual. Use Where to specify the rows and columns whose data you want to monitor.

When someone makes a change, Excel indicates the change by placing a small purple triangle in the upper-left corner of the changed cell. Excel records cell changes in automatically generated cell comments. You can view these comments by moving your mouse pointer over the cells.

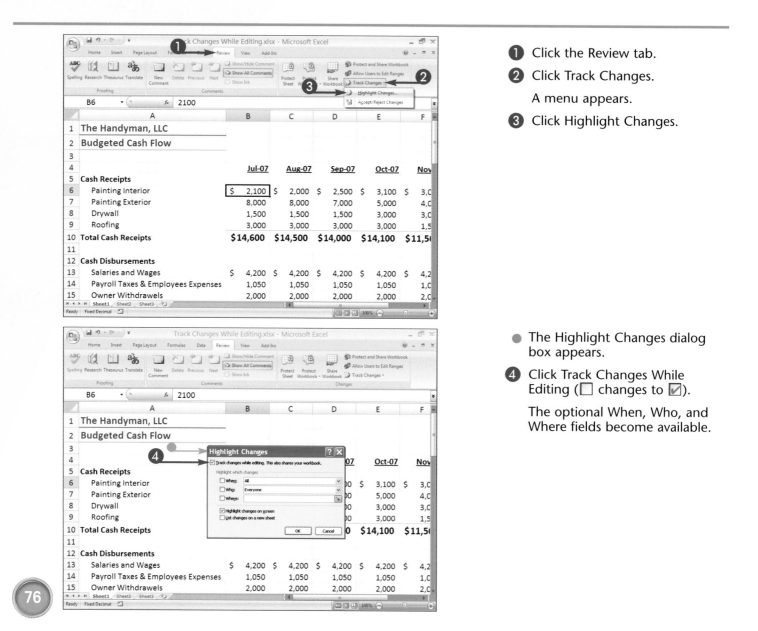

① Click the Review tab.

② Click Track Changes.

A menu appears.

③ Click Highlight Changes.

● The Highlight Changes dialog box appears.

④ Click Track Changes While Editing (☐ changes to ☑).

The optional When, Who, and Where fields become available.

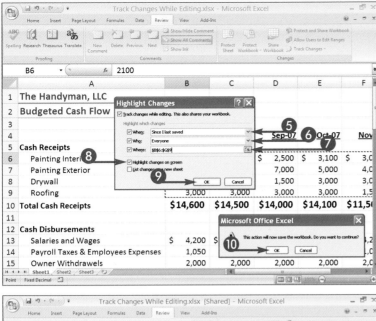

⑤ Click here and select when to track changes.

⑥ Click here and select whose changes to track.

⑦ Type the cell range, or click and drag to select the cells you want to monitor.

⑧ Click Highlight Changes On Screen to insert a purple flag into edited cells (☐ changes to ☑).

⑨ Click OK.

⑩ A message informs you that Excel has saved your workbook. Click OK.

● Purple flags appear in edited cells.

● To view a cell's comment, move your cursor over the cell.

Note: *For more about comments, see Task #7.*

TIPS

Did You Know?

To view all worksheet changes after you or others make edits, open the Highlight Changes dialog box and click the List Changes on a New Sheet option (☐ changes to ☑). For the Who field, click Everyone. Click to uncheck the When and Where fields. Click OK. Excel creates a new worksheet called History that shows each change, the type of change, the values changed, the person who made the change, and so on. You can sort and filter the worksheet.

Did You Know?

You can review every change made to a worksheet and either accept or reject the change. Click the Review tab, click Track Changes, and then click Accept/Reject Changes. The available options let you restrict your review to changes by certain people and at certain times.

CONSOLIDATE
worksheets

If you keep related data in separate worksheets, or for that matter, separate workbooks, you may eventually want to consolidate. For example, if you keep sales information for several regions on separate worksheets, you may want to consolidate the worksheets to find the total sales for all regions. Excel's Consolidate feature allows you to do just that. Excel provides a variety of functions you can use to consolidate including SUM, COUNT, AVERAGE, MAX, MIN, and PRODUCT.

You start the consolidation process by selecting the location for your consolidated data. You may want to format your cells so that the incoming data displays properly. You then select the function you want to use to consolidate you data. The SUM function takes the data from each location you specify and adds it together. You tell Excel the location of the data you want to consolidate. The data can be in the same workbook or another workbook. Excel takes the data and consolidates it.

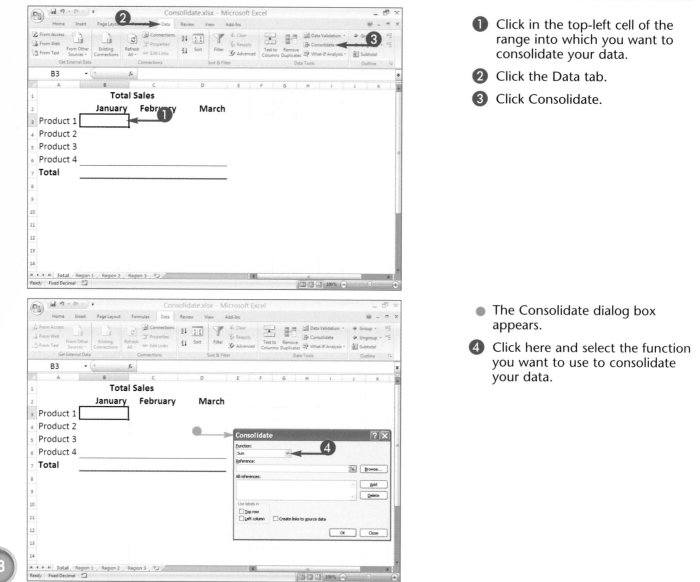

① Click in the top-left cell of the range into which you want to consolidate your data.

② Click the Data tab.

③ Click Consolidate.

● The Consolidate dialog box appears.

④ Click here and select the function you want to use to consolidate your data.

78

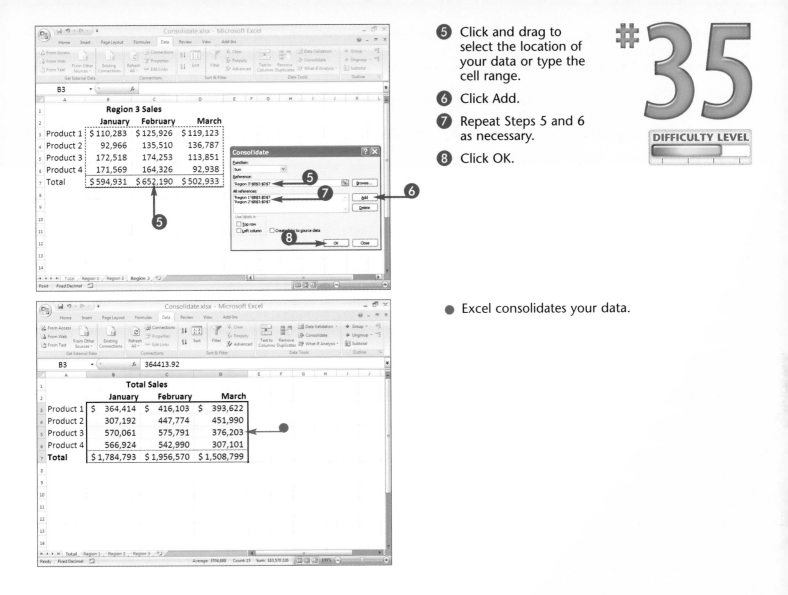

⑤ Click and drag to select the location of your data or type the cell range.

⑥ Click Add.

⑦ Repeat Steps 5 and 6 as necessary.

⑧ Click OK.

● Excel consolidates your data.

TIPS

Did You Know?

To include data from another workbook in your worksheet, open the other workbook. In the Consolidate dialog box in your original workbook, place your cursor in the Reference field. Click the View tab, click Switch Windows, and select the other workbook. Click and drag to specify the data you want to consolidate. Click Add. Click OK. Excel consolidates the data.

Did You Know?

If you click Create Links to Source Data (☐ changes to ☑) in the Consolidate dialog box, Excel updates your consolidated data each time you make a change to the data on which you base your consolidation.

Chapter 4

Manipulate Records

A list is a set of columns and rows. Each column represents a single type of data. For example, a list might have three columns: name, gender, and age. Each row in the list is a record. For each record in the list, the name column contains a name, the gender column contains a gender, and the age column contains an age. When you structure a worksheet as a list, you can tap the Excel database-like capabilities that go beyond what is possible with a simple worksheet.

This chapter shows you how to work with lists and other data that you structure as lists. Much of the chapter focuses on sorting and filtering. To sort means to arrange a list in order, either alphabetically or numerically. You can sort and re-sort lists as necessary and even sort within a sort. To filter means to display only the information that meets certain criteria — temporarily hiding the rest.

Advanced filtering gives you tools for filtering out duplicate records and applying multiple complex filters to your data.

With data formatted as a list, you can count, average, and subtotal parts of your data that meet certain criteria. In a customer survey, for example, you can count the number of senior citizens who prefer a certain sport or compare the time spent online among different age groups in different communities. You carry out calculations by using the Ribbon or by using database functions. Refer to Chapter 2 to learn more about functions.

When you organize data into a list, you have access to lookups, a special way of searching for data. You might use a lookup to retrieve a stock price by typing a stock symbol. You can also create a powerful analytical tool called a PivotTable, which is discussed in Chapter 5.

Top 100

ENTER DATA
with a form

Creating a list is a two-step process: First, you create the structure, which consists of a series of text labels, one per cell, each describing the content of a column. Then you enter the data. Excel enables you to generate a form to simplify data entry.

A form simplifies and speeds up data entry by providing a blank field for each column in your table. You type the data and press the Tab key to move from field to field. After you complete one set of

fields, you enter them into a row in your list and start entering a new set of fields. You can move backward and forward through your list to view or modify your data. The list form also doubles as a search box you can use to retrieve values.

You must add the Form button to the Quick Access toolbar before you can use forms. See Task #95 to learn how to add a button to the Quick Access toolbar.

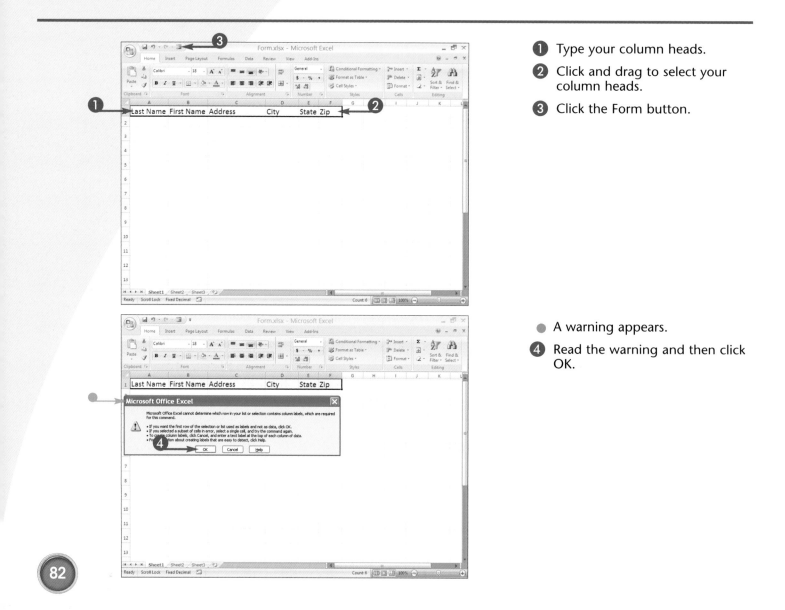

① Type your column heads.

② Click and drag to select your column heads.

③ Click the Form button.

● A warning appears.

④ Read the warning and then click OK.

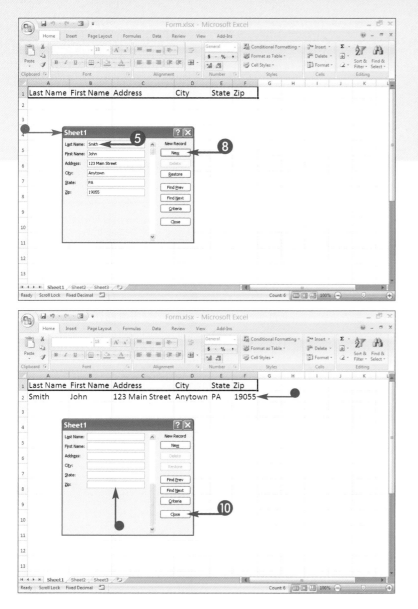

- The data form appears, consisting of one field for each column head you created.

5 Type the requested information in the first field.

6 Press Tab to move to the next field.

7 Repeat Steps 5 and 6 to complete the remaining fields.

8 After completing the first set of fields, click New to start a new record.

- The data fills the worksheet, and the form fields clear, ready for another record.

9 Repeat Steps 5 to 8 for each new record.

10 Click Close after entering all your data.

A list of your data records appears in the worksheet.

TIPS

Did You Know?

You can use the data form to search for and edit your data. With the list and form displayed, click the form's Criteria button. In a blank field, type an operator, such as **=** or **>**, and a value in one or more fields. For example, to find all records for Sally, you would type **="Sally"** in the First Name field and then press Enter. If several records are available, click the Find Prev (Previous) and Find Next buttons as appropriate. If you are looking for text, place the text you are looking for in quotes; if you are looking for a number, do not place the number in quotes.

Did You Know?

You can use a form with an existing list. Just click and drag to select the column heads and then click the Form button on the Quick Access toolbar.

Filter
DUPLICATE RECORDS

Excel provides many tools for managing long lists. With such lists, you may find you need to identify and display unique records. A baseball-card collector, for example, may want to find the number of unique players represented in his collection so he can create a catalog. Alternatively, a store manager may want to know the number of unique individuals represented in her survey to help her make informed decisions about customer needs.

Excel provides tools for displaying only unique records in a list. Start with a worksheet formatted as

a list in which some of the records are duplicates, meaning the values in every column are the same. Use Excel's advanced filtering tools to identify and remove from view the duplicated records. Ordinarily, you use advanced filtering tools to create filters in several columns or even several filters on a single column.

If you want to remove duplicate records permanently, use the Remove Duplicates option on the Data tab.

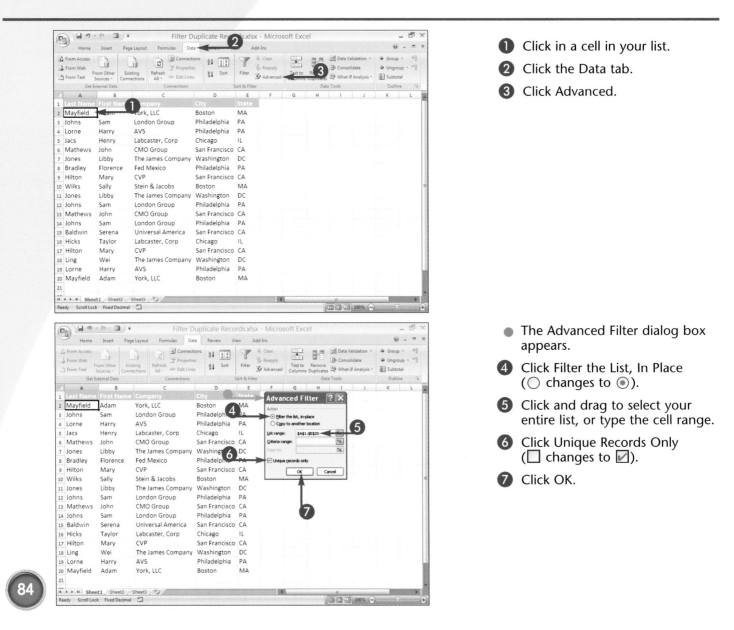

① Click in a cell in your list.

② Click the Data tab.

③ Click Advanced.

● The Advanced Filter dialog box appears.

④ Click Filter the List, In Place (○ changes to ◉).

⑤ Click and drag to select your entire list, or type the cell range.

⑥ Click Unique Records Only (□ changes to ☑).

⑦ Click OK.

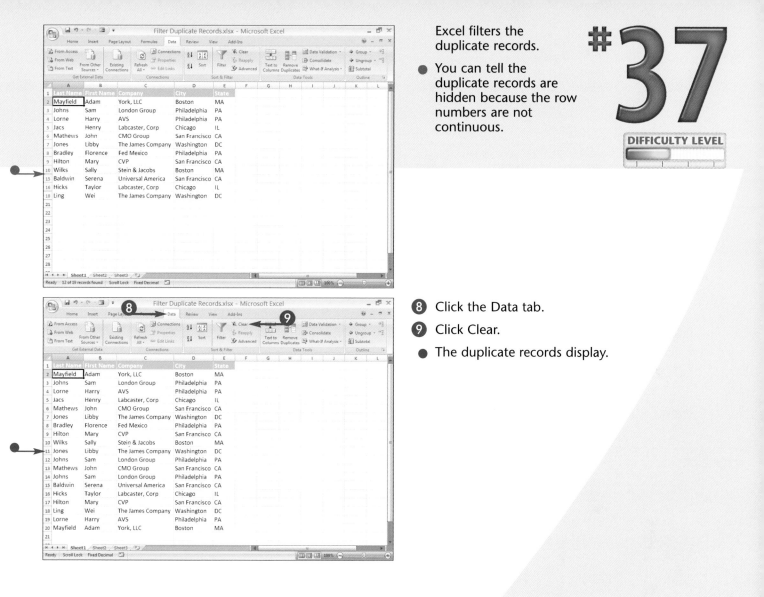

Excel filters the duplicate records.

● You can tell the duplicate records are hidden because the row numbers are not continuous.

DIFFICULTY LEVEL

⑧ Click the Data tab.

⑨ Click Clear.

● The duplicate records display.

TIPS

Did You Know?

If you want to retain you unfiltered list, you can place your filtered list in another area of you worksheet. In the Advanced Filter dialog box, click Copy To Another Location (○ changes to ⦿) and then enter the location where you want to place your filtered list in the Copy To field.

Did You Know?

Filtering duplicate records temporarily removes them from view. If you want to delete duplicate records permanently, select your list, click the Data tab, and then in the Data Tools group click Remove Duplicates. The Remove Duplicates dialog box appears. If your list has headers, click My Data Has Headers (☐ changes to ☑). Select the columns you want to check for duplicates and then click OK. Excel deletes the duplicate records.

Perform simple
SORTS AND FILTERS

Sorting and filtering your lists offers different views of your data. When you sort, you rearrange your data in ascending or descending order.

The meaning of these terms depends on the kind of data you have. Customer data arranged by the date in ascending order shows the earliest record first; descending order shows the latest record first. When you sort by customer name, the names appear in ascending (A to Z) or descending (Z to A) order. When you sort numeric data in ascending order, the

numbers sort from the lowest number to the highest. In descending order, numbers sort from the highest to the lowest. When you sort a list, you can easily find data, group data, and present it meaningfully to others.

Filtering works like a sieve through which you pass your data, displaying only data that meets your criteria. In a customer survey, for example, you can choose to view only customers who live in a certain state or city or are of a certain age or gender.

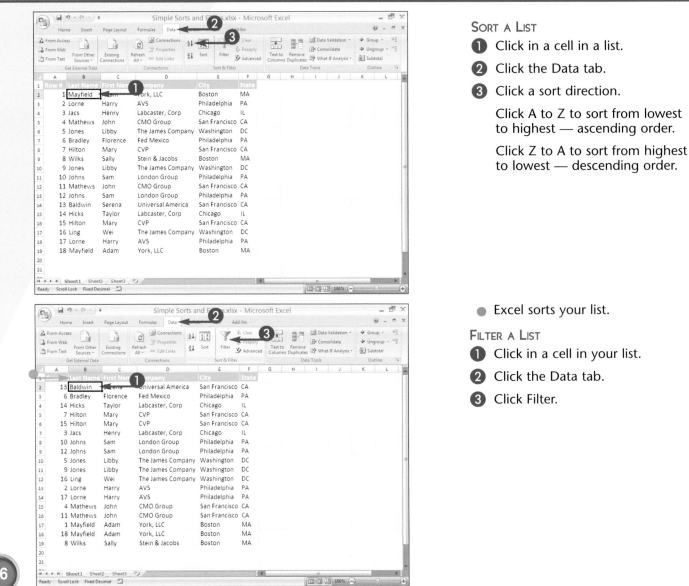

SORT A LIST

1 Click in a cell in a list.

2 Click the Data tab.

3 Click a sort direction.

Click A to Z to sort from lowest to highest — ascending order.

Click Z to A to sort from highest to lowest — descending order.

● Excel sorts your list.

FILTER A LIST

1 Click in a cell in your list.

2 Click the Data tab.

3 Click Filter.

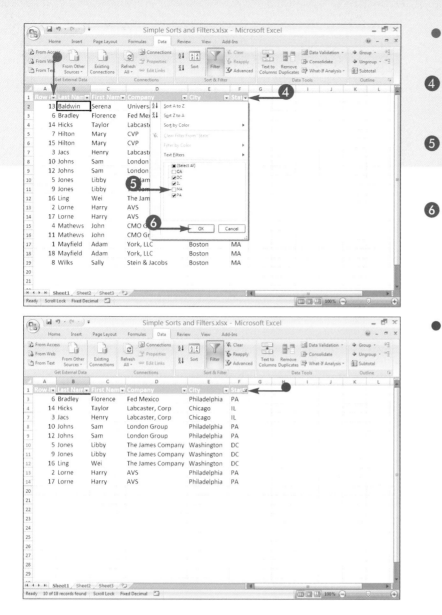

● Down arrows appear next to your field headers.

④ Click a down arrow.

The Sort and Filter dialog box appears.

⑤ Click to deselect the items you do not want to appear (☑ changes to ☐).

⑥ Click OK.

38

● Excel filters your list.

In this example, CA and MA do not appear.

Did You Know?

When you click the down arrow Excel creates when you click Filter, Excel provides options for filtering your data. It also provides options for sorting your data. You can perform simple sorts, complex sorts, or you can sort by cell color, font color, or icon. See Task #s 39 and 40 to learn more about sorting.

Did You Know?

When you perform a filter, Excel places down arrows next to your field headers. Fields you have filtered have a filter button (🔽) on the down arrow. Fields you have sorted in ascending order have an up-arrow button on the down arrow (🔼). Fields you have sorted in descending order have a down-arrow button on the down arrow (🔽).

Perform
COMPLEX SORTS

Sorting a list by one criterion, such as age, arranges your records for easy scanning. You can also sort by multiple criteria — a sort within a sort. When possible, sort first by a discrete category such as gender, community, region, or department. That way, subsequent sorts apply to the multiple values contained within each category.

For example, after sorting your customer records by community, you could sort them by gender to display the communities in which the men and women live. Sorting by a third column, income, would then show how men's and women's incomes differ in each community.

With your data sorted in this way, you can create subtotals, averages, and counts at every break in a category — that is, for all people in a specific community, for men and women in that community, and so on.

You define all sorts in the Sort dialog box. Ascending and descending are not your only choices. In the Sort dialog box, you can click Options to specify a custom order. For example, you could order months chronologically from January to December instead of alphabetically from April to November, which, in most cases, would not be useful.

① Click in a cell in your list.
② Click the Data tab.
③ Click Sort.

● The Sort dialog box appears.
④ Click here and select the column by which you want to sort.
⑤ Click here and select Values.
⑥ Click here and select a sort order.
⑦ Click the Add Level button.

39

- A new level appears.

8 Repeat Steps 4 and 5 to sort by an additional criterion.

9 Click here and select Custom List.

- The Custom Lists dialog box appears.

10 Click to sort by days of the week or months of the year.

11 Click OK to close the Custom Lists dialog box.

12 Click OK to close the Sort dialog box.

- The list sorts according to the sort order specified, along with any options chosen.

Rec No	City	Day of Week	Amount Earned
1	Chicago	Monday	860.00
4	Chicago	Tuesday	3310.00
7	Chicago	Wednesday	1233.00
10	Chicago	Thursday	1225.00
13	Chicago	Friday	2730.00
2	New York	Monday	1970.00
5	New York	Tuesday	2838.00
8	New York	Wednesday	1885.00
11	New York	Thursday	3253.00
14	New York	Friday	2443.00
3	Philadelphia	Monday	1791.00
6	Philadelphia	Tuesday	3152.00
9	Philadelphia	Wednesday	2946.00
12	Philadelphia	Thursday	638.00
15	Philadelphia	Friday	2407.00

TIPS

Did You Know?

Excel defines different sorts as follows. For numbers, ascending order goes from the smallest number to the largest. For text that includes numerals, as in U2 and K12, ascending order places numerals before symbols and symbols before letters. Case does not matter unless you click Options in the Sort dialog box and then click the Case Sensitive check box (☐ changes to ☑).

Did You Know?

In the Sort dialog box, click Delete Level to delete a level of sort. Click Copy Level to copy a level of sort. Click ⬆ to move a sort level up. Click ⬇ to move a sort level down.

SORT
by cell color, font color, or icon

You can use conditional formatting to set criteria and then format your data based on that criteria. For example, you can have the highest ten values in a list appear in a particular color or font or with an icon. You can have values that meet other criteria appear in another color or font or with another icon. See Task #33 to learn how to conditionally format your data. You can then sort your data based on the cell color, font, or icon you assign.

You can also manually assign cells a font or cell color. Then you can sort cells by these colors. Select a single column and then click a sort button on the Ribbon to sort your data. You can nest your sorts. In the Sort dialog box, you can select the color you want to sort by and then tell Excel whether you want to send items of that type to the top or the bottom of the list.

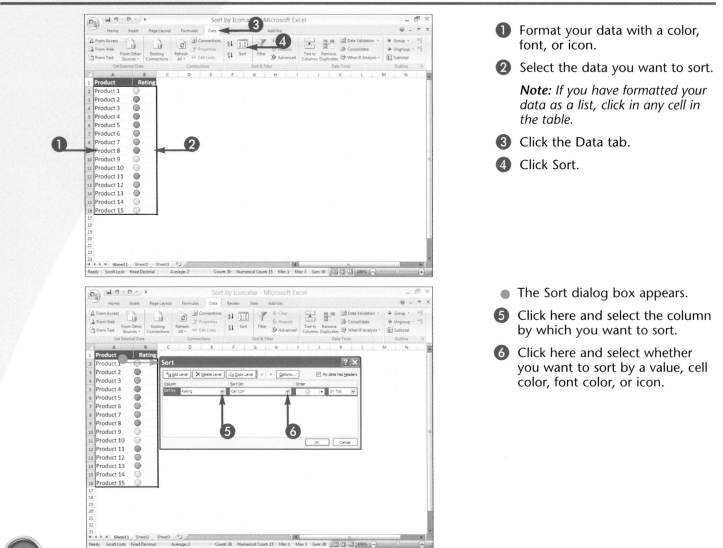

① Format your data with a color, font, or icon.

② Select the data you want to sort.

Note: *If you have formatted your data as a list, click in any cell in the table.*

③ Click the Data tab.

④ Click Sort.

● The Sort dialog box appears.

⑤ Click here and select the column by which you want to sort.

⑥ Click here and select whether you want to sort by a value, cell color, font color, or icon.

40

- If you select Cell Color, Font Color, or Cell Icon, an Order field appears.

⑦ Click here and select a color or icon.

⑧ Click here and select from On Top or On Bottom.

Click On Top to send the items that match the criteria to the top of the list.

Click On Bottom to send the items that match the criteria to the bottom of the list.

⑨ Click the Add Level button to add another level of sort.

Repeat Steps 5 to 8, as necessary.

⑩ Click OK when you finish.

- Excel sorts your data by font, color, or icon.

TIPS

Did You Know?

An alternative way to sort by color, font, or icon is to right-click in any cell that has the color, font, or icon by which you want to sort. A menu appears. Click Sort. Another menu appears. Click to choose from Put Selected Cell Color on Top, Put Selected Font Color on Top, or Put Selected Icon on Top.

Did You Know?

By default, Excel sorts from top to bottom. If you want to sort from left to right, click Options in the Sort dialog box. The Sort Options dialog box appears. Click Sort Left to Right.

Perform
COMPLEX FILTERS

Whereas sorting rearranges all records in ascending or descending order, filtering enables you to see only the records that match your criteria, hiding the rest. Criteria look like this: Age is greater than 65 and State equals Missouri, where Age and State are the names of column heads. When you filter a list, down arrows appear to the right of every column head.

Click a column's arrow to select values, such as Missouri or Age greater than 65. By applying a filter, you display only those records that contain certain values in the column — for example, all customers in

Missouri or all men over 65. You can also create a filter that displays the records for a column's top ten values. With Excel, you can combine filters, applying different criteria to different columns.

By applying several filters, you can quickly narrow down a long list to the few records of interest to you. Criteria that apply to too narrow a range of values, however, might not return any records. To filter a list by multiple criteria, start with a worksheet formatted as a list.

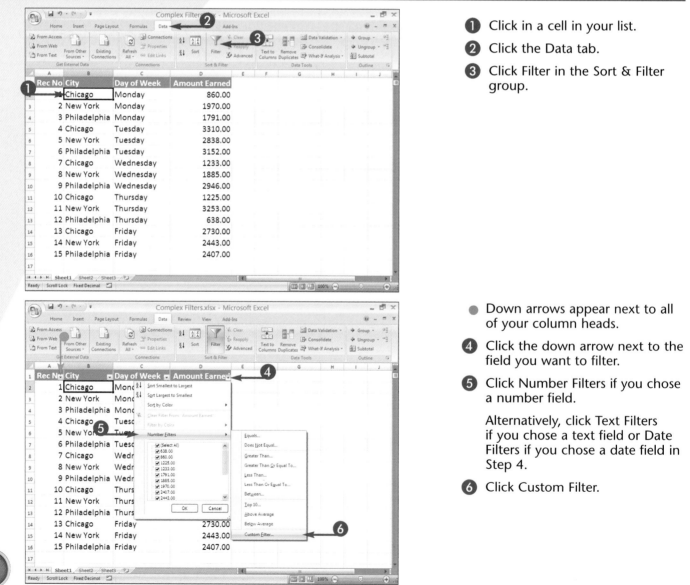

1. Click in a cell in your list.
2. Click the Data tab.
3. Click Filter in the Sort & Filter group.

● Down arrows appear next to all of your column heads.

4. Click the down arrow next to the field you want to filter.

5. Click Number Filters if you chose a number field.

   Alternatively, click Text Filters if you chose a text field or Date Filters if you chose a date field in Step 4.

6. Click Custom Filter.

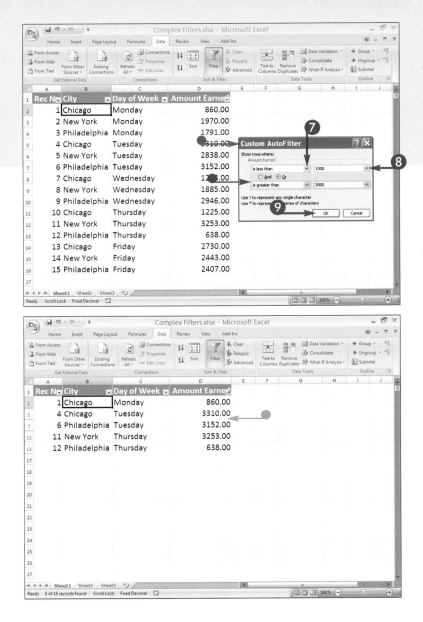

41

- The Custom AutoFilter dialog box appears.

⑦ Click here and select an operator.

⑧ Type a value or select a value.

- You can repeat Steps 7 and 8 if you want to create a second criterion. Choose And if you want both criteria to be met. Choose Or if you want either criteria to be met.

⑨ Click OK.

- The list displays records matching your criteria.

Note: To sort the filtered records, click the Data tab and then click a sort option.

TIP

Did You Know?

You can use a filter to view the top or bottom N values in a list, where N stands for the number of values you want to view. Click the down arrow next to the numeric field you want to filter. A menu appears. Click Number Filters and then click Top Ten. The Top 10 AutoFilter dialog box appears. Select Top if you want to view the Top N values. Click Bottom, if you want to view the bottom N values. Type the number of values you want to view and then select whether you want Excel to return results based on a number or a percentage. Click OK. Excel returns the results you request.

Filter by
MULTIPLE CRITERIA

With advanced filtering, you can go beyond the limitations of the AutoFilter command discussed in Task #41. With advanced filtering, you can create two or more filters and easily coordinate a set of filters between columns. For example, you can filter a survey to find people age 30 or younger who are male and people age 60 or older who are female.

Advanced filtering requires a bit of work, even when you use the Advanced Filter menu command. You must find a block of cells on the worksheet and

create a criteria range. Use one or more column heads from a list. In the cell below each head, type criteria by which to filter each column, such as <=35, to find people 35 and under and = "=M" to find all males.

Using the Advanced Filter dialog box, you specify the cell addresses of the entire list, the criteria range, and a location for the filtered list. The filtered list must be on the same worksheet as the original list.

1 On the worksheet with your list, type the column head names of the columns you want to filter.

2 Type criteria by which you want to filter values.

Note: Use operators to define criteria and place text in quotes. For example, to find all males, type = "=M"; Excel will display =M.

3 Click the Data tab.

4 Click Advanced.

● The Advanced Filter dialog box appears.

⑤ Click to indicate where to place the filtered list (○ changes to ⦿).

You can click Copy To Another Location to copy the list to another location and retain the original list.

⑥ Click and drag to select or type the range for the entire list.

⑦ Click and drag to select or type the range for the criteria defined in Step 2.

⑧ If you chose to copy the filtered list in Step 5, click in the first cell for the filter.

⑨ Click OK.

● The filtered list appears.

You may need to format the results to accommodate wide columns.

TIPS

Did You Know?

A criteria range can have several rows of criteria. When a row consists of two or more criteria, Excel looks through your list and returns only the rows that meet all criteria. If you want Excel to return records that meet either criteria place the criteria on separate rows.

Caution!

Make sure your Copy To range has enough room below it to include all the values that may return in the filtered list. If you place the Copy To range above your original list, the results may overwrite the list and disrupt the filtering. Placing the copy to the side of the list or below it protects your original list.

SUBTOTAL
sorted data

After you sort and group your data into categories such as gender or age, you can perform a calculation on each category. Excel provides the tools for performing simple calculations to compare one category with another. With a sort defined for at least one column, you can find the average, sum, min, max, number of items, and much more for that column or another column. Excel calls the feature that enables you to perform calculations on columns subtotaling, even though you can use it to do more than subtotal.

Subtotaling uses outlining to hide data so you can compare rows or columns. When you calculate the average, sum, or other calculation for a sorted list, outlining enables you to view only the results of the calculation.

Note that with subtotals, you can do a count on a column with text entries. In other circumstances, the COUNT function works only with numbers.

1. Click in a cell in your sorted list.
2. Click the Data tab.
3. Click Subtotal.

- The Subtotal dialog box appears.
4. Click here and select the category by which you want to subtotal.
5. Click here and select the type of calculation you want to perform.
6. Click one or more columns to subtotal (☐ changes to ☑).
7. Click OK.

- The list appears with the outlining controls that enable you to compare the results.

⑧ To compare results in different rows, click the minus signs (-).

 # 43

DIFFICULTY LEVEL

Product Line	Store Location	Projected Sales	Actual Sales
Balls	NJ	15,000	14,279
Balls	DE	2,400	14,279
Balls	PA	150,000	114,369
Balls Max		150,000	114,369
Candy	NJ	23,000	21,569
Candy	DE	8,000	7,654
Candy	PA	46,000	52,639.00
Candy Max		46,000	52,639.00
Dolls	NJ	20,000	19,562.00
Dolls	DE	2,000	19,562
Dolls	PA	40,000	41,876
Dolls Max		40,000	41,876
Games	NJ	75,000	123,000
Games	DE	4,500	123,000
Games	PA	8,000	7,812
Games Max		75,000	123,000
Puzzles	NJ	5,000	2,187
Puzzles	DE	1,000	2,187
Puzzles	PA	46,900	96,521
Puzzles Max		46,900	96,521

- Only the result rows appear.

⑨ To redisplay all results, click the plus signs (+).

All results display.

Product Line	Store Location	Projected Sales	Actual Sales
Balls Max		150,000	114,369
Candy Max		46,000	52,639.00
Dolls Max		40,000	41,876
Games Max		75,000	123,000
Puzzles Max		46,900	96,521
Trucks Max		30,200	32,148
Grand Max		150,000	123,000

TIPS

Did You Know?
You can create several subtotals for a single sorted list. To display all your subtotals, make sure the Replace Current Subtotals check box is not checked when you use the Subtotal dialog box.

Did You Know?
You can remove outlining by clicking the Data tab, and then in the Outline group, clicking Ungroup and Clear Outline.

Did You Know?
Remember that you can do a calculation on a different column from the one defining the sort. For example, if you sort by gender in one column, you can find the average salary or age for men or women and place the results in their respective columns, such as an income column or age column.

Chapter 4: Manipulate Records 97

CHART FILTERED DATA
easily

With Excel, you can quickly create a chart showing the information in a worksheet or list. Charts show trends and anomalies that may otherwise be difficult to detect in columns of numbers. By choosing the appropriate type of chart and formatting chart features, you can share your results with others and convey patterns in your data. For more about charting, see Chapter 6.

To create a chart, select the data you want to chart, click the Insert tab, and then click a chart type.

Excel creates a chart. You can position your chart next to the data on which you base it, so when you change the data you can instantly observe the changes in the chart.

By default, as you filter your data, Excel removes the filtered data from your chart. If you do not want Excel to remove filtered data, select the Show Data in Hidden Fields option in the Hidden and Empty Cell Settings dialog box.

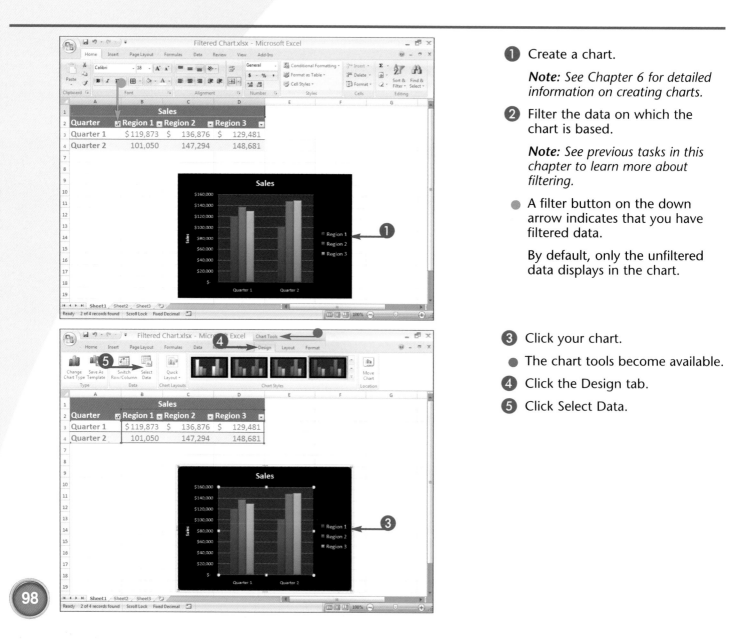

① Create a chart.

Note: See Chapter 6 for detailed information on creating charts.

② Filter the data on which the chart is based.

Note: See previous tasks in this chapter to learn more about filtering.

● A filter button on the down arrow indicates that you have filtered data.

By default, only the unfiltered data displays in the chart.

③ Click your chart.

● The chart tools become available.

④ Click the Design tab.

⑤ Click Select Data.

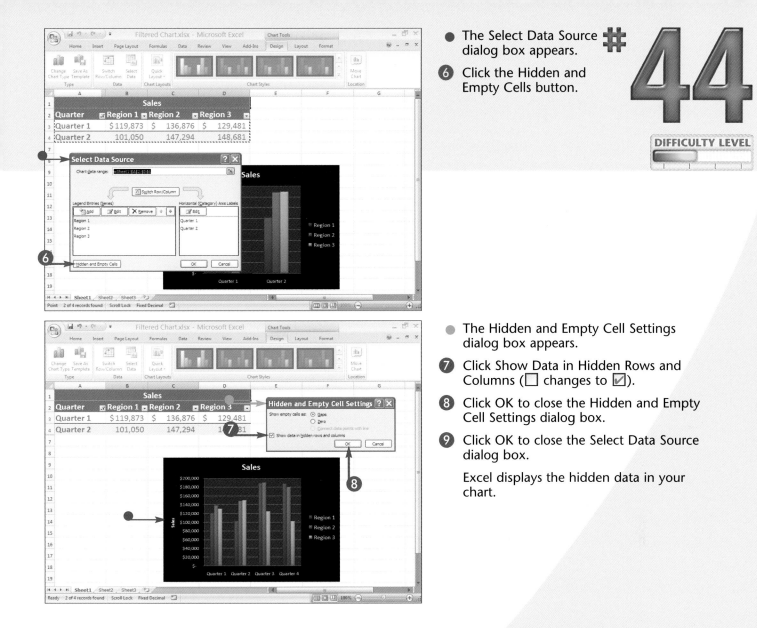

- The Select Data Source dialog box appears.

6 Click the Hidden and Empty Cells button.

- The Hidden and Empty Cell Settings dialog box appears.

7 Click Show Data in Hidden Rows and Columns (☐ changes to ☑).

8 Click OK to close the Hidden and Empty Cell Settings dialog box.

9 Click OK to close the Select Data Source dialog box.

Excel displays the hidden data in your chart.

TIPS

Did You Know?

If you want to reposition a chart, click the chart. A border with triple dots on all four sides of the chart and on the corners appears. Roll your mouse pointer over the dots. When your mouse pointer turns into a four-headed arrow, you can click and drag your chart.

Did You Know?

You can delete the graphical representation of a value from a chart. For example, you can delete the graphical representation of Region 2 in the chart shown in this task. Just click the graphic and then press the Delete key.

COUNT
filtered records

Like the standard worksheet functions, database functions enable you to perform calculations and summarize data patterns. You use database functions with lists. Database functions are especially good at summarizing the subsets of your list. Most database functions combine two tasks: They filter a group of records based on values in a single column, and then they count them or perform another simple operation on the filtered data.

DCOUNT is a database function that counts the number of cells containing a number. DCOUNT takes

three arguments. The first argument, Database, identifies the cell range for the entire list. The second argument, Field, identifies the cell range for the column from which you want to extract data. In the third argument, Criteria, you provide Excel a criterion for extracting information. For example, your criterion in a sales list could be Net Sales>5,000, where Net Sales is the column name. You build the criterion manually, copying a column head and defining a condition in the cell below it.

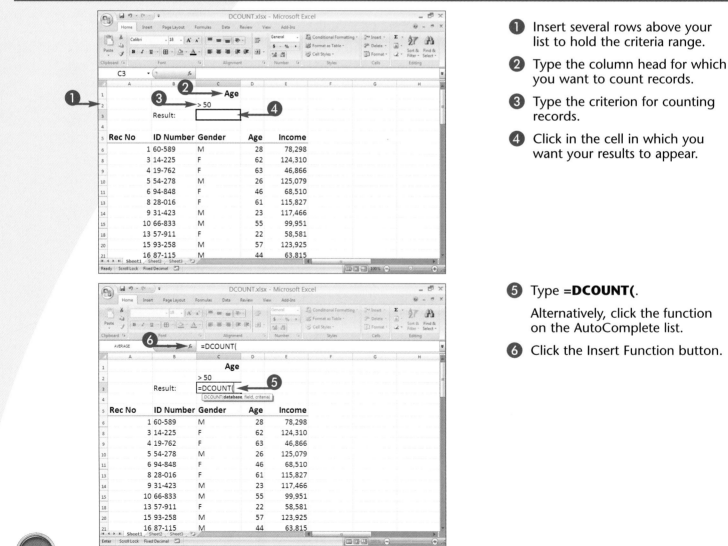

① Insert several rows above your list to hold the criteria range.

② Type the column head for which you want to count records.

③ Type the criterion for counting records.

④ Click in the cell in which you want your results to appear.

⑤ Type **=DCOUNT(**.

Alternatively, click the function on the AutoComplete list.

⑥ Click the Insert Function button.

The Function Arguments dialog box for DCOUNT appears.

⑦ Click and drag all the cells in your list, or type the cell range.

⑧ Type the column name within quotation marks.

Alternatively, you can type the column's number or the column's range.

⑨ Click and drag or type the cell range from Steps 2 and 3.

⑩ Click OK.

● The result appears.

Note: The DCOUNT function counts only cells containing numbers. For nonnumeric data, use the DCOUNTA function.

TIPS

Did You Know?

The names of database functions begin with a D to distinguish them from worksheet functions. As with worksheet functions, you can use the Function Wizard to build database functions. Type the function into a cell, for example =DCOUNT(), and click the Insert Function button.

Did You Know?

You can use the DSUM function to add numbers that match the criteria you specify. You can use DAVERAGE to find the average of numbers that match the criteria you specify. These functions use the same arguments as DCOUNT: database, field, and criteria range.

LOOK UP INFORMATION
in your worksheet

By using the VLOOKUP function, you can enter a product's ID and retrieve its price. Use VLOOKUP when you know one value, such as the product ID, and need to look up another value, such as price.

Before you can use VLOOKUP, you must sort your list in ascending order, and the first column of your list must contain the values you want to use to retrieve another value. Specify the column from which you want to retrieve the corresponding value.

You can use the Function Wizard to enter your VLOOKUP arguments. You must enter three required

arguments: the cell address containing the value you want to use to retrieve another value, the list's cell range, and the column that contains the value you want to retrieve. For simplicity, call the first column in the list 1, the second column 2, and so on.

The VLOOKUP function has an optional fourth argument called range lookup. If you enter TRUE or leave this argument blank, the function looks for the closest match to the value you seek. If you enter FALSE, the function returns only exact matches.

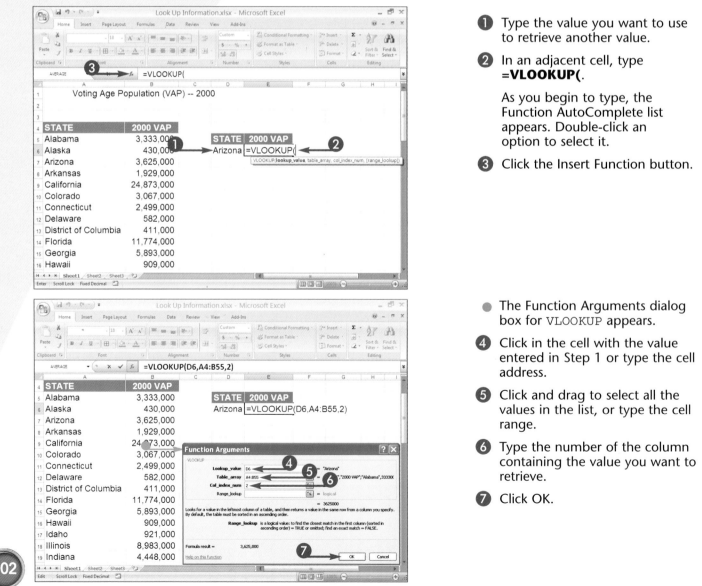

① Type the value you want to use to retrieve another value.

② In an adjacent cell, type **=VLOOKUP(**.

As you begin to type, the Function AutoComplete list appears. Double-click an option to select it.

③ Click the Insert Function button.

● The Function Arguments dialog box for VLOOKUP appears.

④ Click in the cell with the value entered in Step 1 or type the cell address.

⑤ Click and drag to select all the values in the list, or type the cell range.

⑥ Type the number of the column containing the value you want to retrieve.

⑦ Click OK.

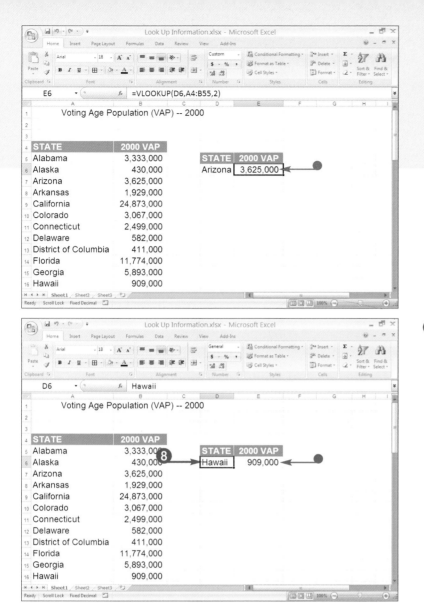

- The cell containing the formula displays the value corresponding to the lookup value.

46

8 Type another lookup value.

- The cell containing the formula displays the value corresponding to the lookup value.

Did You Know?

The closely related but less commonly used HLOOKUP function finds a value in a row based on another value in the same row.

Caution!

When using VLOOKUP, if you are searching text data, make sure the column you are searching does not contain any leading spaces, trailing spaces, inconsistent use of curly and straight quotation marks, or nonprinting characters. These situations can cause VLOOKUP to bring back an incorrect result. For the same reason, if you search dates, make sure you format your dates as dates, not text.

DEFINE DATA
as a table

A table is a set of columns and rows where each column represents a single type of data. For example, your table might have three columns: name, gender, and age. For each row in your table, the name column contains a name, the gender column contains a gender, and the age column contains an age. You can define worksheet rows and columns as a table.

When you define rows and columns as a table, sort and filter drop-down lists are automatically added to each column head, enabling you to readily sort and

filter your data. Defining a table is simple. In fact, you can define an existing worksheet as a table. Before you start, make sure your data is arranged in columns and rows, each with a descriptive column head.

Defining rows and columns as data also makes Design tools available. You can use the design tools to format your table quickly.

You should avoid blank cells and blank spaces at the beginning of a table cell because they make sorting difficult.

① Click and drag to select the data you want to define as a table.

Include column heads.

② Click the Insert tab.

③ Click Table in the Tables group.

● The Create Table dialog box appears.

● The data range you selected appears here.

④ Click here if your table has headers (☐ changes to ☑).

⑤ Click OK.

Excel converts your data to a table.

- The Table tools become available.

- Each column has a drop-down arrow that you can click to sort and filter.

Note: *Refer to the other tasks in this chapter to learn how to sort and filter.*

6 Click the Design tab.

7 Click Total Row
(☐ changes to ☑).

- Excel places a total at the end of your table.

8 Click a field in the Total row.

A down arrow appears next to the field.

9 Click the down arrow and then select how you want to total the column.

Excel totals your column.

TIPS

Did You Know?

An Excel table is primitive when compared with the data management capabilities of Access or server-based databases. You can create worksheets in Excel and then export them into Access, where you can maintain and incorporate the sheets into a set of data tables. For more information, see Task #92.

Did You Know?

You can convert a table back to a regular range of cells. Click anywhere in your table, click the Design tab, and then click Convert to Range in the Tools group. At the prompt, click Yes. Excel converts the table to a normal range and removes the drop-down arrows.

Modify a
TABLE STYLE

Table styles format the rows and columns of your table to make your table easier to read. When you create a table, Excel applies the default style. You can easily change or remove any style applied to your table. Excel provides you with a large gallery of styles from which to choose. As you roll your cursor over each style in the gallery, Excel gives you a quick preview of how each style will appear when applied.

Excel also provides a number of table-style options you can use to modify your table. By choosing banded rows or banded columns, you can have every other row or every other column appear in a different color. You can also apply special formatting to the last column or the first column in your table if you want the titles, totals, or information in those columns to stand out. Table styles make your table more attractive and user friendly.

① Click in any cell in your table.

● The Table tools become available.

② Click the Design tab.

③ Click the down arrow in the Table Styles group.

A gallery of styles becomes available.

④ Click a style to apply the style to your table.

⑤ Click Clear to remove a style from your table.

⑥ Right-click a style.

A menu appears.

⑦ Click Set As Default.

Excel makes the style the default style.

DIFFICULTY LEVEL

⑧ Click to remove banded rows (☑ changes to ☐).

⑨ Click for banded columns (☐ changes to ☑).

⑩ Click to apply special formatting to the first column (☐ changes to ☑).

⑪ Click to apply special formatting to the last column (☐ changes to ☑).

● Excel formats your table.

Did You Know?

You can easily add columns to your table. Click in any cell in your table. The Table tools become available. Click the Design tab and then click Resize Table in the Properties group. The Resize Table dialog box appears. Click and drag to select the new range, or type the range in the Select the New Data Range for Your Table field. Click OK.

Did You Know?

You can create your own table style. The easiest way is to modify an existing style. Click in any cell in your table and then click the Design tab. Click the down arrow in the Table Styles group. A gallery of styles appears. Click the style you want to modify and then right-click. A menu appears. Click Duplicate. The Modify Table Quick Style dialog box appears. Use it to modify your style.

Chapter 5

Explore the Patterns in Your Data

Excel offers you much more than a way of keeping track of your data and doing calculations. It also provides tools to analyze your data and thus to understand it better and make better decisions. In this chapter, you learn about a range of tools that can give you rich insights into your data.

One of the most useful tools, the PivotTable, is also one of the least understood. Similar to cross-tabulation in statistics, a PivotTable shows how data is distributed across categories. For example, you can analyze data and display how different products sell by region and by quarter. Alternatively, you can analyze income distribution or consumer preferences by gender and age bracket. Excel makes it easy for you to answer useful questions about your data.

This chapter also introduces Excel's statistical functions. These statistics were once available only through large, expensive statistical software packages. You will learn to use descriptive statistics to characterize your data and to explore associations between data series by using the correlation function. For the statistically adept, Excel also includes more advanced functions.

Finally, you learn to do two related analytical tasks: what-if analysis and goal seeking. With what-if analysis, you vary an input to find how it affects a result. With goal seeking, you start with a goal and try to achieve it by varying a single factor.

Create a
PIVOTTABLE

PivotTables help you answer questions about your data. PivotTables are based on lists. Lists are made up of rows and columns. You can use a worksheet list or you can connect to a list from another data source, such as Access. For more information on lists, see Chapter 4.

The row and column labels of a PivotTable usually have discrete information, meaning the values fall into categories. For example, gender is a discrete variable because all values are either male or female.

Quarter is another discrete variable because all values fall into one of four quarters — Quarter 1, Quarter 2, Quarter 3, or Quarter 4. Salary and weight are not discrete but continuous because a wide range of values is possible for each.

The body of a PivotTable — the data area — usually has continuous data to show how the data are distributed across rows and columns. For example, you could show how the number of units sold is distributed among sales regions in different quarters.

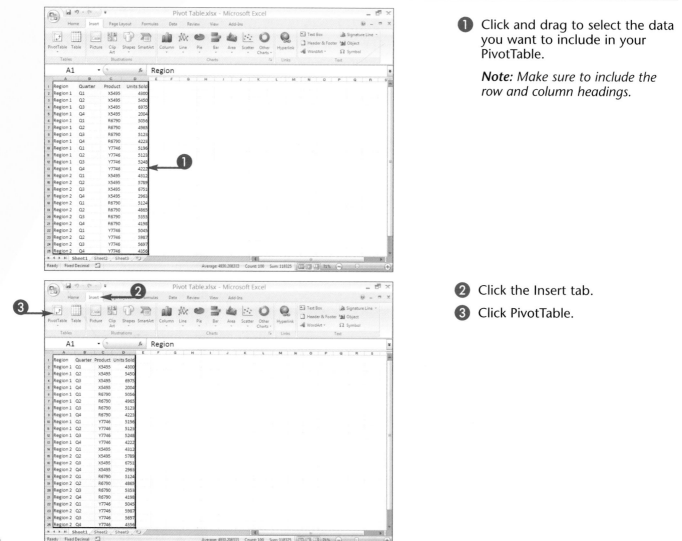

① Click and drag to select the data you want to include in your PivotTable.

Note: *Make sure to include the row and column headings.*

② Click the Insert tab.

③ Click PivotTable.

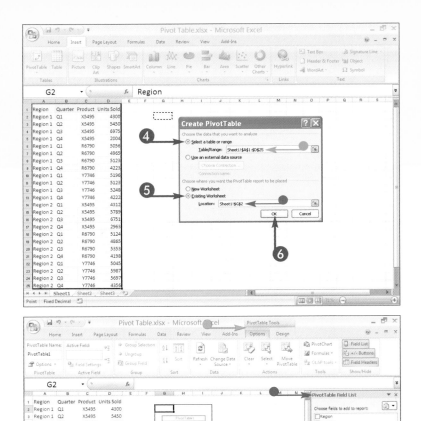

The Create PivotTable dialog box appears.

④ Click a data source (○ changes to ⊙).

● If you selected a range in the current workbook, the range appears here.

⑤ Click to select where to place the report (○ changes to ⊙).

● If you want to place the list in the existing worksheet, click the cell in which you want to place the list, or type a location.

⑥ Click OK.

● Excel opens the PivotTable Field List.

● The PivotTable tools become available.

TIPS

Delete It!
If you want to remove a PivotTable from your worksheet, click anywhere in the PivotTable. The PivotTable tools become available. Click the Options tab. Click Select in the Actions group. A menu appears. Click Entire Table. Excel selects the entire table. Press the Delete key. Excel deletes your PivotTable.

Caution!
PivotTables are based on lists. When creating a PivotTable, do not use a list with blank columns or rows. Excel may not create the PivotTable correctly if the list includes a blank column or row.

Create a
PIVOTTABLE

The PivotTable layout consists of several elements: report filters, data, columns, and rows. Use the PivotTable Field List to organize the elements. When working with a PivotTable, you can bring the Field List into view by clicking anywhere in the PivotTable, clicking the Options tab, and then clicking Field List.

To construct a PivotTable, choose the fields you want to include in your report and then drag fields from the PivotTable Field List into the Report Filter, Column Labels, Row Labels, and Σ Values boxes. You can click

and drag more than one field into an area. Report Filter fields enable you to filter the data that appears in your report. Row Label fields show as row labels down the left side of your PivotTable, and Column Label fields show as column labels across the top of your PivotTable. Place your continuous data fields in the Σ Values box. Fields placed in the Σ Values box make up the data area. You can sort and filter your PivotTable column and row data, and you can arrange and rearrange field layouts.

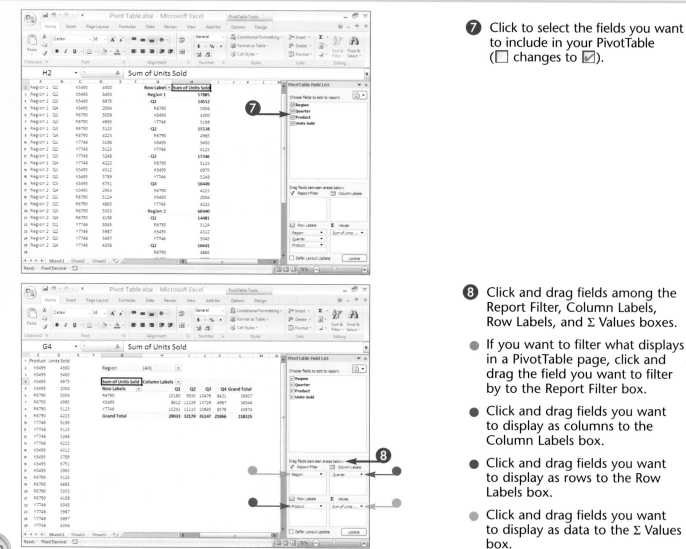

7 Click to select the fields you want to include in your PivotTable (☐ changes to ☑).

8 Click and drag fields among the Report Filter, Column Labels, Row Labels, and Σ Values boxes.

● If you want to filter what displays in a PivotTable page, click and drag the field you want to filter by to the Report Filter box.

● Click and drag fields you want to display as columns to the Column Labels box.

● Click and drag fields you want to display as rows to the Row Labels box.

● Click and drag fields you want to display as data to the Σ Values box.

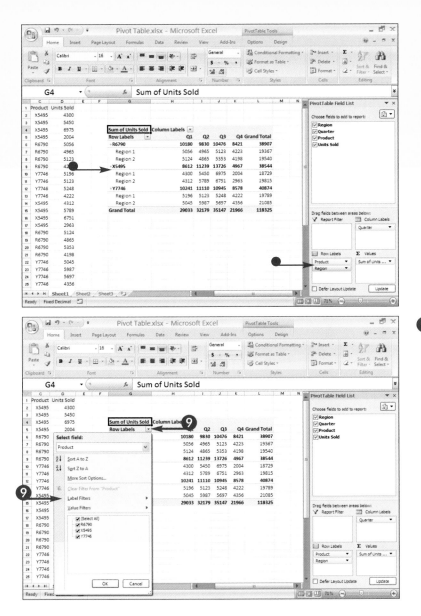

- As you build the PivotTable, your changes instantly appear.

⑨ Click the field header and then choose your sort and filter options.

Note: For more information on sorting and filtering, see Chapter 4.

TIPS

Customize It!

To change the way the PivotTable Field List displays, click the Field List button (⊞ ▾), which is located in the upper right-hand corner of the PivotTable Field List box. A menu appears. Choose from the options listed.

Did You Know?

Field and column labels appear in the order you place them in the Column and Row Labels box. You can change the display order by clicking and dragging the fields within the box.

Modify
PIVOTTABLE DATA AND LAYOUT

PivotTables help you answer essential questions about your data. To extend the value of PivotTables, Excel allows you to change the data on which they are based and the manner in which they are laid out.

PivotTables can easily get quite complex. Fortunately, you need not regenerate and re-edit a table every time the underlying data changes. Instead, you can refresh a table by clicking Refresh.

You can easily change the layout of a PivotTable by clicking the Design tab and choosing the PivotTable style and layout you want. Excel 2007 has many predesigned styles from which you can choose.

You can decide whether you want your PivotTable to have row headers, column headers, banded rows, or banded columns. Excel 2007 also lets you display your table in a compact, tabular, or outline form. Try each form to determine which one displays your data best.

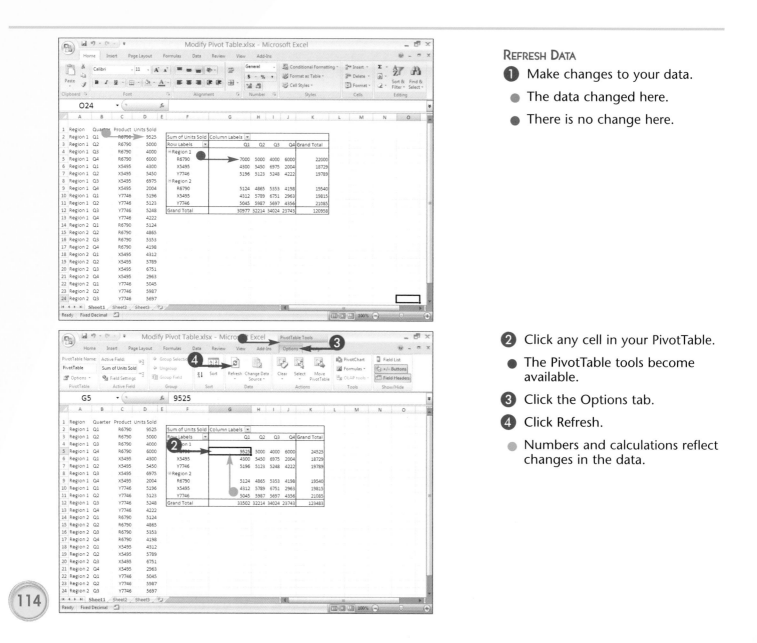

REFRESH DATA

① Make changes to your data.

● The data changed here.

● There is no change here.

② Click any cell in your PivotTable.

● The PivotTable tools become available.

③ Click the Options tab.

④ Click Refresh.

● Numbers and calculations reflect changes in the data.

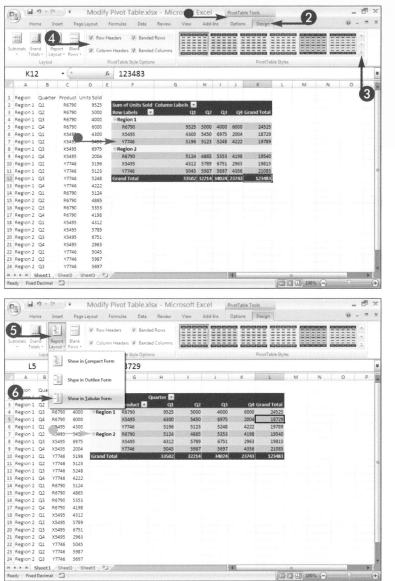

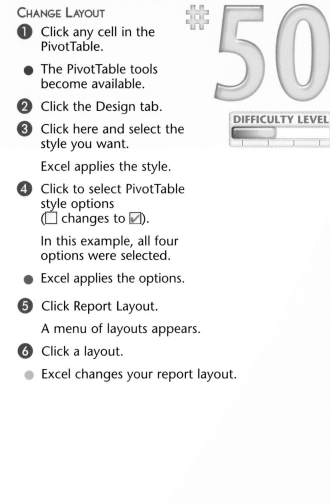

CHANGE LAYOUT

1. Click any cell in the PivotTable.

● The PivotTable tools become available.

2. Click the Design tab.

3. Click here and select the style you want.

   Excel applies the style.

4. Click to select PivotTable style options (☐ changes to ☑).

   In this example, all four options were selected.

● Excel applies the options.

5. Click Report Layout.

   A menu of layouts appears.

6. Click a layout.

● Excel changes your report layout.

TIPS

Did You Know?

By default, Excel creates or modifies your PivotTable as you click and drag fields among the Report Filter, Column Labels, Row Labels, and Σ Values boxes. If you do not want your PivotTable created or modified dynamically, click the Defer Layout Update check box (☐ changes to ☑) at the bottom of the PivotTable Field List and then click the Update button when you are ready to create or modify your PivotTable.

Did You Know?

If you choose the Design tab and then click Blank Rows in the Layout group, you can add — or remove — a blank line after each data group.

Compute PivotTable
SUB AND GRAND TOTALS

You can use PivotTables to compare and contrast the distribution of data across categories. You may need a variety of statistics to examine differences between categories. To aid you, PivotTables can automatically calculate subtotals and grand totals for the columns and rows in your list. When calculating subtotals and grand totals, you have a choice of calculations from which to choose, including sum, average, count, standard deviation, minimum, and maximum.

To change the summary statistic, open the Value Field Settings dialog box and choose the type of

calculation you want to use to summarize your data. Changing the type of calculation used to generate values in a row or column can result in improperly formatted data. To remedy this, use the Number Forward button in the PivotTable Field dialog box to access the number-formatting capabilities of the Format Cells dialog box. You may, for example, want to add a thousands separator so you see 7,236,273 instead of 7236273.

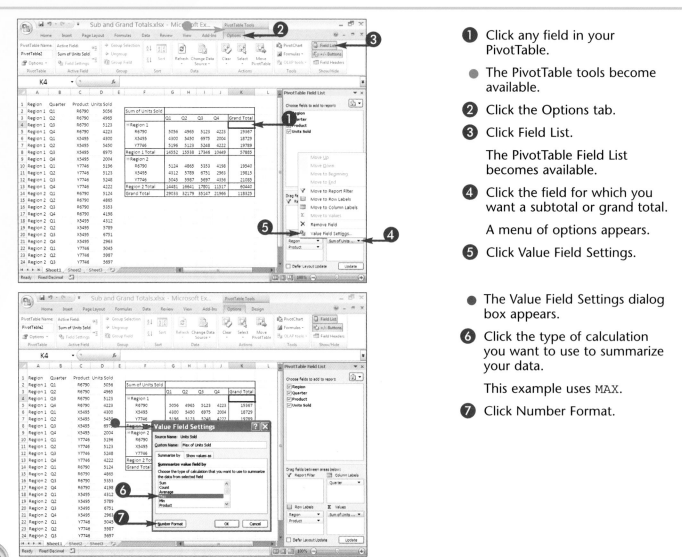

① Click any field in your PivotTable.

● The PivotTable tools become available.

② Click the Options tab.

③ Click Field List.

The PivotTable Field List becomes available.

④ Click the field for which you want a subtotal or grand total.

A menu of options appears.

⑤ Click Value Field Settings.

● The Value Field Settings dialog box appears.

⑥ Click the type of calculation you want to use to summarize your data.

This example uses MAX.

⑦ Click Number Format.

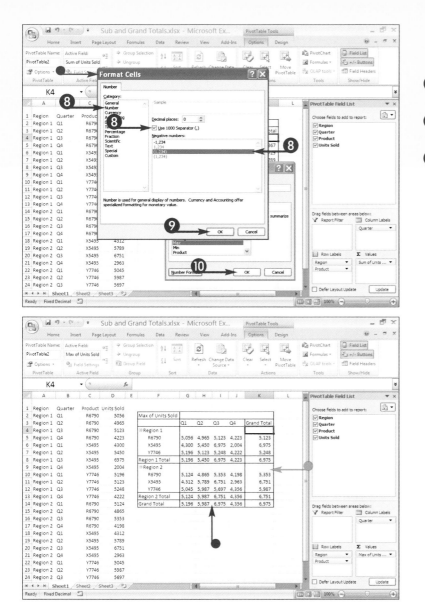

- The Format Cells dialog box appears, displaying only the Number tab.

⑧ Click to select formatting options.

⑨ Click OK to close the Format Cells dialog box.

⑩ Click OK to close the Value Field Settings dialog box.

- Excel recalculates the PivotTable.
- Excel reformats the numbers.

TIPS

Change It!

In the Design tab Layout group, click Subtotals to tell Excel whether you want to show subtotals and whether the subtotals should show at the top or the bottom of the group. Click Grand Totals to tell Excel whether you want to show grand totals for rows and columns, just for rows, or just for columns

Did You Know?

A cell in a PivotTable may summarize several rows of information. To view the underlying data for a cell, double-click it. The rows appear in a new worksheet. Changes you make to the new worksheet have no effect on the original data.

Create a PivotTable
CALCULATED FIELD

Within a PivotTable, you can create new fields, called *calculated fields*, which you base on the values in existing fields. You create a calculated field by performing simple arithmetic on every value in the existing column. Your formula can include functions; operators such as +, −, *, and /; and existing fields, including other calculated fields.

You usually use calculated fields with continuous data such as incomes, prices, miles, and sales. For example, you can multiply each value in a field called

Price by a sales tax rate to create a calculated field called Tax. Use the Insert Calculated Field dialog box to name your calculated field and create the formula you want to use. You can also use this dialog box to modify existing calculated fields or delete fields you no longer want to use.

Your calculated fields are available in the PivotTable Field List for use in your PivotTable. You can use the values in the calculated field only in data cells.

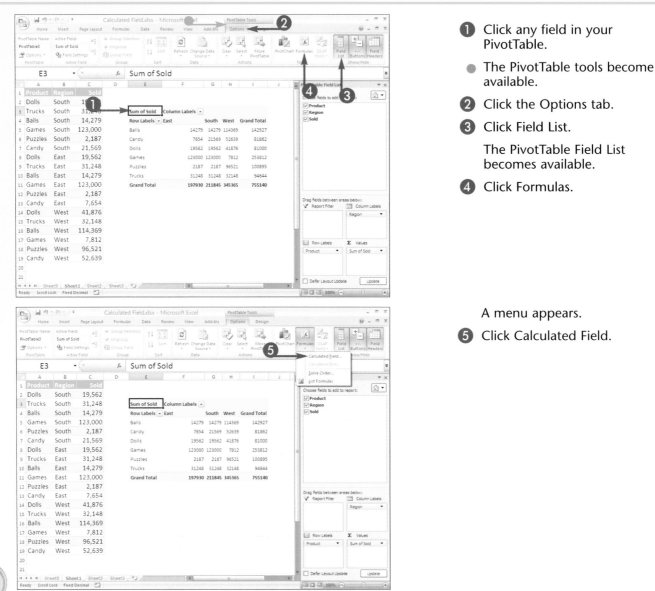

1 Click any field in your PivotTable.

● The PivotTable tools become available.

2 Click the Options tab.

3 Click Field List.

The PivotTable Field List becomes available.

4 Click Formulas.

A menu appears.

5 Click Calculated Field.

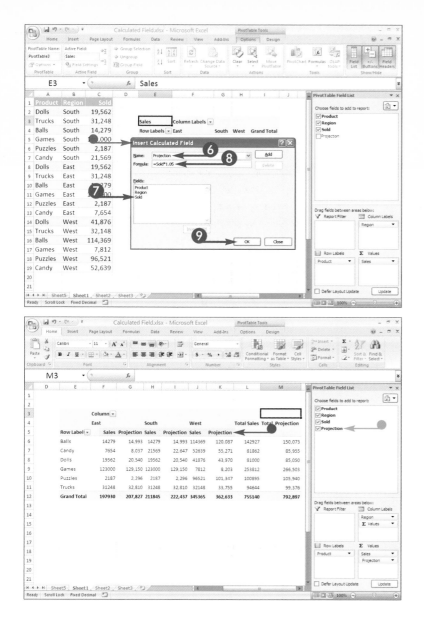

- The Insert Calculated Field dialog box appears.

6 Type a name for the new field.

7 Double-click an existing field to use in defining the field.

8 Type an operator and the value, such as ***1.05**.

9 Click OK.

- Values for the calculated field fill the data area.

- The calculated field appears at the end of the Field List.

TIPS

Did You Know?

You can use the Value Field Settings dialog box to change the name of your field headers. Open the Value Field Settings dialog box and type a new name in the Custom Name field. To remove field headers from your PivotTable, click the Options tab on the Ribbon and then click Field Headers to toggle off the field headers.

Did You Know?

You can change your data source. Click anywhere in your PivotTable to activate the PivotTable tools. On the Ribbon, click Options and then click Change Data Source. The Change PivotTable Data Source dialog box appears. Select a new table or range or change the external data source.

Formatting data changes its appearance, but formatting is not just a matter of cosmetics. Rather, formatting is useful because the details in PivotTables can make it difficult to see data patterns. Formatting improves data legibility.

Two PivotTable formatting options available in Excel are grouping and sorting. With grouping, you can hide detail so you can easily compare groups of data. When you group columns or rows, Excel totals the data, creates a field header, and creates a field with a drill-down button that displays either a plus or a minus sign.

When the drill-down button displays a minus sign, you can click the button to collapse the data. When the drill-down button displays a plus sign, you can click the button to expand the data. If you do not want to display the button, you can click Buttons on the Options tab to toggle the display of buttons to off. If after grouping your data, you want to ungroup it, you can.

① Click and drag the row or column labels to select the rows or columns you want to hide.

● The PivotTable tools become available.

② Click the Options tab.

③ Click Group Selection.

● A new cell appears, with a minus button.

④ Click the minus button.

● The details of the rows or columns are hidden, the total appears, and the minus sign on the button turns into a plus sign.

Note: You can click the plus button to see the hidden cells again.

⑤ Click the cell that contains the group header.

⑥ Click Ungroup.

Excel removes the grouping.

SORT
a PivotTable

DIFFICULTY LEVEL

Sorting enables you to see patterns in your data. You can sort PivotTables by field labels or by data values. When you sort by field labels, the corresponding data values are sorted as well. The opposite is also true: sorting the data values rearranges the field labels.

You can sort your PivotTable in either ascending or descending order. You can also specify the sort direction: top to bottom or left to right. This can get a bit confusing, so the Sort By Value dialog box provides an explanation of the results of your sort selection.

TIP

Did You Know?
You can click the down arrow next to the field header to sort and filter your PivotTable data. For more information on sorting and filtering with field headings, see Chapter 4.

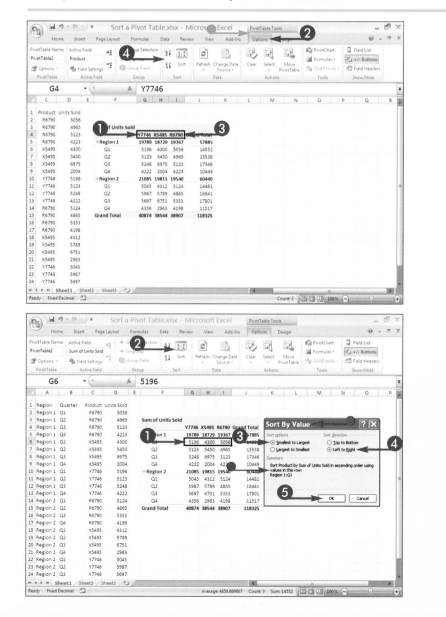

SORT FIELD LABELS

1. Click any field in your PivotTable.
   - The PivotTable tools become available.
2. Click the Options tab.
3. Click and drag to select the field labels you want to sort.
4. Click the ascending or descending button.

   Excel sorts your field labels.

SORT DATA FIELDS

1. Click and drag to select the data you want to sort.
2. Click Sort.
   - The Sort By Value dialog box appears.
3. Click a Sort option (○ changes to ⊙).
4. Click a Sort direction (○ changes to ⊙).
   - The Sort By Value dialog box provides an explanation of what will result from your sort selection.
5. Click OK.

   Excel sorts your data fields.

Create a
PIVOTCHART

PivotTables reveal patterns in your data. PivotCharts, which you base on PivotTables, make patterns even more apparent. Like all charts in Excel, PivotCharts consist of elements such as chart type, axis, legend, and data, all of which you can modify to meet your needs. See Chapter 6 to learn more about working with charts.

When you create a chart from a PivotTable, you can base your chart on summary statistics and you can

adjust the row and column layout. After creating your chart, you can display the PivotTable Field List and change the layout of your PivotTable. As you do, your PivotChart changes automatically.

In addition, PivotCharts have options that regular charts do not have. You can filter the data that appears in your PivotChart. For example, if your data is divided into multiple regions, you can easily specify which regions appear in your PivotChart.

1 Click any cell in your PivotTable.

● The PivotTable tools become available.

2 Click the Options tab.

3 Click PivotChart on the Tools group.

● The Insert Chart dialog box appears.

4 Click to select a chart type.

5 Click to select a chart sub-type.

6 Click OK.

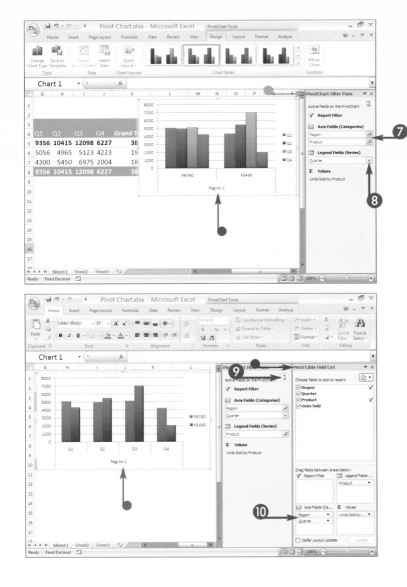

- The PivotChart appears.

- The PivotChart Filter Pane appears.

⑦ Click here and then select the fields you want to appear in your chart.

⑧ Click here and then select the fields you want to appear in your legend.

Excel filters your chart.

⑨ Click the PivotTable Field List button.

- The PivotTable Field List appears.

⑩ Modify your PivotTable layout.

Note: See Task #50 to learn how to modify your layout.

- Excel changes the layout of your chart.

TIPS

Did You Know?

When you use the PivotChart Filter Pane to filter your chart, Excel also filters your PivotTable. As such, information you remove from the PivotChart is also removed from the PivotTable.

Remove It!

To remove all the filters from your PivotChart, click your chart to activate the PivotChart tools. Click the Analyze tab, click Clear, and then click Clear Filters. To clear your PivotChart and your PivotTable, click the chart to activate the PivotChart tools, click the Analyze tab, click Clear, and then click Clear All.

DESCRIBE DATA
with statistics

Excel includes more than 80 statistical functions. You can find these functions by using the Function Wizard in the Statistics category. Some of them are also available in the Descriptive Statistics dialog box. To make additional statistical functions available, install the Excel Analysis Toolpak described in Task #94.

Among the statistical functions, you will find more than a dozen types of descriptive statistics. With these statistics, you characterize both the central tendency of your data, such as mean, mode, and median, and the data's variability, such as sample

variance and standard deviation. The Function Wizard provides individual statistical functions. By using the Descriptive Statistics dialog box, you can apply all descriptive statistics at the same time.

To use descriptive statistics, first display a worksheet with the data you want to analyze. You can generate the worksheet within Excel or import it from Access or another data source. Many functions work only with numeric data.

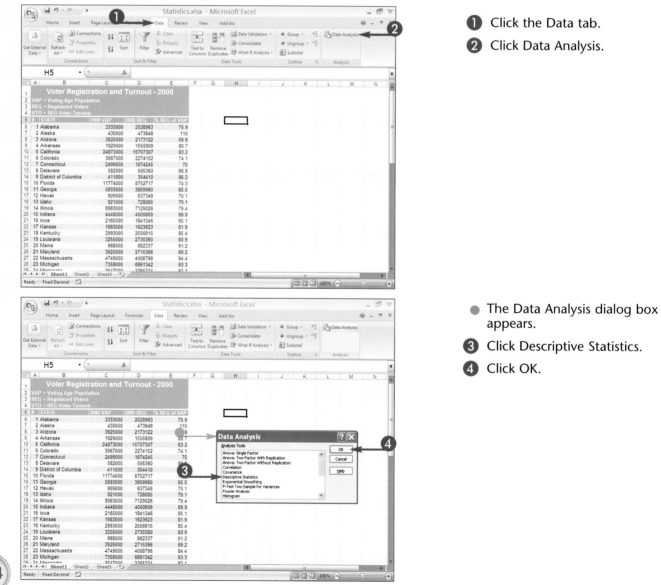

❶ Click the Data tab.

❷ Click Data Analysis.

● The Data Analysis dialog box appears.

❸ Click Descriptive Statistics.

❹ Click OK.

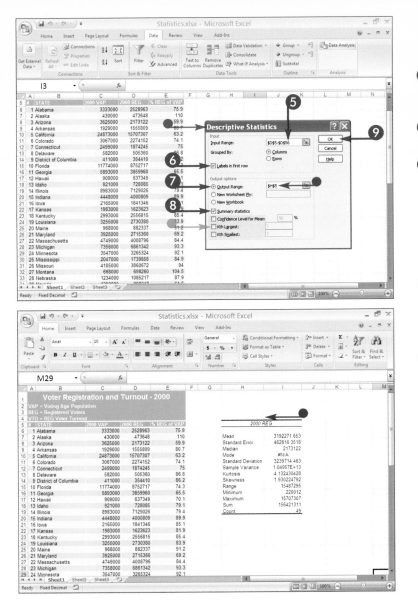

- The Descriptive Statistics dialog box appears.

5 Click and drag the cells you want to describe, or type the cell range.

6 Click if your data has labels (☐ changes to ☑).

7 Click to select where you want the output to appear (○ changes to ⊙).

- If necessary, type a location.

8 Click Summary Statistics (☐ changes to ☑).

- Optionally, you can include other statistics.

9 Click OK.

The statistics appear in a boxed area.

- To see all your statistics, widen the column heads by clicking the border between column letters and dragging.

TIP

Did You Know?

Descriptive statistics are available as Excel functions.

Excel Functions			
Descriptive Statistic	**Excel Function**	**Descriptive Statistic**	**Excel Function**
Mean	AVERAGE()	Skewness	SKEW()
Standard Error	STEYX()	Range	MAX()-MIN()
Median	MEDIAN()	Minimum	MIN()
Mode	MODE()	Maximum	MAX()
Standard Deviation	STDEV()	Sum	SUM()
Sample Variance	VAR()	Count	COUNT()
Kurtosis	KURT()		

Chapter 5: Explore the Patterns in Your Data 125

FIND THE CORRELATION
between variables

With the correlation function, you can measure the relationship between two variables. You can explore questions such as whether baseball players hit fewer home runs as they age.

A correlation does not prove one thing causes another. The most you can say is that one number varies with the other. Their variation may be the result of how your numbers were measured or the result of some factor underlying both variables. When you use correlations, you start with a theory that two things are related. If there is a correlation, you must

then gather evidence and develop plausible reasons for the correlation.

Use the CORREL function to determine a correlation. CORREL takes two arguments: array1 and array2 — the two lists of numbers. The result of the function is a number, r, between –1 and 1. The closer r gets to –1 or 1, the stronger the relationship. If r is negative, the relationship is an inverse relationship — for example, as age increases, batting averages decrease. A positive result suggests that as one variable increases, so does the other.

① Click the cell in which you want to place your answer.

② Type **=correl(** or double-click CORREL on the Function AutoComplete list.

③ Click the Insert Function button.

The Function Arguments dialog box appears.

④ Click and drag to select the first series of numbers, or type the cell range.

⑤ Click and drag to select the second series of numbers, or type the cell range.

Note: *You can select a subset of a list, but make sure the same subset is selected for each list.*

⑥ Click OK.

● The correlation coefficient appears.

Note: *The sign suggests whether the relationship is positive (+) or negative (–).*

TIPS

Did You Know?

When using CORREL, if a reference cell contains text, logical values, or empty cells, Excel ignores those values. However, reference cells that have a value of 0 are included in the calculation. If the number of data points in array1 and array2 are not equal, Excel returns the error message #N/A.

Did You Know?

An *add-in* is software that adds one or more features to Excel. To learn how to install add-ins, see Task #94. The Analysis Toolpak is an add-in that contains a number of statistical tools, including the Correlation tool, which you can use to calculate correlations. Correlations calculated by using the Correlation tool do not automatically update as you update your worksheet.

Explore outcomes with
WHAT-IF ANALYSIS

When you use a function, your purpose is often to find out how one thing influences another. When you use the IRR function, for example, you can find out how a change in the loan amount, payment amount, or payment date — or some combination of these factors — affects the interest received. By typing in different amounts, and payment dates, you can see how different scenarios affect the interest rate.

What-If analysis is a systematic way of finding out how a change in one or more variables affects a

result. Scenario Manager lets you vary one or more inputs to find out how the result changes. The advantage of the Scenario Manager is that it stores a series of values so you can create a single report or table showing how each value or combination of values influences the result — your interest rate, in this example. You can even present this information as a PivotTable, with all the flexibility it offers.

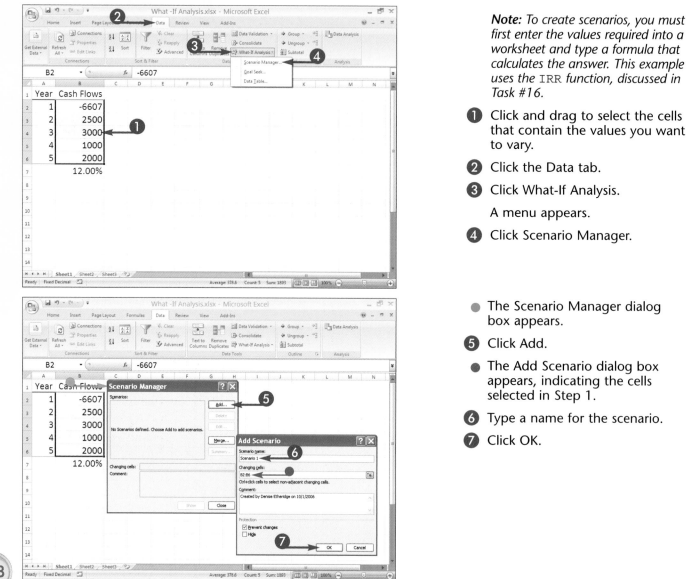

Note: *To create scenarios, you must first enter the values required into a worksheet and type a formula that calculates the answer. This example uses the IRR function, discussed in Task #16.*

1 Click and drag to select the cells that contain the values you want to vary.

2 Click the Data tab.

3 Click What-If Analysis.

A menu appears.

4 Click Scenario Manager.

● The Scenario Manager dialog box appears.

5 Click Add.

● The Add Scenario dialog box appears, indicating the cells selected in Step 1.

6 Type a name for the scenario.

7 Click OK.

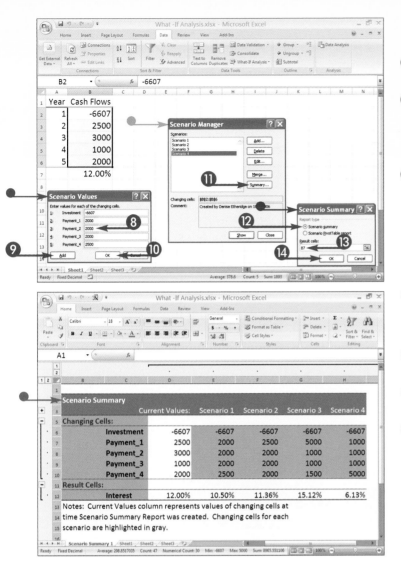

- The Scenario Values dialog box appears.

8 Type the scenario values.

9 Click Add to create more scenarios.

The Add Scenario dialog box reappears.

10 Click OK in the Scenario Values dialog box instead of Add when you finish entering scenarios.

- The Scenario Manager dialog box appears.

11 Click Summary.

- The Scenario Summary dialog box appears.

12 Click to select a report type (○ changes to ◉).

13 Click the field or type the cell address of the field that calculates the results.

14 Click OK.

- The type of report you requested appears on a new worksheet, displaying how each value affects the result.

TIPS

Did You Know?

If you share copies of a workbook and people add their own scenarios, you can merge these scenarios into a single list. To do so, open the workbooks and click Data and then Scenario Manager. In the Scenario Manager, click Merge. In the Merge Scenarios window, select the workbooks and individual worksheets to consolidate. Click OK when you finish selecting.

Did You Know?

If you name the cells in your original worksheet, your Scenario Summary becomes easier to read because Excel displays the cell name instead of the cell address. For example, in this task cell, cell B2 is named Investment, cells B3 through B6 are named Payment_1 through Payment_4, and cell B7 is named Interest_Earned. To learn how to name cells, see Task #11.

Optimize a result with
GOAL SEEK

Excel gives you a powerful tool for finding a way to reach your goals. For example, if you need a loan for a new home your goal might be to pay a specific monthly payment. You can use the Goal Seek feature to show how you can reach your goal by adjusting one of the loan terms such as interest rate or loan amount.

You could also have Goal Seek find the interest rate required to reach your payment goal, given a loan amount, or find the loan amount required to reach your goal, given a specific interest rate. Some goals cannot be met, as when you try to reduce your monthly payment to nothing; the interest rates and loan amounts would be unrealistic.

To vary multiple inputs to achieve a specific goal, you need to use Solver, an add-in. See Task #94 for more about add-ins.

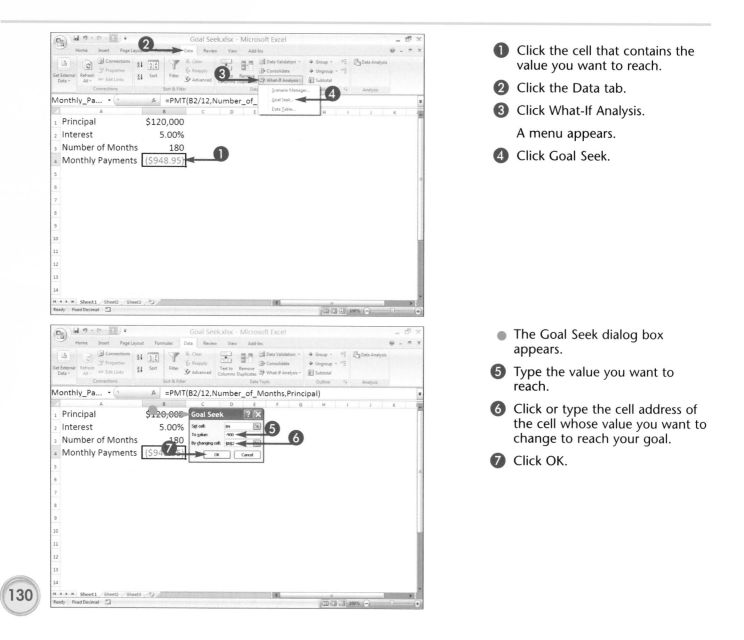

① Click the cell that contains the value you want to reach.

② Click the Data tab.

③ Click What-If Analysis.

A menu appears.

④ Click Goal Seek.

● The Goal Seek dialog box appears.

⑤ Type the value you want to reach.

⑥ Click or type the cell address of the cell whose value you want to change to reach your goal.

⑦ Click OK.

- The result appears in the worksheet.

8 Click OK to accept the change.

- Alternatively, you can click Cancel to restore the original values.

  In this example, principal is kept the same, and the $900 monthly payment can be reached by finding an interest rate of 4.2 percent.

- Repeat Steps 1 to 7 for another value.

TIPS

Did You Know?
The example in this task shows the loan amount required to bring the monthly payment down to $900 ($113,810). If your purchase price is $120,000, you would have to contribute a down payment of just over $6,000 to bring the loan down to that amount. You could construct a worksheet that allows you to enter various down-payment amounts.

Did You Know?
If you are not getting a result, you can try clicking the Office button, Excel Options, and then Formulas. Then in the Calculations Options area, increase the maximum iterations.

Chapter
6

Create Charts

Excel gives you tools for quickly generating a chart, or visual representation, of the numbers in your worksheet. Charts clarify patterns that can get lost in columns of numbers and formulas, and they make your data more accessible to people who are not familiar with or do not want to delve into the details.

Charts can make a greater impression than rows and columns of numbers because the mind perceives, processes, and recalls visual information more quickly than textual or numerical information. In addition, shapes and colors have real impact. This effectiveness, however, can be a liability when charts emphasize unimportant or misleading patterns. This chapter helps you become comfortable with the Excel charting tools, so you can communicate your content as effectively as possible.

In this chapter, you learn how to generate a chart quickly. You then learn to add chart details, change the chart type, and remove data series. One task shows you how to create a trendline. A trendline visually summarizes the direction and magnitude of change over time.

Anyone who uses Excel to manage and analyze experimental data can benefit from the section in this chapter on error bars. Several tasks provide insight into specific types of charts. For example, you can use histograms to show frequencies.

Top 100

CREATE A CHART
that has visual appeal

With Excel 2007, you can create charts with dramatic visual appeal quickly and easily. Simply select the data you want to chart and then choose a chart type from the Insert tab's Chart group. Excel provides several chart types from which to choose, including column, line, pie, bar, area, and scatter charts. In addition, each chart type has a number of subtype options.

After you create your chart, Excel makes Chart tools available to you through the Design, Layout, and

Format contextual tabs. Using the Chart tools, you can choose a chart style and layout. You can change the color scheme of your chart with chart styles and use layouts to add a chart title, axis labels, a legend, or a data table to your chart. A chart title summarizes chart content; axis labels explain each axis; a legend explains the colors used to represent data; and a data table displays the data presented in the chart. Chart tools make changing row data to column data, or vice versa, as simple as clicking a button.

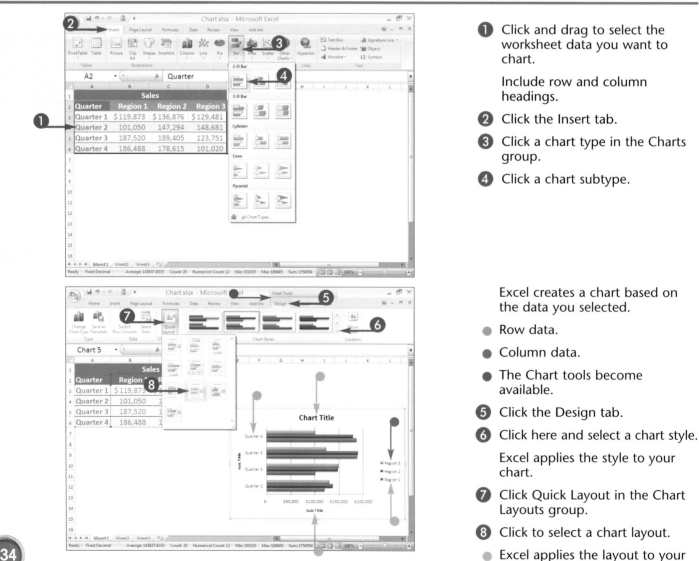

① Click and drag to select the worksheet data you want to chart.

Include row and column headings.

② Click the Insert tab.

③ Click a chart type in the Charts group.

④ Click a chart subtype.

Excel creates a chart based on the data you selected.

● Row data.

● Column data.

● The Chart tools become available.

⑤ Click the Design tab.

⑥ Click here and select a chart style.

Excel applies the style to your chart.

⑦ Click Quick Layout in the Chart Layouts group.

⑧ Click to select a chart layout.

● Excel applies the layout to your chart.

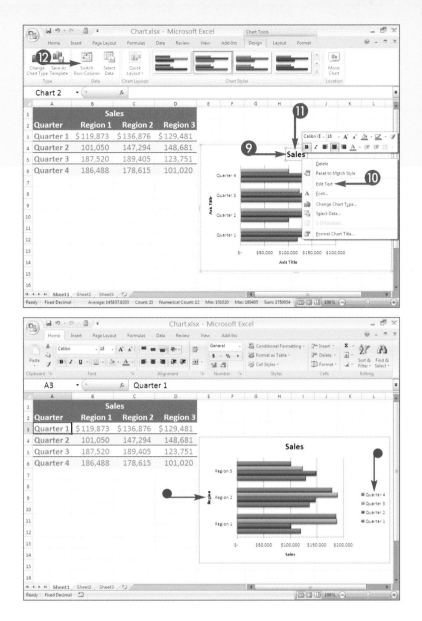

9 Right-click the chart title or an axis title.

A menu appears.

10 Click Edit Text.

11 Type to change the title or axis label.

12 Click Switch Row/Column in the Data group.

#60

DIFFICULTY LEVEL

● Excel switches the data row and column.

Did You Know?

The Column chart is the default chart type. You can change the default chart type by clicking the launcher in the Insert tab's Chart group to open the Insert Chart dialog box. Click a chart type and a subtype, and then click the Set as Default Chart button located at the bottom of the Insert Chart dialog box.

Did You Know?

The fastest way to create a chart using all of Excel's charting defaults is to select the data you want to chart and then press F11. Excel creates a chart on a new worksheet. You can then modify the chart by using any of the Chart tools.

Add
CHART DETAILS

After you create your chart, Excel makes is easy for you to modify it or add details. In fact, you can modify virtually all the elements of a chart. For example, when you create a chart, Excel places it on the same worksheet as the data from which you created it. You can move the chart to another worksheet or to a special chart sheet.

To make a 3-D chart easier to read, you can use the X and Y fields in the 3-D Rotation dialog box to

change the chart rotation. The X field rotates the horizontal axis of your chart and the Y field rotates the vertical axis of your chart. In addition to changing your chart's rotation, you may also want to change your chart's perspective. Changing the perspective is useful if the bars in the front of your chart hide bars in the back of your chart. Use the Perspective field in the 3-D Rotation dialog box to change the perspective.

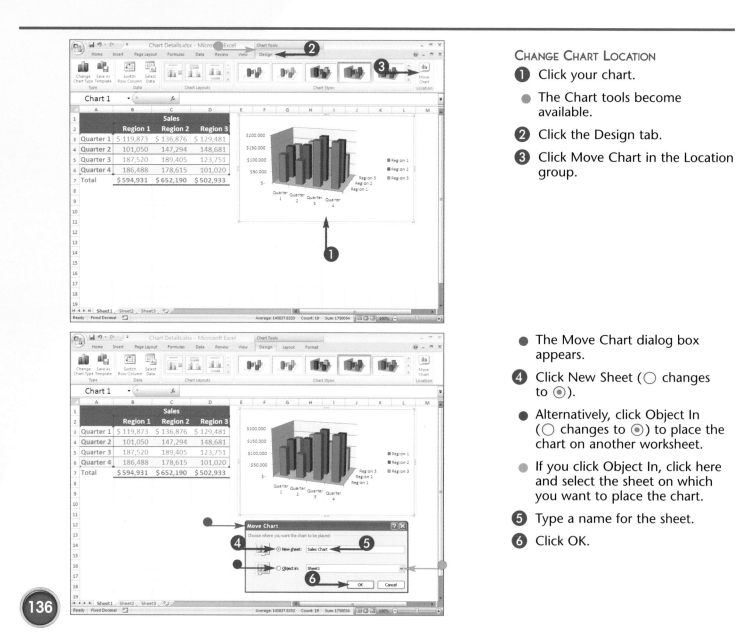

CHANGE CHART LOCATION

1 Click your chart.

● The Chart tools become available.

2 Click the Design tab.

3 Click Move Chart in the Location group.

● The Move Chart dialog box appears.

4 Click New Sheet (○ changes to ◉).

● Alternatively, click Object In (○ changes to ◉) to place the chart on another worksheet.

● If you click Object In, click here and select the sheet on which you want to place the chart.

5 Type a name for the sheet.

6 Click OK.

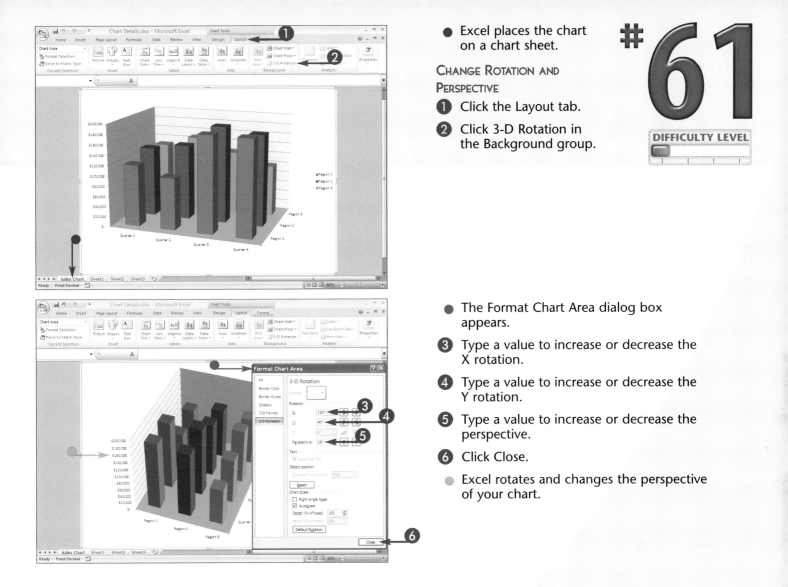

- Excel places the chart on a chart sheet.

CHANGE ROTATION AND PERSPECTIVE

1. Click the Layout tab.

2. Click 3-D Rotation in the Background group.

61

- The Format Chart Area dialog box appears.

3. Type a value to increase or decrease the X rotation.

4. Type a value to increase or decrease the Y rotation.

5. Type a value to increase or decrease the perspective.

6. Click Close.

- Excel rotates and changes the perspective of your chart.

TIPS

Did You Know?

You can add, remove, or change the plot area's fill when working with two-dimensional charts. Just click your chart, click the Layout tab, and then click Plot Area in the Background group. A menu of options appears. You can use the menu to change the color and style of the plot area of your chart.

Did You Know?

You can edit any element in your chart by right-clicking it. A menu appears, sometimes with a mini-toolbar. Use the menu and mini-toolbar to delete elements, add elements, change the font, change the font size, change the alignment, or edit the data source.

Add
CHART DETAILS

To make your chart more readable, you may want to change some of the attributes of your chart. You can easily change the walls and floor of your three-dimensional charts. The walls are the side and back of your chart and the floor is the bottom of your chart. You can choose to show the chart walls and/or floor; fill the chart walls and/or floor with a color, gradient, or other item; or not show the walls and/or floor at all.

Excel bases axis values on the range of values in your data. Axis values encompass the range. Axis

labels describe the data displayed on each axis. Excel provides several options for choosing whether to display axis values and how to display the axis values and labels on each axis, including the horizontal, vertical, and depth axes.

When you create a chart in Excel, Excel creates horizontal and vertical gridlines to mark major intervals in your data series. You can remove the gridlines, display major gridlines only, display minor gridlines, or display major and minor gridlines.

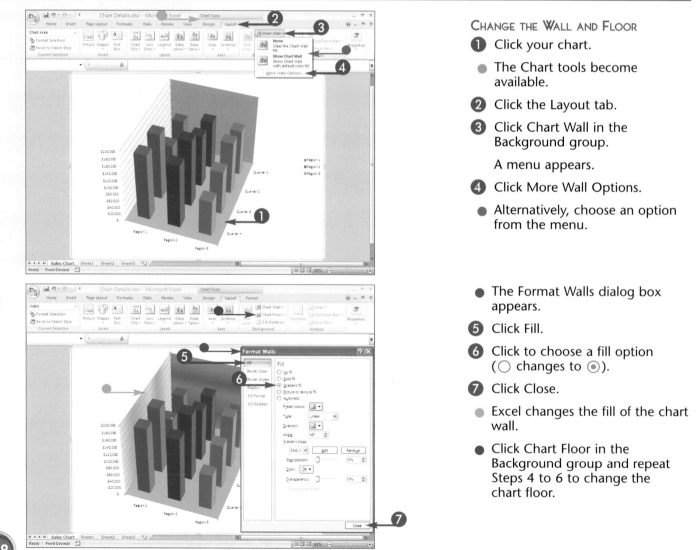

CHANGE THE WALL AND FLOOR

1 Click your chart.

● The Chart tools become available.

2 Click the Layout tab.

3 Click Chart Wall in the Background group.

A menu appears.

4 Click More Wall Options.

● Alternatively, choose an option from the menu.

● The Format Walls dialog box appears.

5 Click Fill.

6 Click to choose a fill option (○ changes to ◉).

7 Click Close.

● Excel changes the fill of the chart wall.

● Click Chart Floor in the Background group and repeat Steps 4 to 6 to change the chart floor.

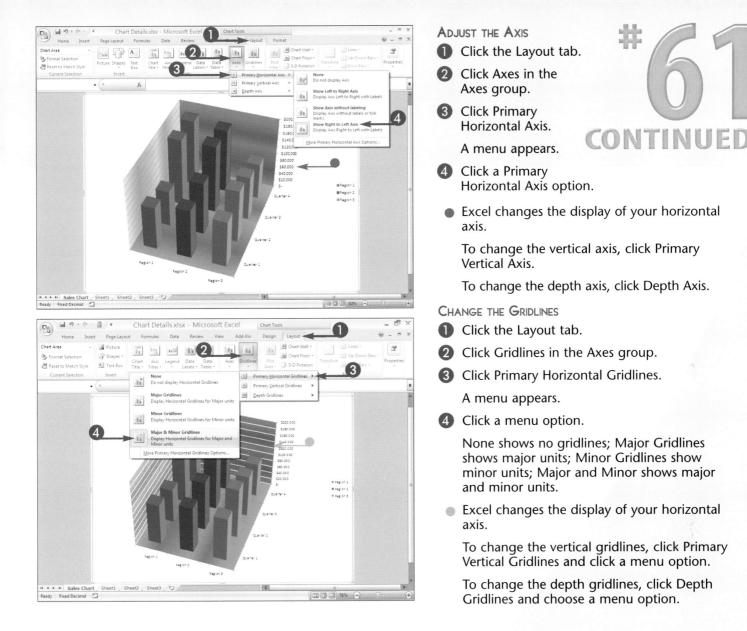

ADJUST THE AXIS

1 Click the Layout tab.

2 Click Axes in the Axes group.

3 Click Primary Horizontal Axis.

A menu appears.

4 Click a Primary Horizontal Axis option.

● Excel changes the display of your horizontal axis.

To change the vertical axis, click Primary Vertical Axis.

To change the depth axis, click Depth Axis.

CHANGE THE GRIDLINES

1 Click the Layout tab.

2 Click Gridlines in the Axes group.

3 Click Primary Horizontal Gridlines.

A menu appears.

4 Click a menu option.

None shows no gridlines; Major Gridlines shows major units; Minor Gridlines show minor units; Major and Minor shows major and minor units.

● Excel changes the display of your horizontal axis.

To change the vertical gridlines, click Primary Vertical Gridlines and click a menu option.

To change the depth gridlines, click Depth Gridlines and choose a menu option.

Caution!

To resize a chart, click the chart. A border surrounds it, with dots on the sides and corners. Place the cursor over the dots. When a double arrow appears, click and drag to resize the chart. Be careful when resizing, because resizing may skew the chart and distort the presentation of the content.

Did You Know?

You can use the options in the Labels group on the Layout tab to add or modify a chart title, axis titles, legend, data labels, or data tables.

Did You Know?

You can use the Shapes options in the Insert group on the Layout tab to add pictures, shapes, and text boxes to your chart.

Change the
CHART TYPE

Excel provides a variety of chart types and subtypes from which to choose. Choose the chart type that best explains your data.

You can use a column or bar chart to plot data arranged in rows and columns. Both types are useful when you have data that changes over time or when you want to compare data values.

Area and line charts are also good for plotting data organized into columns and rows. Use an area chart

to show how values change over time and how each part of the whole contributes to the change. Line charts are ideal for showing trends in your data; consider using a line chart to show changes measured at regular intervals.

Pie charts are useful when you want to display data arranged in one column or one row. Each data point in a pie chart represents a percentage of the whole pie.

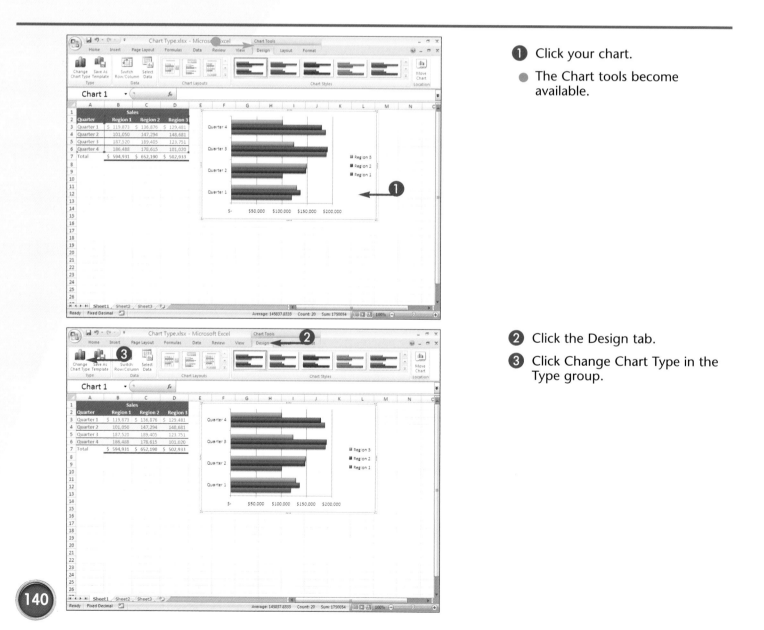

① Click your chart.

● The Chart tools become available.

② Click the Design tab.

③ Click Change Chart Type in the Type group.

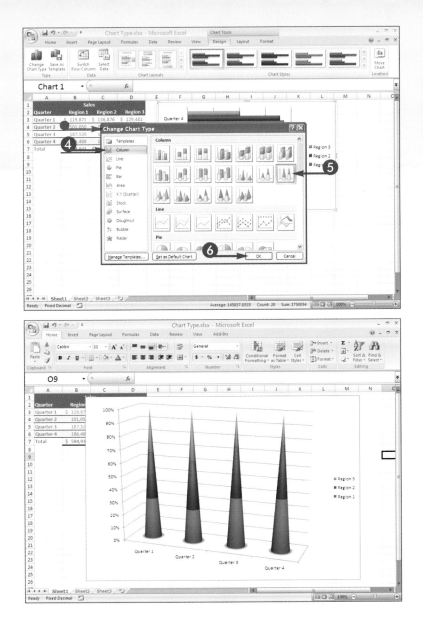

● The Change Chart Type dialog box appears.

④ Click a new chart type.

⑤ Click a subtype.

⑥ Click OK.

The chart appears, formatted in the new chart type and subtype.

TIPS

Did You Know?

If you show more than two data series in a single chart, you can change the chart type for one or more series and create a combination chart. Using different chart types can make it easier to distinguish different categories of data shown in the same chart.

Do It!

To create a combination chart, right-click a representation of a data series in the current chart. For example, right-click one of the bars in a bar chart. Then choose Change Series Chart Type from the menu that appears. The Change Chart Type dialog box appears. Choose a new chart type, and then click OK.

Add a
TRENDLINE

With Excel, you can add trendlines to your charts. Trendlines help you see both the size and direction of changes in your data and you can use them to forecast future or past values based on available data. By creating a trendline, you can answer questions such as, "Is there a pattern in the recent surge of new orders?"

You can add a trendline to any chart type except 3-D, stacked, radar, pie, surface, or doughnut charts. Excel superimposes the trendline over your chart.

A trendline is the line through your data series that is as close as possible to every point in the data series. Excel provides the following trendline types: linear, logarithmic, polynomial, power, exponential, and moving average. The type of trendline you choose should be based on the type of data you have. Excel generates a statistic called R-squared that indicates how well a given trendline fits your data. The closer R-squared is to 1, the better the line fits your data. You can choose to have the R-squared value appear on your chart.

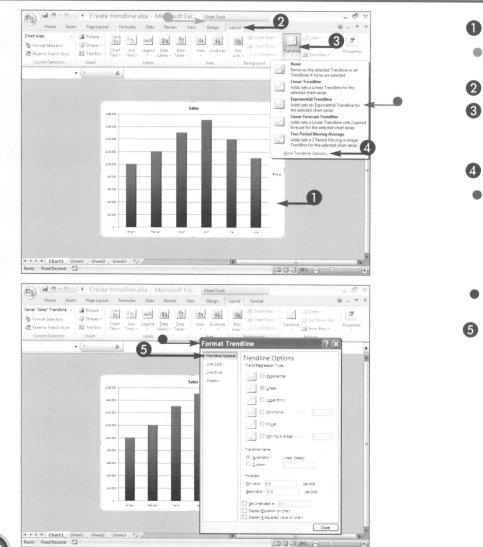

① Click your chart.

● The Chart tools become available.

② Click the Layout tab.

③ Click Trendline in the Analysis group.

A menu appears.

④ Click More Trendline Options.

● Alternatively, click a menu option to choose the type of trendline you want to apply.

● The Format Trendline dialog box appears.

⑤ Click Trendline Options.

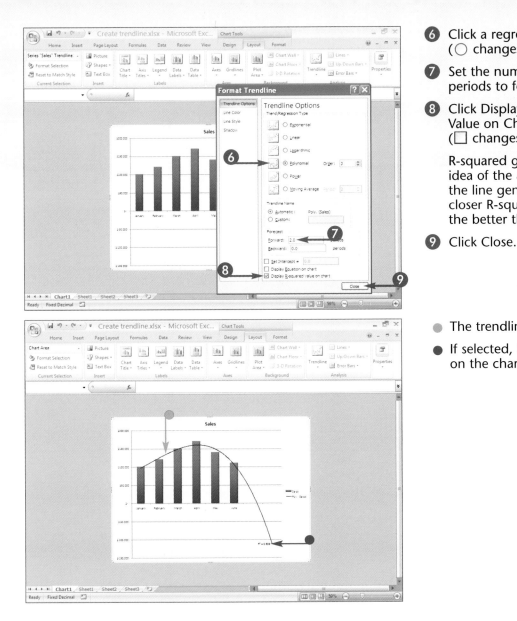

6 Click a regression type
(○ changes to ⦿).

7 Set the number of
periods to forecast.

8 Click Display R-squared
Value on Chart
(☐ changes to ☑).

R-squared gives you an
idea of the accuracy of
the line generated. The
closer R-squared is to 1,
the better the fit.

9 Click Close.

● The trendline appears on the chart.

● If selected, the R-squared value appears
on the chart.

![TIPS]

Did You Know?

If you want to project future
values for a simple linear trend,
you can use the fill handle. Select
at least the last two rows in your
data and then drag the fill handle.

Did You Know?

You can project values that fit a
straight-line trend by using the
TREND function. You can project
values that fit an exponential
trend by using the GROWTH
function. See the Excel Help files
for more about these functions.

Did You Know?

You can use the Forecast section
of the Format Trendline dialog
box to forecast future and past
data. To open the Format
Trendline dialog box, click your
chart, the Layout tab, Trendline,
More Trendline Options, and then
Trendline Options.

Add and remove
CHART DATA

If you want to include new data in your chart or exclude data from your chart, you can use the Edit Data Source dialog box to add and remove entire columns or rows of information or change your data series entirely without changing your chart's type or other properties.

You can also add data to an existing data series. Use the Edit Data Source dialog box's Legend Entries (Series) to select the cell addresses that define your

data series label and your data series. You can also use the Legend Entry (Series) box to add or remove a data series. Click Switch Row/Column if you need to switch your column and row data.

If you update the data on which your chart is based, you do not have to regenerate your chart. Excel charts automatically update to reflect changes you make to your data.

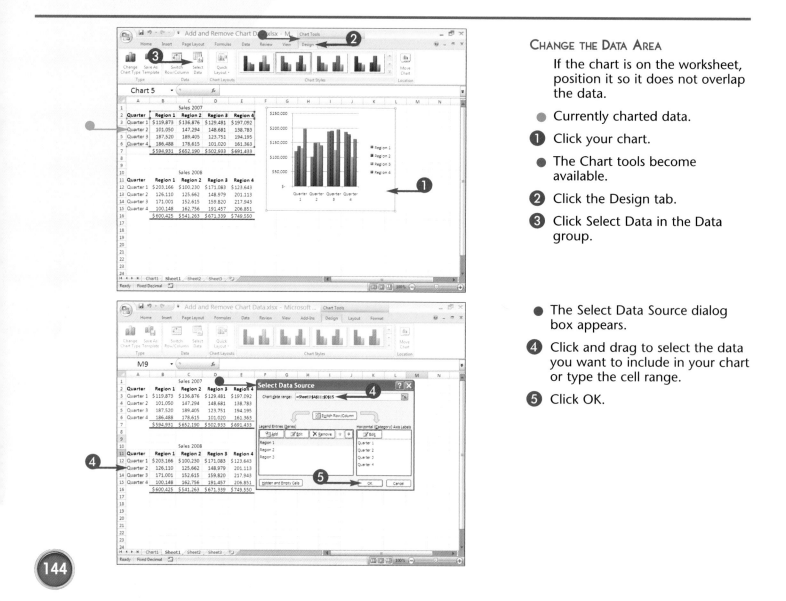

CHANGE THE DATA AREA

If the chart is on the worksheet, position it so it does not overlap the data.

● Currently charted data.

① Click your chart.

● The Chart tools become available.

② Click the Design tab.

③ Click Select Data in the Data group.

● The Select Data Source dialog box appears.

④ Click and drag to select the data you want to include in your chart or type the cell range.

⑤ Click OK.

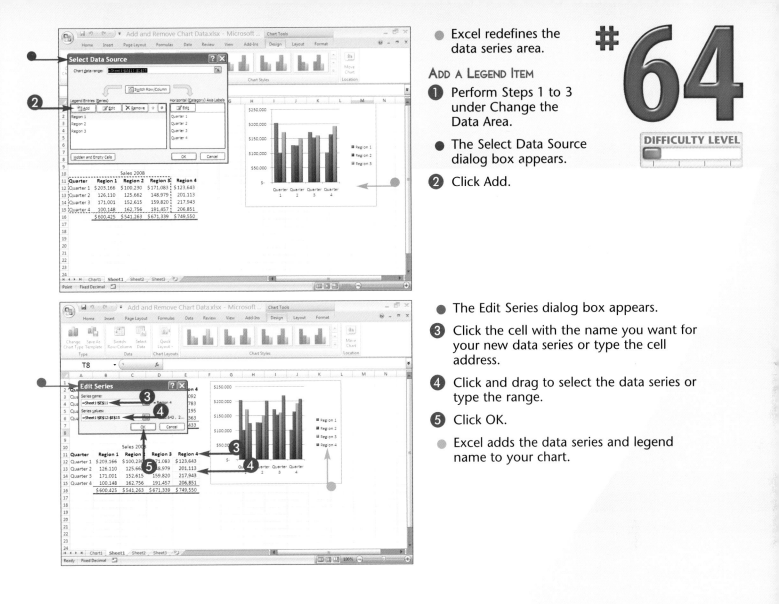

- Excel redefines the data series area.

ADD A LEGEND ITEM

1 Perform Steps 1 to 3 under Change the Data Area.

- The Select Data Source dialog box appears.

2 Click Add.

- The Edit Series dialog box appears.

3 Click the cell with the name you want for your new data series or type the cell address.

4 Click and drag to select the data series or type the range.

5 Click OK.

- Excel adds the data series and legend name to your chart.

TIPS

Delete It!

To delete data from your chart, click the data you want to delete in the Legend Series box of the Select Data Source dialog box and then click Remove. Or, click the legend item on the chart and then press the Delete key.

Did You Know?

Here is a quick way to add data to a chart. Click and drag to select the data you want to include in the chart. Click the Copy button on the Home tab. Click the chart to select it and click Paste on the Home tab. The chart reflects the added data series.

Add
ERROR BARS

With Excel, you can easily generate error bars to provide an estimate of the potential error in experimental or sampled data. In science, marketing, polling, and other fields, people make conclusions about populations by sampling the population or devising controlled experiments. When data is sampled or generated in laboratory conditions, the resulting numbers approximate the larger reality you are exploring. An error bar shows the range of possible values for these experimentally derived numbers. With Excel, you can show the range of

possible values in several ways: as a fixed number, measured in the same units used to measure data, above or below each data point in your data series; as a percentage of the data point; or in terms of standard deviation units.

Standard deviation units indicate whether an experimental number is reasonably close to the population characteristic being studied. For example, you can have a confidence level of 95 percent that the population mean falls within two standard deviation units of the sampled mean, which you know.

① Click your chart.

● The Chart tools become available.

② Click the Layout tab.

③ Click Error Bars in the Analysis group.

A menu appears.

④ Click More Error Bars Options.

● Alternatively, click the appropriate menu option.

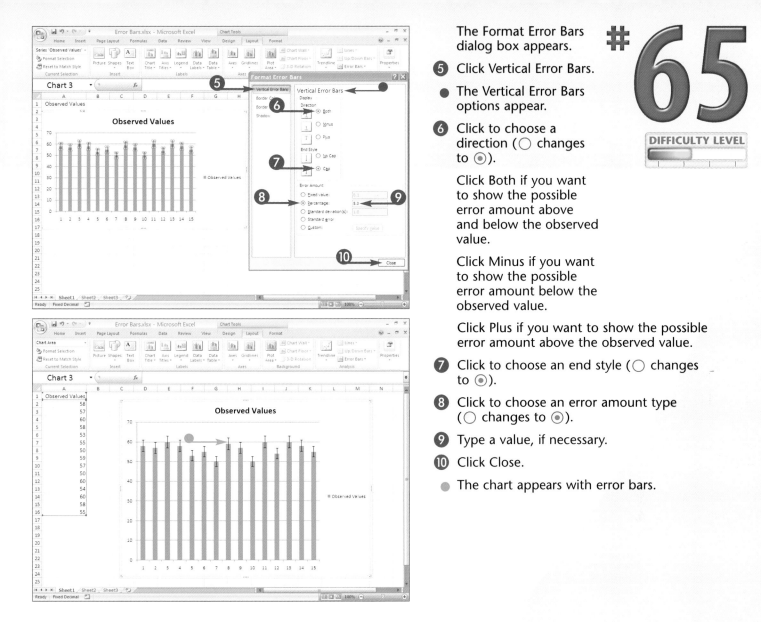

The Format Error Bars dialog box appears.

5 Click Vertical Error Bars.

● The Vertical Error Bars options appear.

6 Click to choose a direction (○ changes to ◉).

Click Both if you want to show the possible error amount above and below the observed value.

Click Minus if you want to show the possible error amount below the observed value.

Click Plus if you want to show the possible error amount above the observed value.

7 Click to choose an end style (○ changes to ◉).

8 Click to choose an error amount type (○ changes to ◉).

9 Type a value, if necessary.

10 Click Close.

● The chart appears with error bars.

TIPS

Did You Know?

Your confidence level in estimating population characteristics assumes that the sampled values are normally (evenly) distributed around the mean, as in a bell curve.

Did You Know?

You can add trendlines and error bars to a PivotChart. However, if you make changes to your PivotChart, Excel may remove the trendlines or error bars. Changes that may result in the loss of trendlines or error bars include changing the layout, removing fields, and hiding or displaying items.

Did You Know?

Only certain chart types support error bars, including 2-D area, bar, column, line, and XY scatter charts. These types let you create error bars for the values measured by the y axis. For the scatter chart, you can create both X and Y error bars.

Create a
HISTOGRAM

With Excel, you can use histograms to group a list of values into categories and compare the categories. Excel calls these categories bins. To display the test scores for a group of students, for example, your first bin might be <=60, representing scores of 60 percent or under; your second bin might be 70; and so on up to a bin for test scores over 100 percent. Excel counts the number of occurrences in each bin.

When creating a histogram, you must provide three pieces of information. First, define the raw data you want to sort. Then define the bins. Finally, specify

the cell in which you want the result to appear. Your bins must be in lowest to highest order. The results can appear in the current worksheet, in a new worksheet, or in a new workbook. As you make changes to your data, Excel does not automatically make changes to your histogram. You must regenerate your histogram when you make changes to your data.

The histogram tool is part of the Analysis Toolpak, which you may need to install as explained in Task #94.

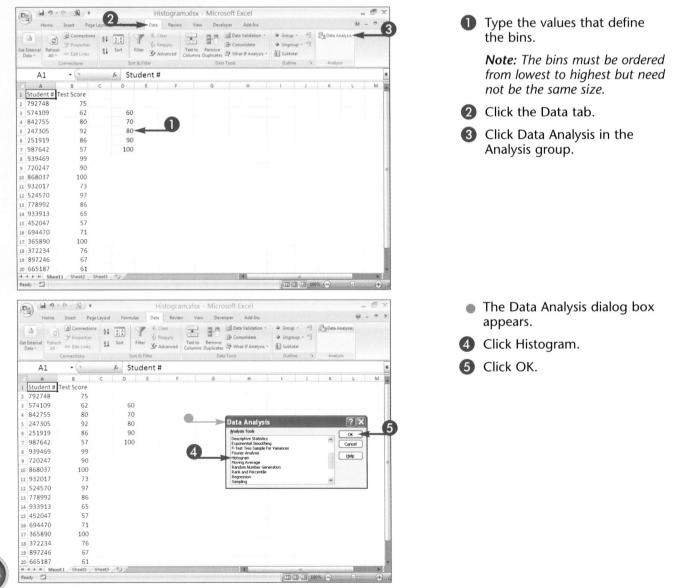

① Type the values that define the bins.

Note: The bins must be ordered from lowest to highest but need not be the same size.

② Click the Data tab.

③ Click Data Analysis in the Analysis group.

● The Data Analysis dialog box appears.

④ Click Histogram.

⑤ Click OK.

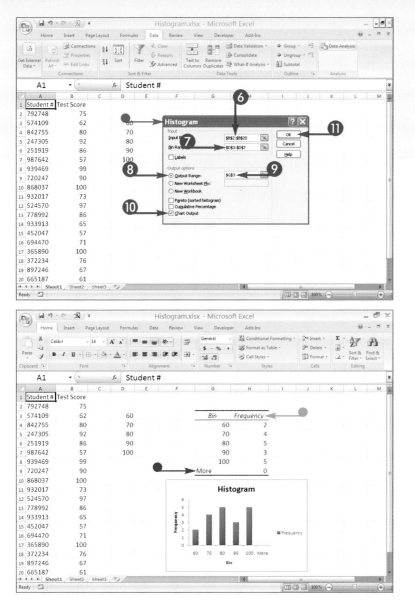

- The Histogram dialog box appears.

6 Click and drag the range of numbers to categorize, or type the cell range.

7 Click and drag the range of bins created in Step 1, or type the cell range.

8 Click where you want to place your output.

9 Click the cell where you want the results to start, or type the cell address.

10 Select options.

Pareto sorts data from highest to lowest.

Cumulative shows cumulative percentage.

Chart Output displays a chart.

11 Click OK.

The results appear on the same worksheet as the original data.

- Frequency means number of values per bin.

- More refers to the uncategorized values above the highest bin.

TIPS

Did You Know?

Click the Chart Output option (☐ changes to ☑) in the Histogram dialog box to create a histogram and a chart at the same time. You can modify the chart just as you would any other chart.

Did You Know?

You can click the Cumulative Percentage option (☐ changes to ☑) in the Histogram dialog box to create a histogram output table that includes cumulative percentages. You can click the Pareto (sorted histogram) option (☐ changes to ☑) to create a histogram output table that includes your data sorted in descending order based on frequency.

Did You Know?

The FREQUENCY function gives you the same capabilities as the histogram tool. However, when you use the FREQUENCY function, your bins are automatically updated as you update your data. See the Excel Help files for more about this function.

Create a
COMBINATION CHART

If you show more than two data series in a single chart, you can change the chart type for one or more series and create a combination chart. Using different chart types can make it easier to distinguish different categories of data shown in the same chart. For example, you can create a combination chart that shows the number of homes sold as a line chart and the average sales price as a column chart.

When you plot two different types of data in the same chart, the range of values can vary wildly. For example, the range of values for homes sold might be between 9 and 15 while the range of values for the average sales price might be between 760,577 and 936,966. You can plot each of these data series on a different vertical axis to make it easier for the user to see values for the associated series. In the example, you could plot average sales prices on one vertical axis and number of homes sold on the other vertical axis.

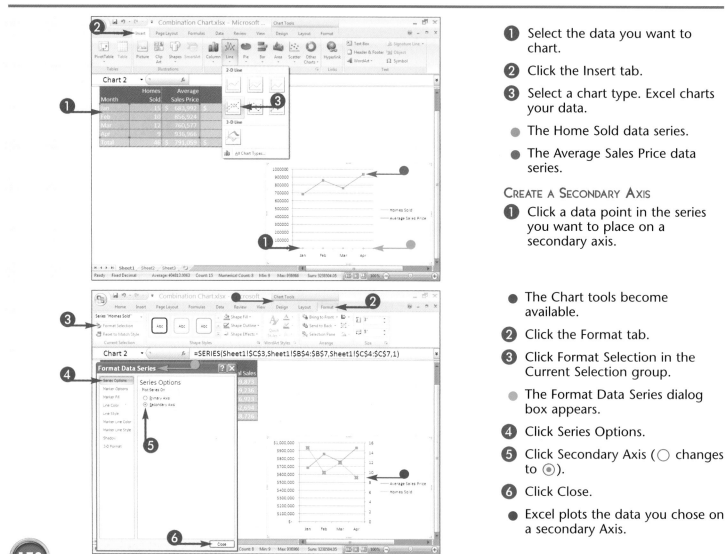

① Select the data you want to chart.

② Click the Insert tab.

③ Select a chart type. Excel charts your data.

● The Home Sold data series.

● The Average Sales Price data series.

CREATE A SECONDARY AXIS

① Click a data point in the series you want to place on a secondary axis.

● The Chart tools become available.

② Click the Format tab.

③ Click Format Selection in the Current Selection group.

● The Format Data Series dialog box appears.

④ Click Series Options.

⑤ Click Secondary Axis (○ changes to ⊙).

⑥ Click Close.

● Excel plots the data you chose on a secondary Axis.

CHANGE CHART TYPE

1. Click a data point in the series for which you want to change the data series.

● The Chart tools become available.

2. Click the Design tab.

3. Click Change Chart Type.

● The Change Chart Type dialog box appears.

4. Click a new chart type.

5. Click a new chart subtype.

6. Click OK.

● Excel changes the chart type for the series.

TIP

Did You Know?

You can add a title to your secondary axis. Click anywhere in your chart. The Chart tools become available. Click the Layout tab, click Axis Titles in the Labels group, click Secondary Vertical Axis Title, and then choose an option from the menu. Choose None if you do not want to display an Axis Title. Choose Rotated if you want to display a Rotated axis title and you want Excel to resize the chart. Choose Vertical if you want to display vertical text and you want Excel to resize the chart. Choose Horizontal if you want to display horizontal text and you want Excel to resize the chart.

Chapter
7

Present Worksheets

With Excel, you can adjust almost every aspect of how your worksheets appear. Such control results in more than making text bold or coloring cells blue. Formatting makes your worksheets easier to read and understand and thus more useful to others.

This chapter provides tips on formatting. You learn how to format numbers and cells manually and then how to apply formats quickly with Format Painter. Format Painter speeds your work. With Format Painter, in just a few clicks, you can copy a format from one cell to other cells.

Excel gives you several tools to simplify the work of formatting. The Home tab and the Format Cells dialog box provide all the controls

you need to change the look and properties of both cells and numbers. You can adjust the color, border, and numerous other cell properties, and you can choose from a variety of formats for numbers, dates, and times.

With shapes, text boxes, and pictures, Excel goes even further, giving you the ability to integrate graphics into your worksheet. It also supplies prepackaged styles you can apply to your graphics to give them a distinctive flair.

You can place background images behind your data to get people's attention or to enhance the content itself. You can also take a picture of your worksheet and use the resulting graphic in Excel or another software product.

Top 100

FORMAT
numbers, dates, and times

Excel provides a variety of options for formatting numbers, dates, and times. Formatting makes your data easier to read and helps you conform to company, country, or industry standards for formatting.

The Home tab in the Number group has a number of buttons you can use to format numbers quickly. If you cannot find the format you need, you can click the Number group's launcher to open the Format Cells dialog box.

The Format Cells dialog box has four categories you can use to format numbers: General, Number,

Currency, and Accounting. The General format is the default format. It displays the numbers exactly the way you type them.

The Number format lets you apply special formats to your numbers. You can set the number of decimal places, specify whether your number should display a thousands separator, and determine how to display negative numbers. You can choose from four choices for negative numbers: preceded by a negative sign (–), in red, in parentheses, or in red and in parentheses.

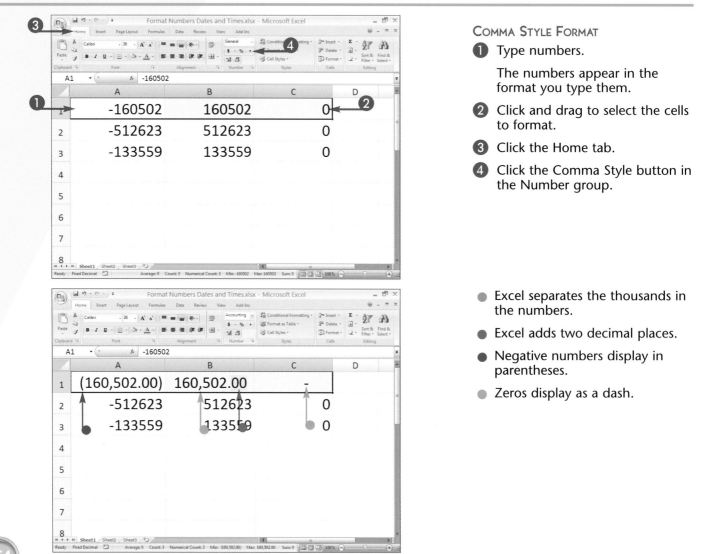

COMMA STYLE FORMAT

1. Type numbers.

   The numbers appear in the format you type them.

2. Click and drag to select the cells to format.

3. Click the Home tab.

4. Click the Comma Style button in the Number group.

● Excel separates the thousands in the numbers.

● Excel adds two decimal places.

● Negative numbers display in parentheses.

● Zeros display as a dash.

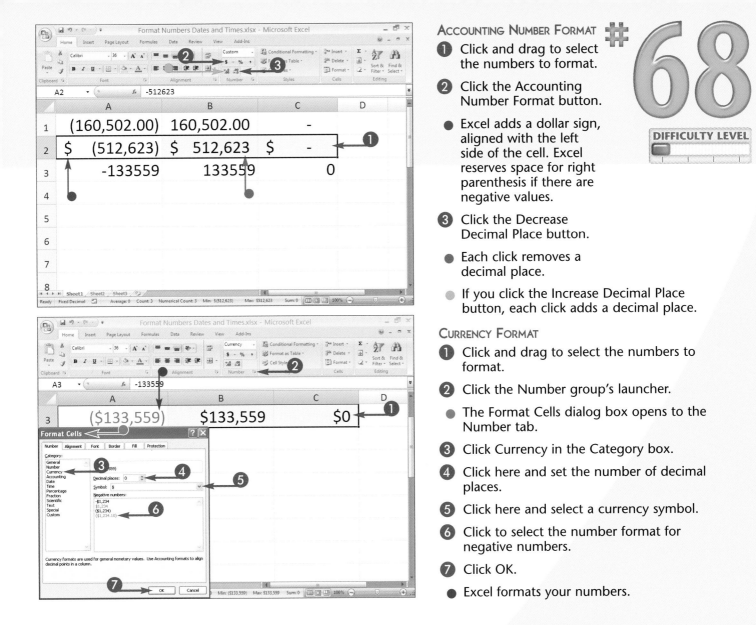

① Click and drag to select the numbers to format.

② Click the Accounting Number Format button.

● Excel adds a dollar sign, aligned with the left side of the cell. Excel reserves space for right parenthesis if there are negative values.

③ Click the Decrease Decimal Place button.

● Each click removes a decimal place.

● If you click the Increase Decimal Place button, each click adds a decimal place.

CURRENCY FORMAT

① Click and drag to select the numbers to format.

② Click the Number group's launcher.

● The Format Cells dialog box opens to the Number tab.

③ Click Currency in the Category box.

④ Click here and set the number of decimal places.

⑤ Click here and select a currency symbol.

⑥ Click to select the number format for negative numbers.

⑦ Click OK.

● Excel formats your numbers.

TIPS

Did You Know?

Changing a number format can increase the contents of the cell. If your number is too long to fit in its cell, Excel fills the cells with pound signs (#####). To view the number, at the top of the column, double-click the line that separates columns or click and drag the line to make the cell wider.

Did You Know?

You can use the Text format in the Format Cells dialog box to convert a number to text. Numbers formatted as text should not be used in mathematical calculations. Certain numbers — for example, employee numbers — are never used in mathematical calculations and should be formatted as text. If you want to format a number as text as you type it, precede the number with an apostrophe (').

FORMAT
numbers, dates, and times

The Currency format offers you the same options as the Number format except you can choose to display a currency symbol. The currency symbol you choose determines the options you have for displaying negative numbers. If you choose the dollar sign ($), thousands are separated by commas by default.

Excel designed the Accounting format to comply with accounting standards. If you use the dollar sign symbol ($), the dollar sign displays aligned with the left side of the cell, decimal points are aligned, a dash (–) displays instead of a zero, and negative values display in parentheses.

Countries vary in the way they display dates and times. Use the Date and Time format option to choose a locale. If you choose English (U.S.), you have more than 15 ways to display a date and a variety of ways to display time. To learn more about dates and times, see Task #s 22 and 23.

The percentage option converts numbers to a percent. You can choose the number of decimal places you want to display. The fraction option converts numbers to a fraction.

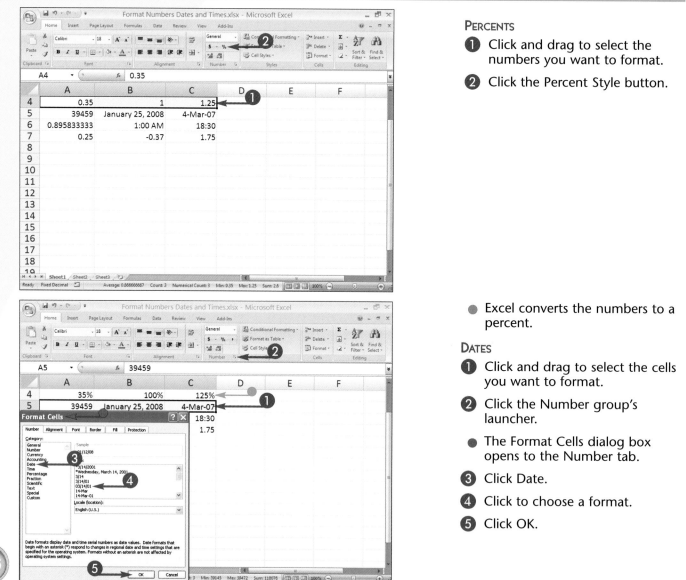

PERCENTS

1 Click and drag to select the numbers you want to format.

2 Click the Percent Style button.

● Excel converts the numbers to a percent.

DATES

1 Click and drag to select the cells you want to format.

2 Click the Number group's launcher.

● The Format Cells dialog box opens to the Number tab.

3 Click Date.

4 Click to choose a format.

5 Click OK.

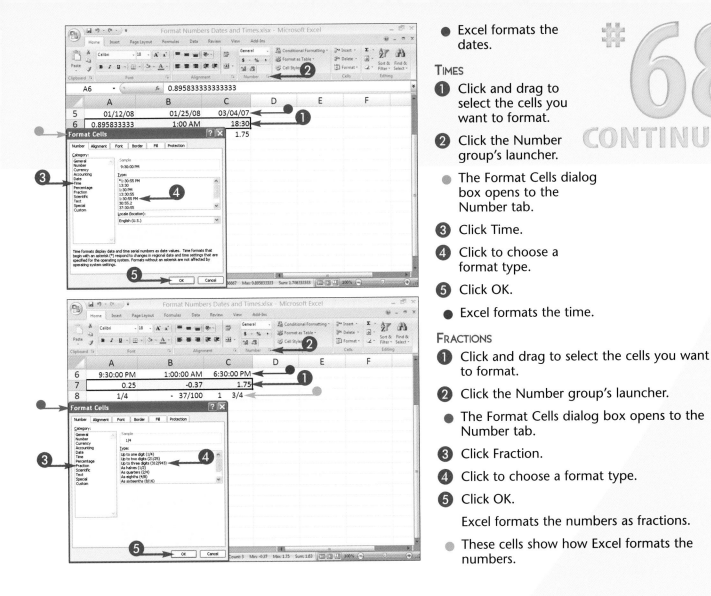

- Excel formats the dates.

TIMES

① Click and drag to select the cells you want to format.

② Click the Number group's launcher.

- The Format Cells dialog box opens to the Number tab.

③ Click Time.

④ Click to choose a format type.

⑤ Click OK.

- Excel formats the time.

FRACTIONS

① Click and drag to select the cells you want to format.

② Click the Number group's launcher.

- The Format Cells dialog box opens to the Number tab.

③ Click Fraction.

④ Click to choose a format type.

⑤ Click OK.

Excel formats the numbers as fractions.

- These cells show how Excel formats the numbers.

#68

CONTINUED

TIPS

Did You Know?

You can set the default number of decimal places Excel applies when you type a number into a worksheet. Click the Office button. A menu appears. Click Excel Options in the lower-right corner. Click Advanced. Make sure the Automatically Insert Decimal Point check box is checked (☐ changes to ☑). Type the number of decimal places you want in the Places field. Click OK.

Did You Know?

If you right-click in any cell that contains a number, you can choose number formatting options from the Mini-Toolbar or you can click Format Cells from the contextual menu to open the Format Cells dialog box.

APPLY FORMATS
to cells

Formatting enhances the presentation of reports. Rows of column headings provide a visual orientation to your data and highlight important information about the structure and content of your data.

By using the Home tab, you can format cells in a variety of ways. Clicking the launcher in the Font or Alignment group opens the Format Cells dialog box, which you can use to format numbers, align data within or across cells, apply a variety of formats to fonts, add borders, and fill cells with color. Many of

the options available to you in the Format Cells dialog box are also available in the Ribbon. By using the Ribbon, you can frequently apply a format with a single click.

You can set off cells by applying a colored background and changing the font color. You can set off columns or other important information by applying borders. When applying a border, you can choose the color, style, and placement of the border.

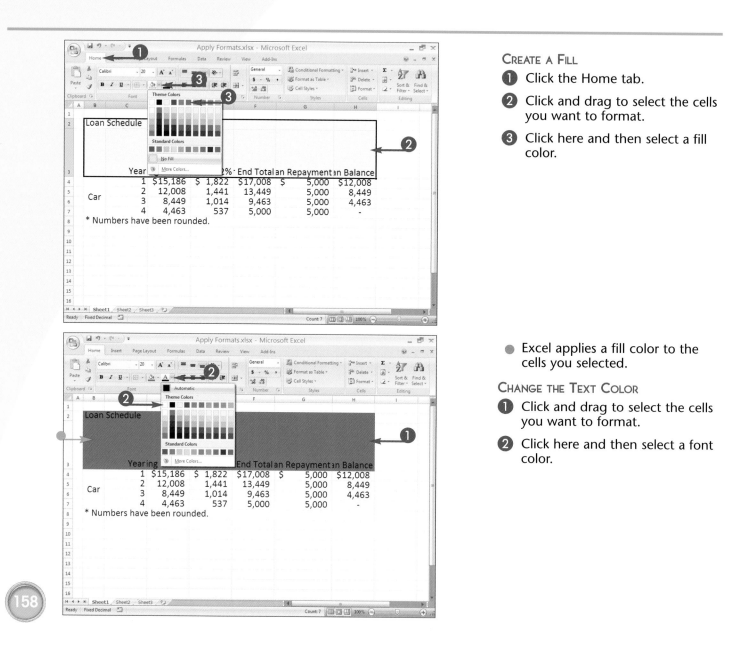

CREATE A FILL

❶ Click the Home tab.

❷ Click and drag to select the cells you want to format.

❸ Click here and then select a fill color.

● Excel applies a fill color to the cells you selected.

CHANGE THE TEXT COLOR

❶ Click and drag to select the cells you want to format.

❷ Click here and then select a font color.

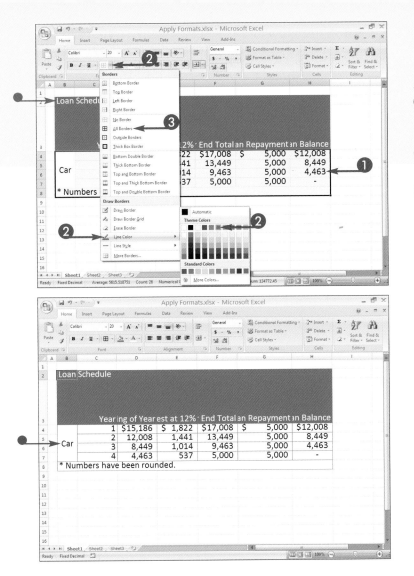

- Excel applies the font color to the cells you selected.

ADD A BORDER

1. Click and drag to select the cells you want to format.

2. Click here and then select a border color.

3. Click to select a border style.

DIFFICULTY LEVEL

- Excel adds a border to your cells.

TIPS

Did You Know?
On the Home tab, in the Font group, Excel provides an Increase Font Size button (A˄) and a Decrease Font Size button (A˅). Click the Increase Font Size button to make your font larger. Click the Decrease Font Size button to make your font smaller.

Did You Know?
Clicking the down arrow next to the Border button, Fill Color button, and the Font Color button provides you with a menu of choices. The choice you make becomes the default format for the button until you change it. When you want to reapply the format, just click the appropriate button.

APPLY FORMATS
to cells

Titles provide a brief summary of your data and you often center them over the data they summarize. To center text within a cell, click the Center button. To center text across several cells, click the Merge and Center button to merge all the cells you select and center the text in the merged cells.

If the text you enter is too long to fit in a single cell, Excel allows the text to spill over into adjacent cells. If you place text or data in the adjacent cells, Excel cuts the text off and you can no longer read the text

that spilt into the adjacent cell. You can click the Wrap Text button to wrap the text in the cell in which you typed it and thereby make it readable.

By default, data or text you enter in a cell displays from left to right. You can change the default display by clicking the Orientation button and selecting a new orientation. You can angle your text or have your text display vertically.

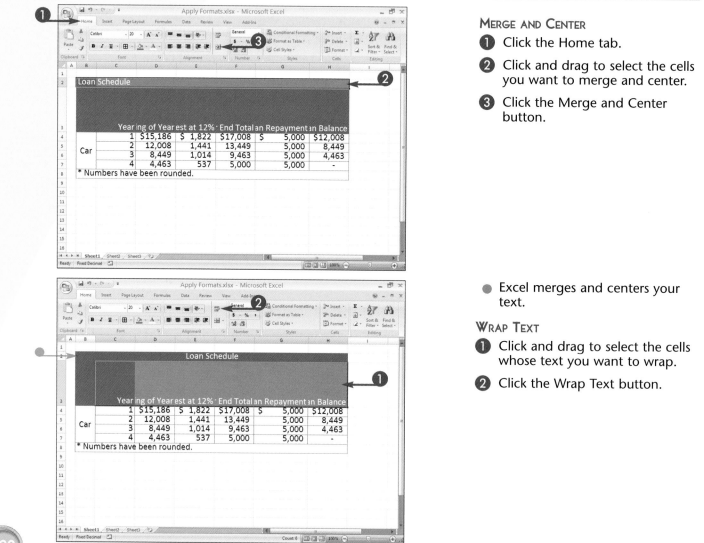

MERGE AND CENTER

1 Click the Home tab.

2 Click and drag to select the cells you want to merge and center.

3 Click the Merge and Center button.

● Excel merges and centers your text.

WRAP TEXT

1 Click and drag to select the cells whose text you want to wrap.

2 Click the Wrap Text button.

● Excel wraps your text.

ORIENTATION

① Click the cell or cells whose orientation you want to change.

② Click here and then select an orientation.

● Excel changes the orientation of your text.

69 CONTINUED

TIPS

Did You Know?

Excel has several buttons you can use to align data within a cell. Use the Align Left button (⊞) to align your data with the left side of the cell, use the Align Right button (⊞) to align your data with the right side of the cell, and use the Center button (⊞) to center your data in the cell.

Did You Know?

Excel has buttons you can use to place data at the top, bottom, or middle of the cell. Use the Top Align button (⊞) to place data at the top of the cell, use the Middle Align button (⊞) to place data in the middle of the cell, and use the Bottom Align button (⊞) to place data at the bottom of the cell.

Fill with a
GRADIENT

You can add a two-color effect to your fills by using Excel's gradient fill feature. A gradient is a blending of colors — one color gradually changes to another color.

In Excel, you choose the two colors you want to use to create your gradient. You then choose from one of the following shading styles: Horizontal, Vertical, Diagonal Up, Diagonal Down, From Corner, or From Center. Each shading style has several Variants — ways in which you can create your gradient. The Sample box provides you with a preview of what your gradient will look like when applied.

The Horizontal shading style provides horizontal bands of color, the Vertical shading style provides vertical bands of color, and Diagonal Up and Diagonal Down shading styles provide diagonal bands of color. In the Variants box, you can choose the color with which the gradient starts and ends.

The From Corner style starts with Color 1 and blends to Color 2. In the Variants box, you choose the corner in which Color 1 starts. The From Center style starts with Color 1 in the center and blends outward to Color 2.

① Select the cells you want to format.

② Click the Home tab.

③ Click the launcher in the Font group.

● The Format Cells dialog box appears.

④ Click the Fill tab.

⑤ Click Fill Effects.

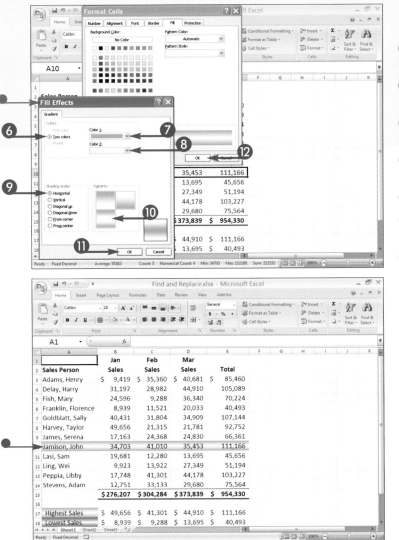

- The Fill Effects dialog box appears.

6 Click Two Colors (○ changes to ◉).

7 Click here and then select Color 1.

8 Click here and then select Color 2.

9 Click to select a Shading style (○ changes to ◉).

10 Click to select a Variant.

11 Click OK to close the Fill Effects dialog box.

12 Click OK to close the Format Cells dialog box.

- Excel fills the cells with the gradient you created.

TIPS

Did You Know?

You can clear the formats you apply to cells. Select the cells you want to clear, click the Home tab, and then click the Clear button (🖉) in the Editing group. A menu appears. Click Clear Formats. Excel removes the formats you applied to the selected cells.

Did You Know?

You can give your fill a professional look by adding a pattern to your fill. Patterns consist of dots or hatches. To add patterns, use the Fill tab in the Format Cells dialog box. In the Pattern Color field, select a color. In the Pattern Style field, select a pattern. Click OK. Excel adds the pattern to selected cells.

Format quickly with
FORMAT PAINTER

Excel can save you time when you need to reapply formats that already exist in your worksheet. The easiest way to apply a cell's format to another cell or to a range of cells is by using the Format Painter. Use the Format Painter for one-time copying of formats within a workbook. Use styles, discussed in Task #s 31 and 32, when you plan to apply common formats throughout a workbook and across workbooks.

You can find the Format Painter tool on the Home tab in the Clipboard group. To use it, first click in a cell

with the format you want to copy. Then click the Format Painter button. Finally, click in a cell or cells that you want to receive the formatting. You can apply a format to many cells at the same time. Excel applies formats instantly. Use the Format Painter to copy and apply both cell and number formats. If you make a mistake, you can undo the formats by pressing Ctrl+Z.

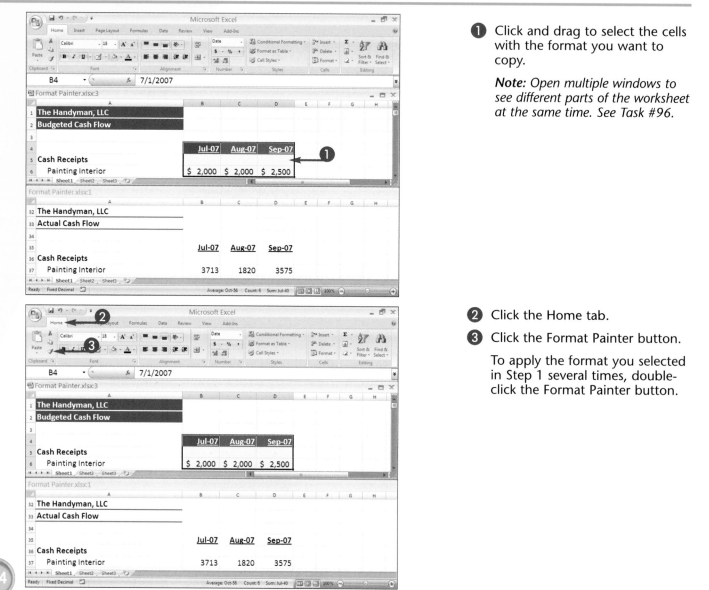

① Click and drag to select the cells with the format you want to copy.

Note: Open multiple windows to see different parts of the worksheet at the same time. See Task #96.

② Click the Home tab.

③ Click the Format Painter button.

To apply the format you selected in Step 1 several times, double-click the Format Painter button.

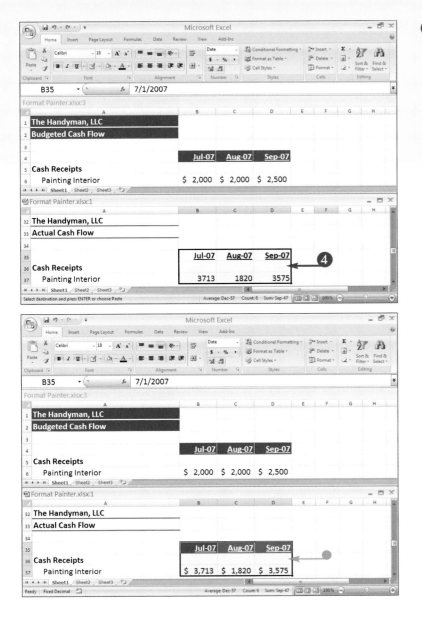

④ Click in the cell or cells in which you want to apply the format.

You can also click and drag to select a range of cells you want to format.

● The cell or cell range instantly takes on the formatting of the cell.

TIPS

Did You Know?
You can only apply a format once if you click the Format Painter tool. If you want to copy a format more than once, applying one format to several nonadjacent cells, double-click the tool instead of single-clicking it in Step 2.

Did You Know?
You can use the Format Painter to transfer properties from one image, such as clip art, to another image. The properties you transfer include background color, text flow around the image, and so on. Click the formatted graphic, click the Format Painter button, and then click the graphic you want to format.

INSERT SHAPES
into your worksheet

Shapes have a variety of purposes. Arrows point out relationships between data. Flowchart elements convey the structure of your data. Excel provides a variety of shapes, including lines, rectangles, arrows, flowchart elements, stars, banners, and callouts — all of which you can use in your worksheet.

You can rotate, resize, move, and reshape shapes. You can also apply predefined styles to your shapes. Excel provides many predefined styles from which to choose. As you roll your cursor over each shape style, Excel provides a quick preview of how the style appears when applied.

In many cases, you can add text to your shape. You can reformat the text on your shape and change its font, size, color, and alignment. Simply select the text and then click commands on the Home tab to make your changes.

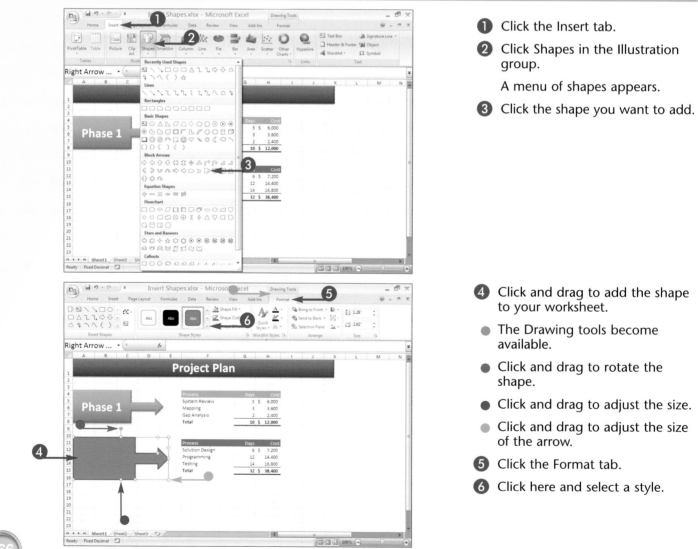

① Click the Insert tab.

② Click Shapes in the Illustration group.

A menu of shapes appears.

③ Click the shape you want to add.

④ Click and drag to add the shape to your worksheet.

● The Drawing tools become available.

● Click and drag to rotate the shape.

● Click and drag to adjust the size.

● Click and drag to adjust the size of the arrow.

⑤ Click the Format tab.

⑥ Click here and select a style.

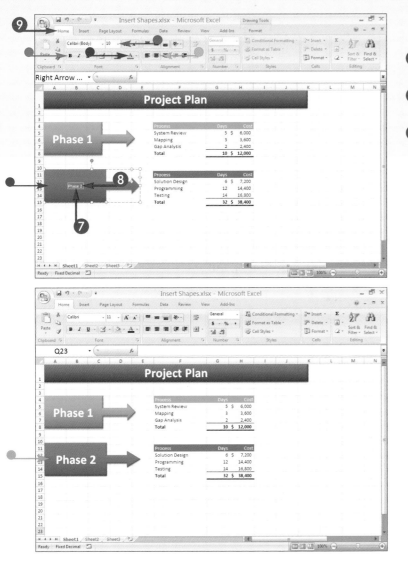

- Excel formats your shape.

7. Click your shape and type your text.

8. Click and drag to the left to select your text.

9. Click the Home tab.

- Click to adjust the size of your text.

- Click to align your text.

- Click to format your text.

- Click to change the color of your text.

- Excel applies your changes.

TIPS

Did You Know?

You can copy and paste shapes. Select your shape. Click the Home tab. Click the Copy button (📋). Click Paste. A menu appears. Click Paste Special. The Paste Special Dialog box appears. In the As box, click Microsoft Office Drawing Object and then click OK. A copy of your shape appears in your worksheet.

Did You Know?

You can use the buttons to format your text.

Format Options			
Button	**Function**	**Button**	**Function**
B	Bold	I	Italicize
U	Underline	▷	Rotate
▤	Increase Indent	▤	Decrease Indent
Calibri	Change Font		

INSERT TEXT BOXES
into your worksheet

By using a text graphic, you can create logos, add text to pictures, or add text to your worksheet. You can create text with shadows, reflections, glows, bevels, 3-D rotations, and transforms. For each option, you can choose from several sub-options, and you can apply multiple effects to the same piece of text.

By using the various options, you can create the style you want or select a predefined style. As you roll your cursor over the predefined styles, Excel provides a quick preview of how the styles appear when applied to your text.

Use the Text Fill button to change the color of your text and the Text Outline button to change the color that outlines your text.

As with all graphics, you can resize, rotate, and reposition text boxes. You can also change the font size, alignment, and format. Use the same methods you use to change text added to a shape. To learn more, see Task #72.

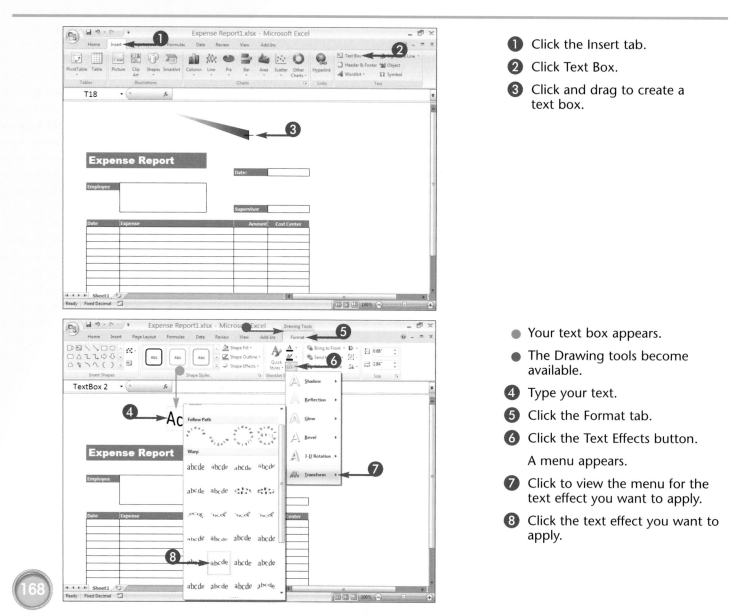

① Click the Insert tab.

② Click Text Box.

③ Click and drag to create a text box.

● Your text box appears.

● The Drawing tools become available.

④ Type your text.

⑤ Click the Format tab.

⑥ Click the Text Effects button.

A menu appears.

⑦ Click to view the menu for the text effect you want to apply.

⑧ Click the text effect you want to apply.

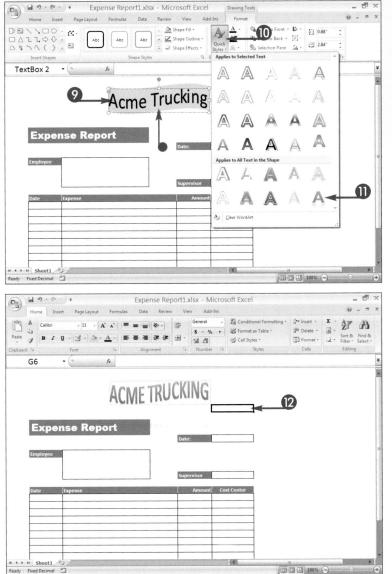

- Excel applies the effect.

⑨ Click and drag to the left to select your text.

You can also press Shift+Home.

⑩ Click Quick Styles.

A menu of choices appears.

⑪ Click the style you want to apply.

⑫ Click outside your text box.

Excel applies your formats.

Note: *As you roll your cursor over your text box, a four-sided arrow appears. When you see the four-sided arrow, click and drag to reposition your text.*

TIPS

Did You Know?

You can format a text box as columns. Use the launcher on the Format tab in the Shape Styles group to open the Format Shapes dialog box. Click Text Box. The Text Box Pane appears. Click the Columns button. The Columns dialog box appears. In the Number field, enter the number of columns you want. In the Spacing field, enter the amount of space you want to create between each column.

Did You Know?

You can use WordArt to create a text graphic. Click the Insert tab. Click WordArt. A list of options appears. Click the text style you want. A text box appears with text. Type your text. You can modify the WordArt text just as you would any other text box.

INSERT PHOTOGRAPHS
into your worksheet

Photographs can enhance your worksheet, illustrate your point, and emphasize your message. Adding a photograph to Excel is easy. Just locate the photograph and insert it.

After you insert your photograph, you can choose from many options to enhance the display of your photo. Use picture styles to angle; add borders, shadows, and reflections; and otherwise stylize your photograph. As you roll your cursor over the various picture styles, Excel provides a preview of how the styles appear when applied.

You can change the color of your picture border and adjust your photo's brightness and contrast. You can even crop your photo to show only the portion you want.

You can manipulate your photograph the same way you manipulate any other graphic. You can move it, rotate it, and resize it. When resizing, drag the corner handles to resize your photo proportionately. Drag the side handles to make your picture wider. Drag the top and bottom handles to make your picture taller.

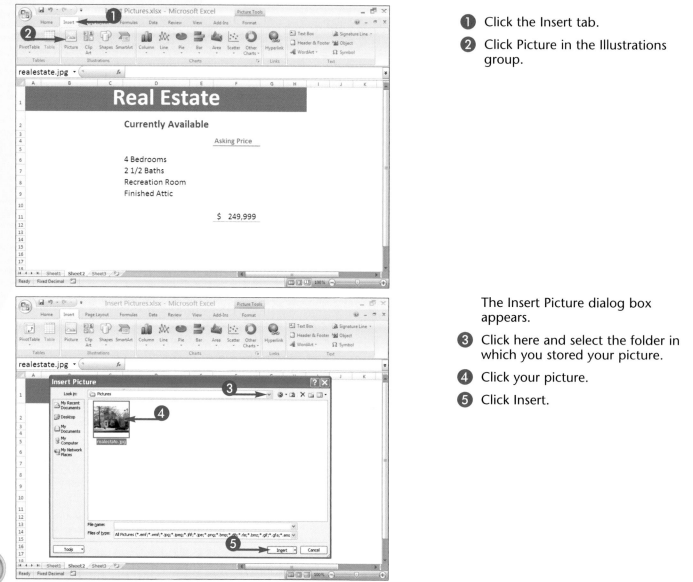

① Click the Insert tab.

② Click Picture in the Illustrations group.

The Insert Picture dialog box appears.

③ Click here and select the folder in which you stored your picture.

④ Click your picture.

⑤ Click Insert.

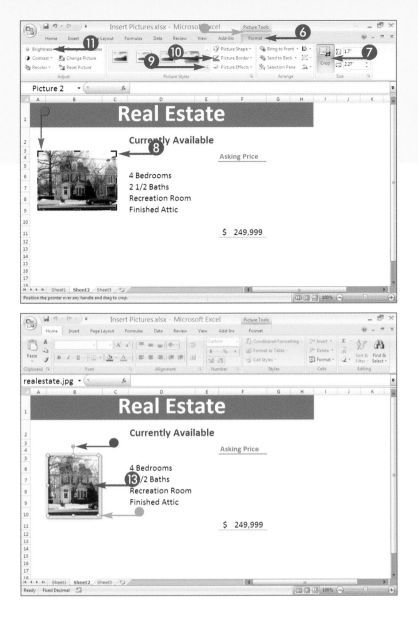

The picture appears in your worksheet.

● The Picture tools become available.

6 Click the Format tab.

7 Click Crop.

● Black markings appear on your photo.

8 Click and drag the markings to crop your photo.

9 Click here and select a picture style.

10 Click here and select a color for your picture's border.

11 Click here and select a brightness adjustment.

12 Click outside your photo.

Excel applies the options you selected.

13 Click your photo.

● Click and drag to rotate.

● Click and drag to resize.

Excel adjusts your photo.

74

DIFFICULTY LEVEL

TIPS

Did You Know?
You can also add clip art to your worksheet. Click the Insert tab and then click Clip Art. The Clip Art dialog box appears. In the Search For field, type the category in which the item for which you are looking falls and then click Go. Excel finds all the clip art in that category and displays them. Double-click the image you want. It appears in your worksheet.

Did You Know?
You can use Excel to colorize your photographs. Click your photo. Click the Format tab and then click Recolor in the Adjust group. Among other choices, you can change your photo to grayscale or to a sepia tone.

ARRANGE THE GRAPHICS
in your worksheet

When you place a shape, text box, photograph, clip art, or any other type of graphic into your Excel worksheet, Excel stacks it. When graphics overlap, graphics that are higher in the stack appear to be on top of graphics that are lower in the stack. This can cause problems. For example, the text you want to place on a shape could actually appear behind the shape. Fortunately, you can change the stacking order. You can use the Selection and Visibility Pane to choose the exact stack order in which your graphics display.

Excel names each graphic as you create or add it to your worksheet. When you open the Selection and Visibility Pane, these names display. You can change the Excel-generated names to names that are more meaningful.

Excel also provides tools to help you arrange graphics on your worksheet. You can select graphics and then align or rotate them.

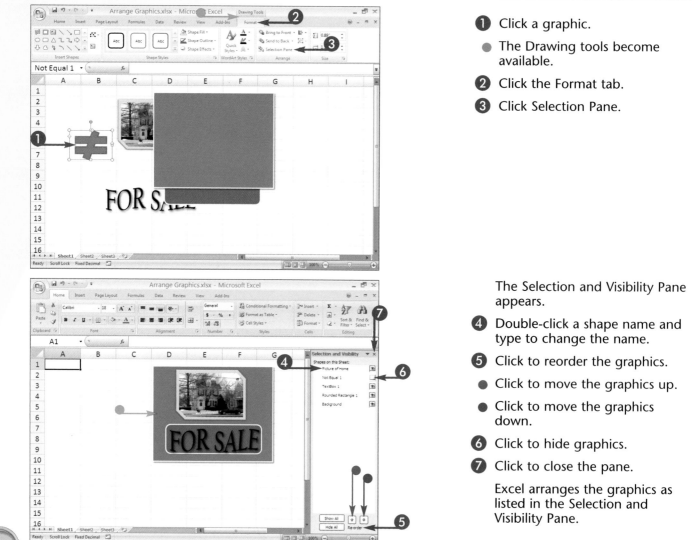

① Click a graphic.

● The Drawing tools become available.

② Click the Format tab.

③ Click Selection Pane.

The Selection and Visibility Pane appears.

④ Double-click a shape name and type to change the name.

⑤ Click to reorder the graphics.

● Click to move the graphics up.

● Click to move the graphics down.

⑥ Click to hide graphics.

⑦ Click to close the pane.

Excel arranges the graphics as listed in the Selection and Visibility Pane.

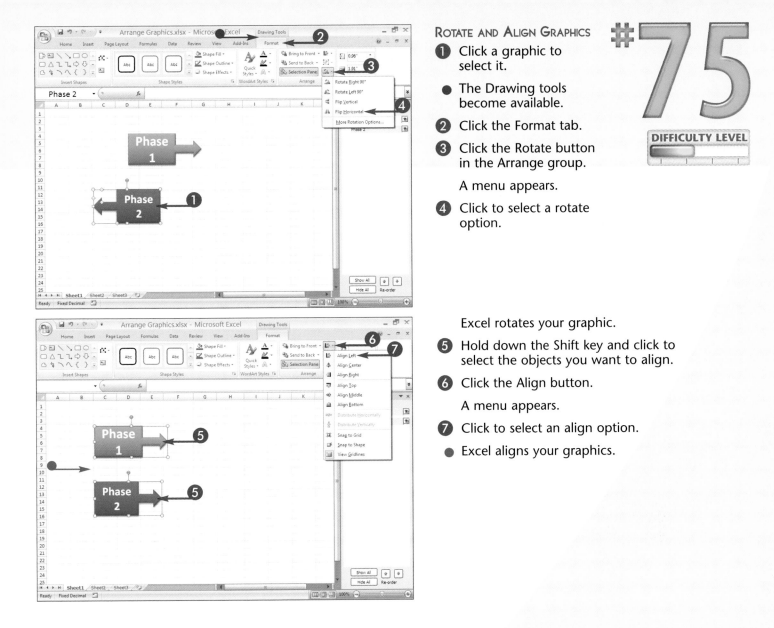

75

DIFFICULTY LEVEL

1. Click a graphic to select it.

● The Drawing tools become available.

2. Click the Format tab.

3. Click the Rotate button in the Arrange group.

A menu appears.

4. Click to select a rotate option.

Excel rotates your graphic.

5. Hold down the Shift key and click to select the objects you want to align.

6. Click the Align button.

A menu appears.

7. Click to select an align option.

● Excel aligns your graphics.

TIPS

Did You Know?

You can group your graphics. Grouping graphics allows you to treat two or more graphics as if they are one. As you move one graphic in a group, all the other graphics in the same group move with it. To group, hold down the Shift key and click each graphic you want to group. Click the Format tab, click the Group button ( ), and then click Group.

Did You Know?

You can use the Bring to Front and Send to Back options on the Format tab in the Arrange group to change the stacking order of your graphics. Send to Back sends your graphic to the bottom of the stack. Send Back moves it down one level. Bring to Front brings your graphic to the top of the stack. Bring Forward brings it up one level.

Insert a
BACKGROUND IMAGE

Placing a background image behind a worksheet can draw attention to and enhance the appearance of otherwise drab columns of numbers. In other words, backgrounds can set the tone. Using a company logo, for example, can convey official status. Backgrounds can also create a dramatic or decorative effect related to worksheet content. For example, you can place pale red hearts behind a worksheet showing trends in the sale of Valentine's Day cards.

A background shows a color or image under the text and covers the entire surface of the worksheet. You

can use images in any standard format, such as JPG, BMP, PNG, or GIF. Excel tiles your worksheet with the image.

Background images are for display in Excel only. When you print your worksheet or publish your worksheet as a Web page, the image is not printed or displayed on the Web page.

If you include your worksheet in a presentation, you may want to view it in Full Screen mode.

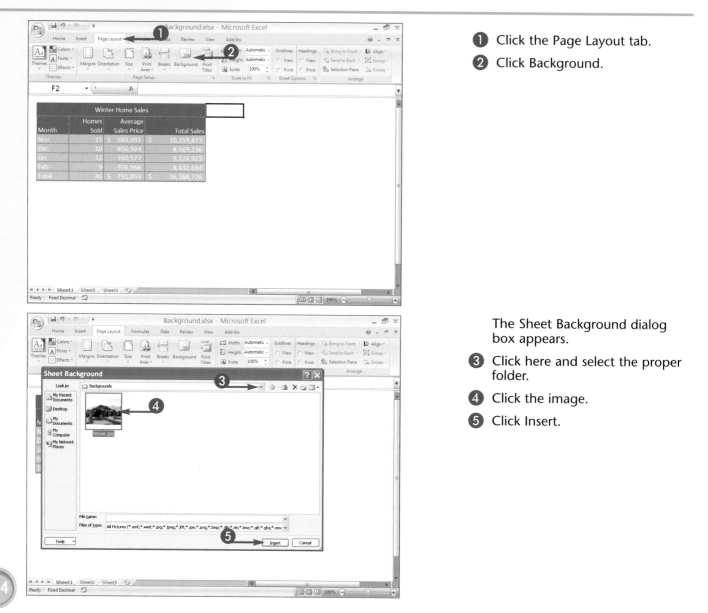

1 Click the Page Layout tab.

2 Click Background.

The Sheet Background dialog box appears.

3 Click here and select the proper folder.

4 Click the image.

5 Click Insert.

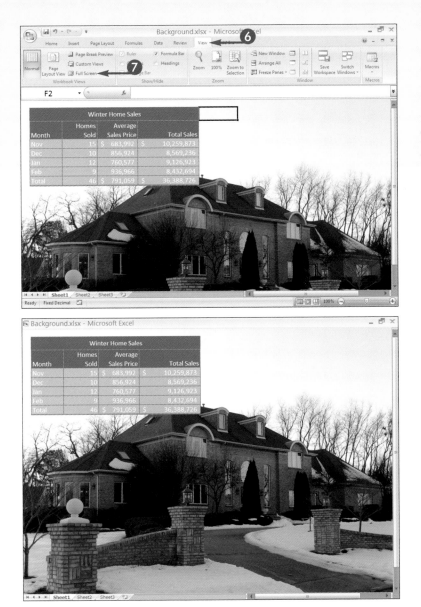

The image appears in your worksheet.

Note: *Click Delete Background on the Page Layout tab to remove the image.*

6 Click View.

7 Click Full Screen in the Workbook views group.

76

Your worksheet displays in Full Screen mode.

Note: *Press the Esc key to return to normal mode.*

TIPS

Did You Know?

If you do not want to see the formula bar, headings, or gridlines when you present your worksheet, you can hide them. Click the View tab and then, in the Show/Hide group, deselect the options you want to hide (☑ changes to ☐).

Did You Know?

You can apply backgrounds to other objects in Excel. To place a background behind a chart, right-click near the chart border. A menu appears. Click Format Chart Area. The Format Chart Area dialog box appears. Click Fill and then click the File button to import a picture or other background.

TAKE A PICTURE
of your worksheet

Using Excel's Copy as Picture feature, you can take snapshots of cell ranges in your worksheet. The Copy as Picture feature turns whatever you copy into a graphic that you can manipulate just as you would any other graphic. In fact, you can apply styles, shapes, borders, and picture effects to the graphic. You can also adjust the brightness and the contrast, and you can recolor your graphic. You can copy your graphic to the Clipboard and paste it into other Office

products such as Word or non-Office products such as Photoshop.

Using the Copy as Picture feature is as simple as copying and pasting. When you copy as a picture, you do not retain information such as formulas. The result is a graphical image with which you can work. You can resize the image and drag it to a new location, but you cannot edit the values represented in the image.

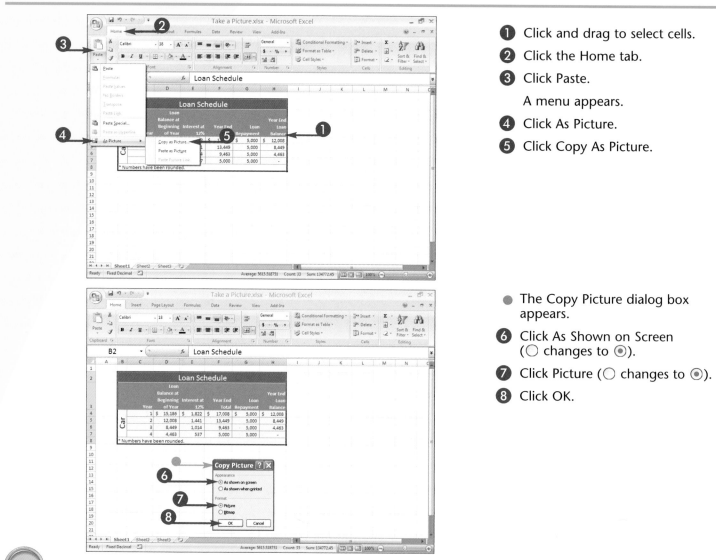

① Click and drag to select cells.

② Click the Home tab.

③ Click Paste.

A menu appears.

④ Click As Picture.

⑤ Click Copy As Picture.

● The Copy Picture dialog box appears.

⑥ Click As Shown on Screen (○ changes to ◉).

⑦ Click Picture (○ changes to ◉).

⑧ Click OK.

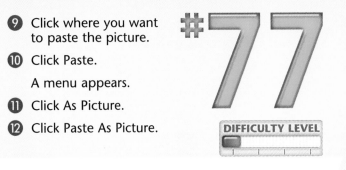

9 Click where you want to paste the picture.

10 Click Paste.

A menu appears.

11 Click As Picture.

12 Click Paste As Picture.

DIFFICULTY LEVEL

● Excel pastes the cells as a picture.

● The Picture tools become available.

TIPS

Did You Know?

You can add the Camera button (⬚) to the Quick Access toolbar and use it to take pictures of your worksheet. You select the cells, click the Camera button, and then click the location where you want to paste the picture. You cannot use the Picture tools with graphics created with the Camera button. See Task #95 to learn how to add a button to the Quick Access toolbar.

Did You Know?

You can copy cell images as pictures into other Office applications and use them in presentations and reports; however, the copies lose their live connection to the Excel data. With a live connection, updates occur in Word, for example, as you update your data in Excel.

Protect, Save, and Print

After you complete the work of entering, formatting, analyzing, and charting your data, you can share it with others. Sharing data usually means either saving it and sharing the file, or saving it and sharing a printout. The tips in this chapter make it easier to share your work with others.

You can protect your worksheet so others can view and print it but cannot make changes to it. You can also save your workbook as a template. By saving your workbook as a template, you eliminate the chore of re-creating a special-purpose worksheet each time you need to use it. In addition, you can save documents in many formats; in this chapter, you review a few document formats and the advantages of each are explained.

The printing tips in this chapter focus on printing multiple-page worksheets and multiple-sheet workbooks. You find out how to select noncontiguous cell ranges and print them and how to repeat row and column labels across several pages.

The two key printing tools are the Page Setup dialog box and the Print Preview window. Familiarize yourself with the many choices they offer.

Chapter 9 carries forward the themes introduced in this chapter. There you learn more about exchanging data between Excel and other applications.

PROTECT
your worksheet

If you share your worksheets with others, you can protect them so others can view and print them, but cannot make changes to them. Even if you do not share your worksheets, you may want to lock certain areas so you do not inadvertently make changes. Locking your worksheet enables users to make certain types of changes while disallowing others. For example, you can allow users to make changes to formats; insert or delete columns, rows, or hyperlinks; sort; filter; use PivotTables; and/or edit objects or scenarios.

By default, when you lock a worksheet, Excel locks every cell in the worksheet, and the formulas are visible to anyone who uses the worksheet. You can specify the cells that remain unlocked, and you can hide formulas.

To protect your worksheet, enter a password in the Protect Sheet dialog box. Keep a list of your worksheet passwords in a safe place because a worksheet password cannot be recovered. If you lose or forget your password, you can no longer access the locked areas of your worksheet.

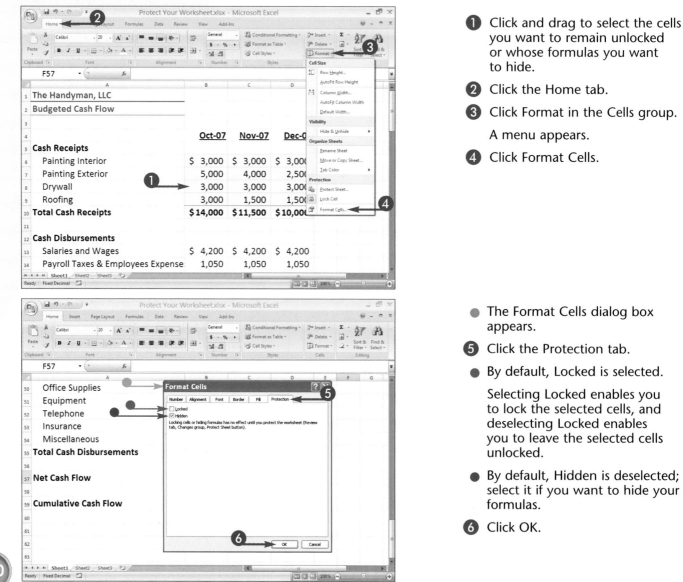

① Click and drag to select the cells you want to remain unlocked or whose formulas you want to hide.

② Click the Home tab.

③ Click Format in the Cells group.

A menu appears.

④ Click Format Cells.

● The Format Cells dialog box appears.

⑤ Click the Protection tab.

● By default, Locked is selected.

Selecting Locked enables you to lock the selected cells, and deselecting Locked enables you to leave the selected cells unlocked.

● By default, Hidden is deselected; select it if you want to hide your formulas.

⑥ Click OK.

⑦ Click Format in the Cells group.

A menu appears.

⑧ Click Protect Sheet.

● The Protect Sheet dialog box appears.

⑨ Enter a password, if you wish to password-protect your worksheet.

⑩ Click to select the options you want to allow the users to perform (☐ changes to ☑).

⑪ Click OK.

● The Confirm Password dialog box appears.

⑫ Reenter your password.

⑬ Click OK.

Excel locks the cells in your worksheet and hides the formulas in the selected cells.

● Users receive a message if they attempt to change data.

TIPS

Did You Know?

You can protect a workbook from unwanted changes. Click the Review tab, click Protect Workbook in the Changes group, and then click Protect Structure and Windows. The Protect Structure and Windows dialog box appears. Select Structure (☐ changes to ☑) to protect your workbook from the moving, addition, and deletion of worksheets. Select Windows (☐ changes to ☑) to protect your workbook from changes in the size and position of windows. Optionally, require a password to remove these protections.

Did You Know?

If you click the Review tab and then click Allow Users to Edit Ranges in the Changes group, the Allow Users to Edit Ranges dialog box appears. Use this dialog box to specify the ranges users can modify. Click the New button and complete the fields in the New Range dialog box. You can password-protect each range you allow.

Save a workbook as
A TEMPLATE

Templates are special-purpose workbooks you use to create new worksheets. They can contain formats, styles, and specific content such as images, column heads, and date ranges you want to reuse in other worksheets. Templates save you the work of re-creating workbooks for recurring purposes such as filling out invoices and preparing monthly reports.

When you work with a template, you edit a copy, not the original, so you retain the original template for use in structuring other worksheets. Excel 2007 worksheets ordinarily have an .xlsx file extension.

Saving an Excel worksheet as a template creates a file with an .xltx extension.

Your custom template includes all the changes you have made to your workbook, including formats, formulas, and such changes as opening multiple windows or deleting tabs. Saving formulas with your template causes your worksheet to calculate automatically. Saving formats saves you from having to re-create them.

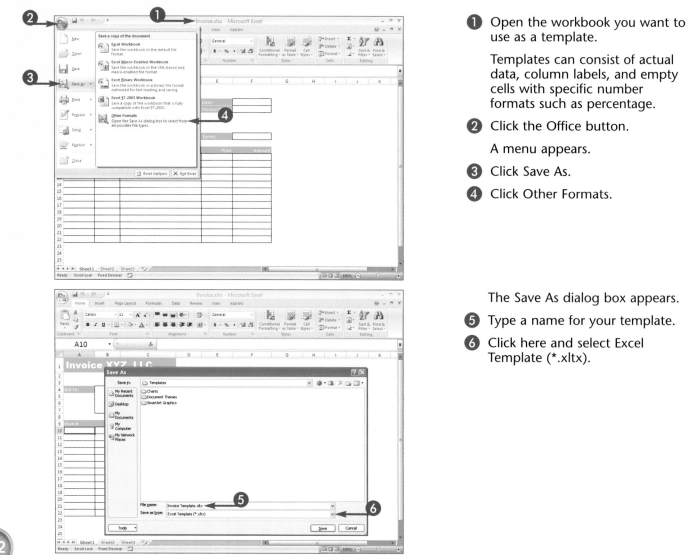

① Open the workbook you want to use as a template.

Templates can consist of actual data, column labels, and empty cells with specific number formats such as percentage.

② Click the Office button.

A menu appears.

③ Click Save As.

④ Click Other Formats.

The Save As dialog box appears.

⑤ Type a name for your template.

⑥ Click here and select Excel Template (*.xltx).

- The Save In folder changes to Templates.

7 Click Save.

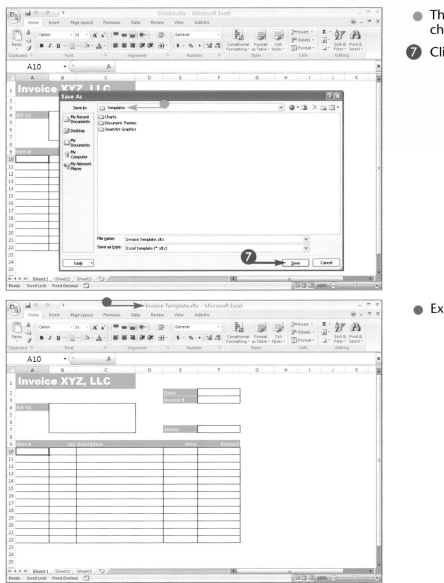

- Excel creates the template.

Did You Know?

To use a template you have created, click the Office button and then click New. The New Workbook dialog box appears. Click My Templates. The New dialog box appears. Click the template you want to open and then click OK. Excel opens your template. When you save your modified file, save it as a regular file with an .xlsx extension so you do not overwrite your template.

Did You Know?

Excel comes with ready-made templates that serve basic business purposes such as invoicing. To open and use one of these templates, click the Office button and then click New. The New Workbook dialog box appears. Click Installed Templates. Click the template you want to open and then click Create.

CHOOSE A FORMAT
when saving a workbook

After you create an Excel 2007 worksheet, you may want to share it with others. The file format you choose when you save your file can aid you. The default format for Office 2007 is Excel Workbook (.xlsx). This file format is new to Office 2007. It creates smaller files that are easily accessible in other software programs because the files are in XML format, which is a data-exchange standard.

Previous versions of Excel did not use XML as the default format. These files have an .xls extension. If you want to share your documents with people who

use Excel 97-2003, you can save your file as an Excel 97-2003 workbook (.xls). Features that are not supported in earlier versions of Excel are lost when you save your file as an Excel 97-2003 workbook.

You can also save your worksheet in other file formats, including several text-based formats such as Text (Tab delimited), Text (Macintosh), and CSV (comma delimited). These formats save the worksheet as text that can be read into other applications.

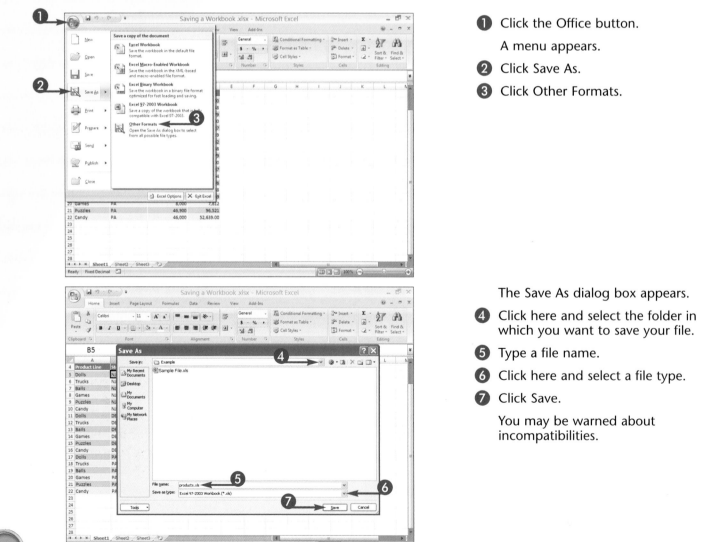

1 Click the Office button.

A menu appears.

2 Click Save As.

3 Click Other Formats.

The Save As dialog box appears.

4 Click here and select the folder in which you want to save your file.

5 Type a file name.

6 Click here and select a file type.

7 Click Save.

You may be warned about incompatibilities.

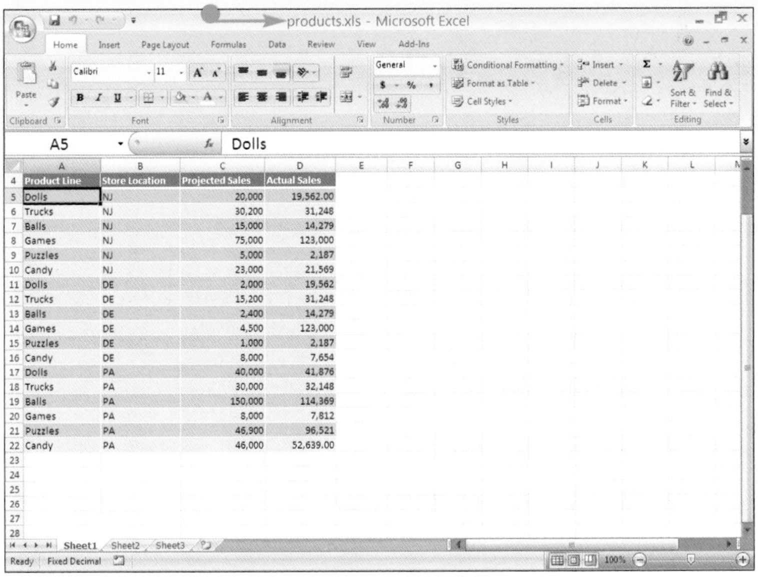

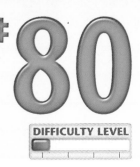

Excel saves your worksheet in the format you specify.

- This example shows the worksheet saved in Office 2003.

#80

DIFFICULTY LEVEL

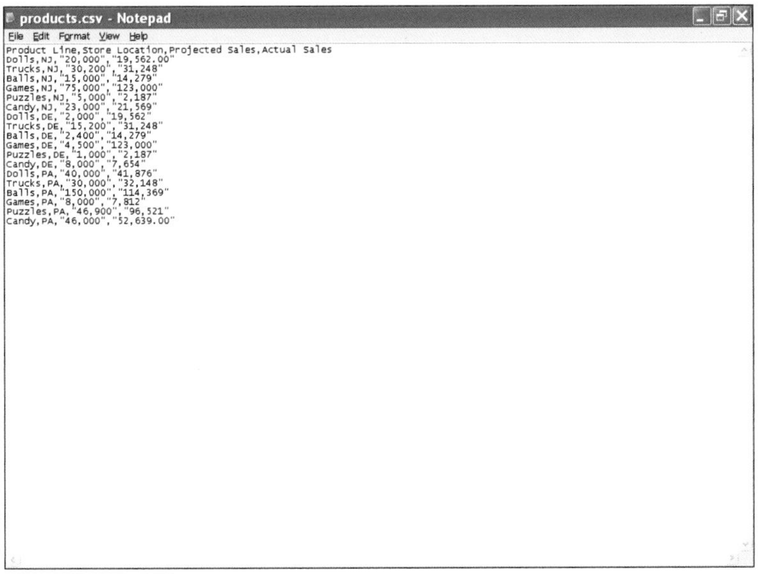

This example shows the file saved in CSV format.

TIPS

Did You Know?

If you want to see the XML layout for an Excel 2007 file, change the file extension on the file to .zip and then double-click the file. The file opens and several folders and files appear. Double-click the files to open and view them.

Did You Know?

If you have a computer with Excel 97-2003 installed, you can go to the Office Update Web site and download the 2007 Microsoft Office system Compatibility Pack for Excel. Once you install the Compatibility Pack, you can open Excel 2007 files in Excel 97-2003. Excel features and formatting may not display in the earlier version, but they are still available when you open the file again in Excel 2007.

PRINT MULTIPLE AREAS
of a workbook

You can print noncontiguous areas of your worksheet, thereby limiting your printing to the information that is of relevance. This feature involves little more than selecting the cells you want to print.

There are many reasons why you may want to print noncontiguous areas of your worksheet. For example, if you have sales data for several products, each in a column, you can select and print only the columns that are of interest to you. You select noncontiguous areas of the worksheet by pressing and holding the

Ctrl key as you click and drag. After you select areas, you set them as the print area.

When printing noncontiguous areas of your worksheet, you may have column headings or row labels you want to print with each selection. You can specify the rows you want to repeat at the top or the columns you want to repeat down the side of every page you print.

When you print a worksheet with multiple selected areas, each area prints on its own page.

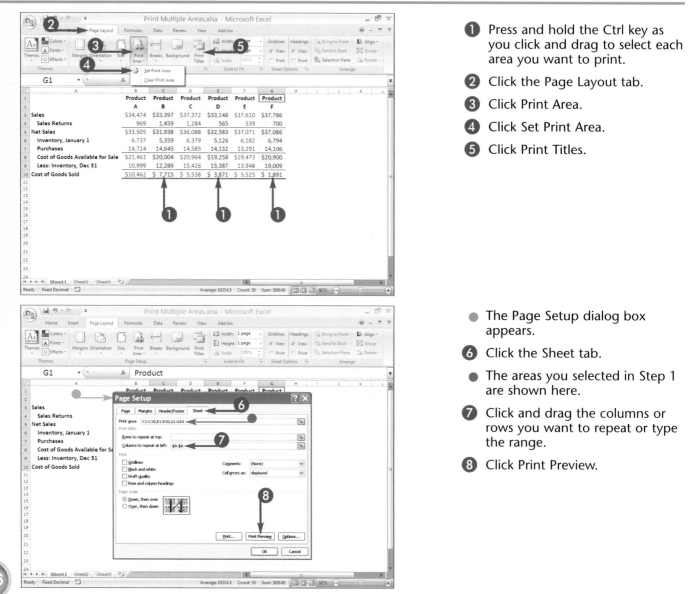

① Press and hold the Ctrl key as you click and drag to select each area you want to print.

② Click the Page Layout tab.

③ Click Print Area.

④ Click Set Print Area.

⑤ Click Print Titles.

● The Page Setup dialog box appears.

⑥ Click the Sheet tab.

● The areas you selected in Step 1 are shown here.

⑦ Click and drag the columns or rows you want to repeat or type the range.

⑧ Click Print Preview.

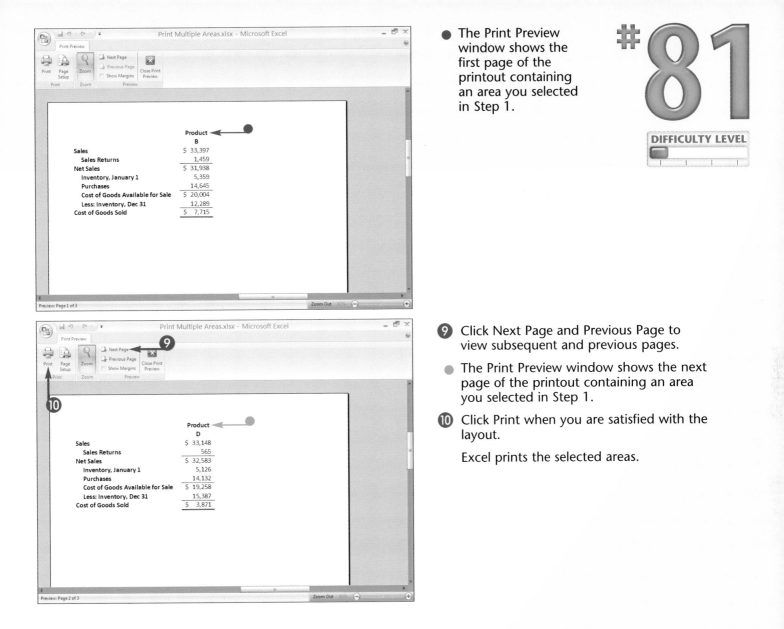

- The Print Preview window shows the first page of the printout containing an area you selected in Step 1.

9 Click Next Page and Previous Page to view subsequent and previous pages.

- The Print Preview window shows the next page of the printout containing an area you selected in Step 1.

10 Click Print when you are satisfied with the layout.

Excel prints the selected areas.

TIPS

Delete It!
To clear the print area, click Page Layout and then click Print Area. A menu appears. Click Clear Print Area. Print Areas stay in effect until you clear them. You can add to the print area by selecting a range and clicking Page Layout, Print Area, and then Add to Print Area.

Did You Know?
To open the Page Setup dialog box, click the launcher in the Page Setup group. You can use the Header/Footer tab in the dialog box to add page numbers as well as both a header and a footer. Click Custom Header or Custom Footer to create dates and page numbers on each page, or even add an image to the header or footer.

PRINT MULTIPLE WORKSHEETS
from a workbook

By default, Excel prints either the entire active worksheet or a selected print area within the active worksheet. However, you can select several worksheets and print them all at the same time. You may want to use this option if you have a workbook with data or charts on several separate sheets.

To select two or more adjacent sheets for printing, press and hold the Shift key and click the tab for each sheet you want to print. To select several nonadjacent worksheets, press and hold the Ctrl key and click the

tab for each sheet you want to print. To print every worksheet in the workbook, right-click any tab. A menu appears. Click Select All Sheets.

Selecting multiple tabs groups the sheets. While the sheets are grouped, any data you type into any sheet or any changes you make to the structure of sheets are also typed into or changed in all the other sheets in the group. To ungroup sheets, click any unselected sheet. If no unselected sheet is visible, right-click any sheet. A menu appears. Click Ungroup Sheets.

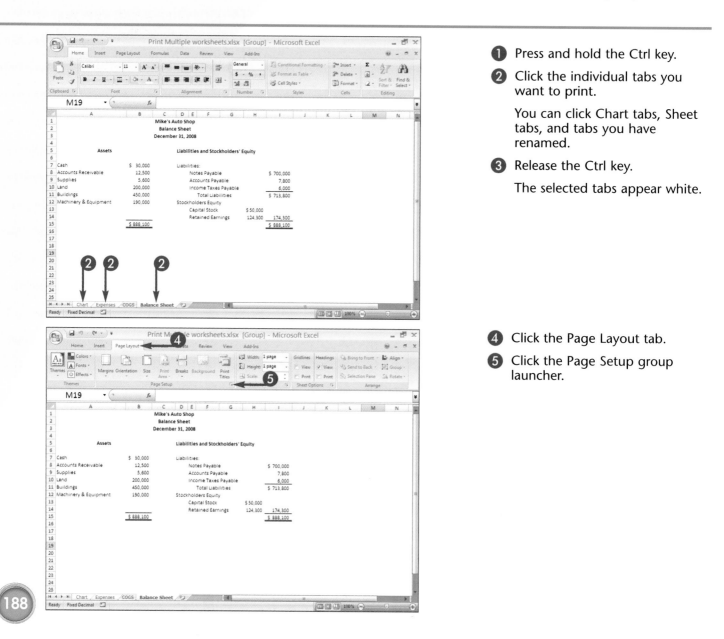

1 Press and hold the Ctrl key.

2 Click the individual tabs you want to print.

You can click Chart tabs, Sheet tabs, and tabs you have renamed.

3 Release the Ctrl key.

The selected tabs appear white.

4 Click the Page Layout tab.

5 Click the Page Setup group launcher.

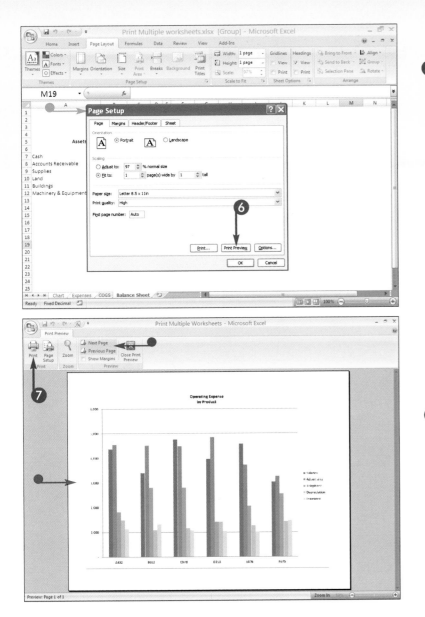

● The Page Setup dialog box appears.

⑥ Click Print Preview.

● Each worksheet appears on its own page. The first worksheet you selected in Step 2 appears first.

● Click Previous Page and Next Page to review the selected sheets.

⑦ Click Print when you are ready to print.

Excel prints the selected worksheets.

TIPS

Did You Know?

You can print row numbers and column letters on every page. Click the Launcher in the Page Setup group on the Page Layout tab to open the Page Setup dialog box. On the Sheet tab, click Row and Column Headings (☐ changes to ☑) before printing your worksheet. To print comments, select an option in the Comments field. You can print comments adjacent to their cells or gather them at the end of the report.

Did You Know?

To print several workbooks at the same time, click the Office button and then click Open. In the Open dialog box, press and hold the Ctrl key and click the workbooks you want to print. Click the Tools drop-down menu in the lower-right corner and then click Print.

Chapter 9

Extend Excel

In Excel, you can do more than create and maintain workbooks and worksheets. Through data exchange, you can extend Excel in two ways. First, you can use data from other programs within Excel and thereby apply Excel's extensive worksheet capabilities to other programs' data. Second, you can use Excel data within other programs, thereby extending your ability to use, analyze, and present your Excel data. This chapter focuses on the many techniques for integrating Excel with Word, PowerPoint, and Access; querying Web sites; importing data; exporting data; and querying Access databases from Excel.

With queries, you can bring non-Excel data, such as a Microsoft Access table, into Excel. As you create a query, you can sort and filter the data. Later you can analyze and chart the data as you would any other worksheet data.

Queries are a powerful database tool for analyzing data sets. With minor changes, you can extend the tasks in this chapter to exchange data with corporate databases based on Oracle, SQL Server, and other such products.

Less known to Excel users are the query features that enable you to query a Web site within Excel. You can query a Web site and import Web content into Excel. For example, you can import statistics presented in HTML tables.

You can create links from your worksheets to other worksheets and other programs. For example, you can use a link to open a related workbook or a related Word document.

Top 100

PASTE LINK
into Word or PowerPoint

By paste linking Excel worksheets into Word or PowerPoint, you can add sophisticated calculations created in Excel to documents created in Word or PowerPoint. In Word, for example, you can use Excel worksheets to present quarterly reports or other financial documents.

When you paste link, if you alter Excel data while in Word or PowerPoint, Office automatically updates the Excel worksheet. The opposite is also true. When you alter paste-linked data while in Excel, Office automatically updates the paste-linked Word or PowerPoint document. Paste linking enables you to keep your documents in sync, because you do not have to worry about manually coordinating the changes to one document with the other document.

To update a paste-linked Excel worksheet while in Word or PowerPoint, double-click the worksheet to edit it. When you do, Microsoft Word or PowerPoint automatically opens the document in Excel so you have all the Excel commands available to you as you edit your document.

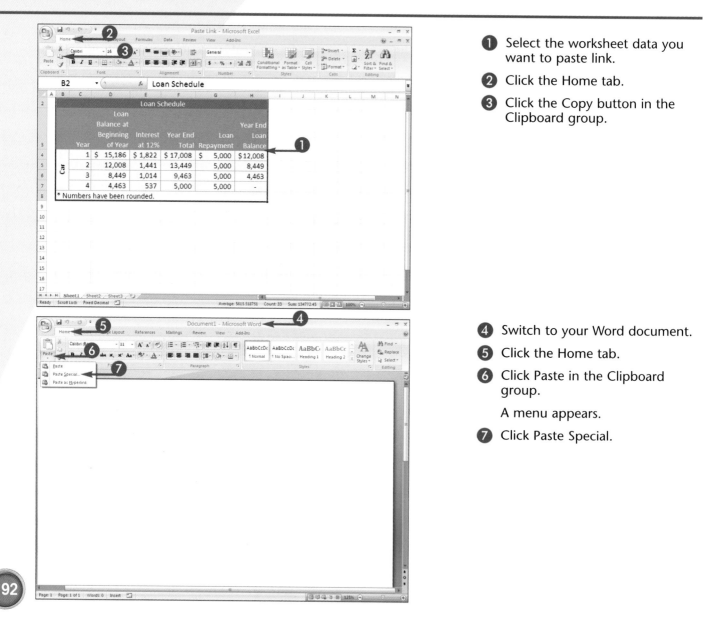

1 Select the worksheet data you want to paste link.

2 Click the Home tab.

3 Click the Copy button in the Clipboard group.

4 Switch to your Word document.

5 Click the Home tab.

6 Click Paste in the Clipboard group.

A menu appears.

7 Click Paste Special.

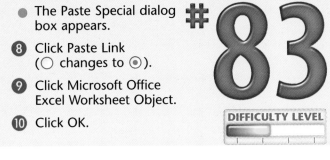

- The Paste Special dialog box appears.

8 Click Paste Link (○ changes to ◉).

9 Click Microsoft Office Excel Worksheet Object.

10 Click OK.

DIFFICULTY LEVEL

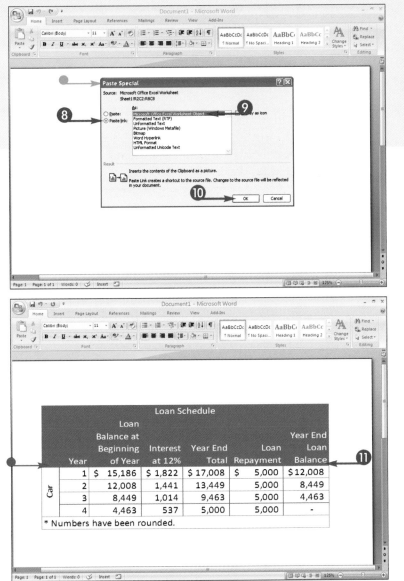

- The worksheet appears in Word.

11 Double-click the worksheet to edit it.

Your worksheet opens in Excel and you can make any necessary edits.

When you finish your edits, save and close Excel and return to your Word document.

TIPS

Did You Know?

The example paste links Excel into Word. You can follow the same steps to paste link an Excel worksheet into PowerPoint; just switch to PowerPoint instead of Word in Step 4.

Did You Know?

You can paste link a Word document into Excel. The procedure is the same except you select the data in Word you want to paste link and click the Word Copy button (📋). Then move to Excel and click the Home tab, Paste, and Paste Special. The Paste Special dialog box appears. Click Paste Link (○ changes to ◉). Click Microsoft Office Word Document Object and then OK. Your Word document appears in Excel. Double-click your Word document to edit it.

EMBED
a worksheet

You can create a PowerPoint presentation or a Word document that contains an Excel worksheet you can edit without leaving PowerPoint or Word. This means you can demonstrate different business scenarios as you give your PowerPoint presentation or do sophisticated mathematical calculations while in Word. To use this feature, you must embed your worksheet into your PowerPoint or Word file. You can use an existing Excel file or generate a new Excel file entirely within PowerPoint or Word.

When you embed Excel documents, the Excel worksheet becomes part of the PowerPoint or Word document and is accessible only through PowerPoint or Word. Embedding differs from paste linking. When you make changes to an Excel worksheet embedded into PowerPoint or Word, changes you make only affect the PowerPoint or Word file. When you paste link a worksheet into PowerPoint or Word and make changes to your file from Word or PowerPoint, Office also updates the Excel file.

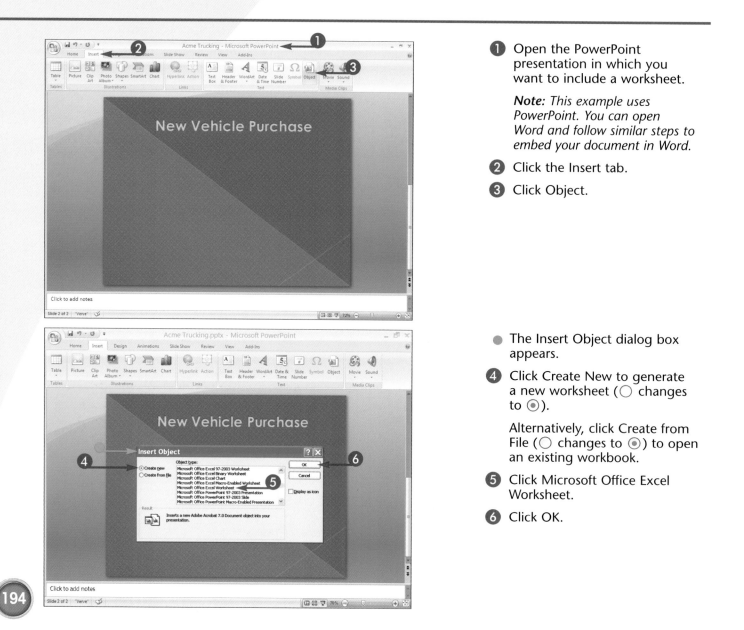

① Open the PowerPoint presentation in which you want to include a worksheet.

Note: This example uses PowerPoint. You can open Word and follow similar steps to embed your document in Word.

② Click the Insert tab.

③ Click Object.

● The Insert Object dialog box appears.

④ Click Create New to generate a new worksheet (○ changes to ⊙).

Alternatively, click Create from File (○ changes to ⊙) to open an existing workbook.

⑤ Click Microsoft Office Excel Worksheet.

⑥ Click OK.

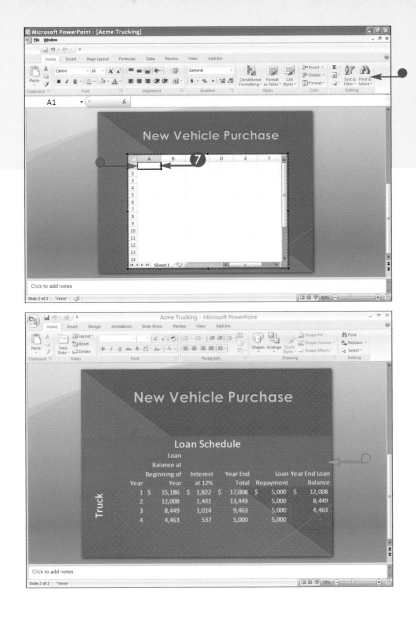

- A blank worksheet appears.
- All of the Microsoft Excel commands are available to you.

⑦ Create your worksheet.

Click outside the worksheet when you finish.

DIFFICULTY LEVEL

- Excel adds the worksheet to your PowerPoint presentation.

TIPS

Did You Know?

When you create a new Excel chart in PowerPoint, you see a fake data set and associated chart. Change the data and replace it with your own, either by typing new data or by copying and pasting data from an existing Excel worksheet. You can use the new or copied data as the basis for a chart that you can modify as you would any chart. For more information on creating charts, see Chapter 6.

Did You Know?

You can embed an existing worksheet. Click Create from File (○ changes to ◉) in Step 4 of the example. The dialog box changes and prompts you to type a file name or to click Browse to select a workbook to embed.

CREATE A LINK
from an Excel workbook

You may be familiar with the many benefits of links as a result of using the Internet. On the Internet, when you click a link, you jump to a new Web page with more links, creating an enormous and seamless web of information. Like most Office applications, Excel lets you create links. These links can take you to a place in the same worksheet or workbook, to a document created by another Office application, or even to a Web page.

Linking a document is different from paste linking. Instead of pulling data created by another application into Excel, a link enables you to move from a worksheet to a related document.

You can use links to jump directly to a chart or PivotTable based on the worksheet. Or, you can link a worksheet to a Word document providing detailed information or identifying the assumptions used in the worksheet. You can also create e-mail address links. This option is useful if you are going to save your file as a Web page and you want readers to be able to click a link to e-mail you.

❶ Click the cell in which you want the link to appear.

❷ Click the Insert tab.

❸ Click Hyperlink.

● The Insert Hyperlink dialog box appears.

❹ Click a Link To location.

This example uses Existing File or Web Page.

❺ Type the text you want to display in the worksheet field.

❻ Click here and select the folder in which the file you want to link to is located.

❼ Click the file to which you want to link.

❽ Click OK.

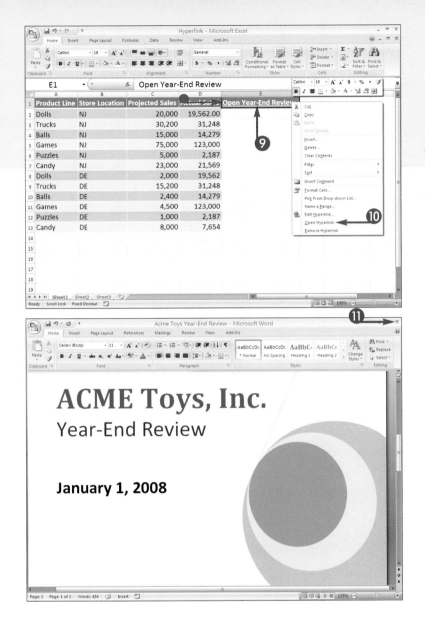

- The cell content appears as a link.

  You can pass your mouse over the link without clicking to see the name of the linked-to file.

⑨ Right-click the new link.

  A menu appears.

⑩ Click Open Hyperlink.

The linked-to document appears.

⑪ Close the document to return to your original document.

To remove the link, right-click the linked worksheet cell and then click Remove Hyperlink.

TIPS

Did You Know?

Creating a link to a Word document provides an alternative to annotating worksheets by using comments and text boxes. Unlike comments, Word links can be of any length and complexity. Unlike text boxes, hyperlinks do not obstruct worksheets or distract readers.

Did You Know?

You can create links from workbook graphics such as shapes, pictures, clip art, and WordArt. Click the graphic, click the Insert tab, and then click Hyperlink. Use the Insert Hyperlink dialog box to select a destination in the same document, in another document, or on the Web.

Query a
WEB SITE

You can use Excel to query Web data so you can analyze the Web data in Excel. You can find structured data in many forms on the Web, including online Excel worksheets. Excel considers ordinary Web pages structured if they contain tabular content — that is, rows and columns of numbers or other data.

Excel gives you two options for opening and using Web-based tabular data. You can click the Office button and then click Open. The Open dialog box appears. Type the Web address in the File Name field and then click Open. Or, click the Data tab and, in

the Get External Data group, click the From Web option to query a Web page.

Both techniques allow you to view and edit numbers, but querying a Web site has advantages. Importing data as a query enables you to filter the data, viewing only records of interest. A query also lets you refresh data if it is subject to updates. With the data in Excel, you have complete access to data analysis and presentation tools, including functions, PivotTables, and charts.

① Open a new Excel worksheet.

② Click the Data tab.

③ Click From Web in the Get External Data group.

The New Web Query dialog box appears.

④ Type the Web address for the site from which you want data.

This example uses www.fec.gov/pages/96to.htm.

⑤ Click Go.

The Web page appears in the dialog box.

⑥ Click the elements you want to appear in your query.

● A check mark indicates you want to query an element. An arrow indicates you do not want to query it.

⑦ Click Import.

Voter Registration and Turnout - 1996

STATE	1996 VAP	1996 REG	% REG of VAP	TURNOUT*	% T/O of VAP
Alabama	3,220,000	2,470,766	76.73%	1,534,349	47.65%
Alaska	425,000	414,815	97.60%	241,620	56.85%
Arizona	3,145,000	2,244,672	71.37%	1,404,405	44.66%
Arkansas	1,873,000	1,369,459	73.12%	884,262	47.21%
California	22,826,000	15,662,075	68.62%	10,019,484.00	43.90%

● The Import Data dialog box appears.

⑧ Click to select where you want to put the imported data (○ changes to ◉).

Choose from Existing Worksheet or New Worksheet.

⑨ Click the cell address or type a range if you selected Existing Worksheet.

⑩ Click OK.

● The selected Web elements appear within Excel, ready for analysis, charting, and so on.

	A	B	C	D	E	F
1	STATE	1996 VAP	1996 REG	% REG of VAP	TURNOUT*	% T/O of VAP
2	Alabama	3,220,000	2,470,766	76.73%	1,534,349	47.65%
3	Alaska	425,000	414,815	97.60%	241,620	56.85%
4	Arizona	3,145,000	2,244,672	71.37%	1,404,405	44.66%
5	Arkansas	1,873,000	1,369,459	73.12%	884,262	47.21%
6	California	22,826,000	15,662,075	68.62%	10,019,484.00	43.90%
7	Colorado	2,862,000	2,346,253	81.98%	1,510,70	52.78%
8	Conn.	2,479,000	1,881,323	75.89%	1,392,614	56.16%
9	Delaware	548,000	421,710	76.95%	810	49.42%
10	District of Columbia	422,000	361,419	85.64%	185,726	44.01%
11	Florida	11,043,000	8,077,877	73.15%	5,300,927	48.00%
12	Georgia	5,418,000	3,811,284	70.34%	2,298,899	42.43%
13	Hawaii	890,000	544,916	61.23%	360,120	40.46%
14	Idaho	858,000	700,430	81.64%	489,481	57.05%
15	Illinois	8,754,000	6,663,301	76.12%	4,311,391	49.25%
16	Indiana	4,374,000	3,488,088	79.75%	2,135,431	48.82%
17	Iowa	2,138,000	1,776,433	83.09%	1,234,075	57.72%
18	Kansas	1,897,000	1,436,418	75.72%	1,063,452	56.06%
19	Kentucky	2,928,000	2,396,086	81.83%	1,387,999	47.40%
20	Louisiana	3,131,000	2,559,352	81.74%	1,783,959	56.98%
21	Maine	945,000	1,001,292	105.96%	679,499	71.90%
22	Maryland	3,820,000	2,587,978	67.75%	1,780,870	46.62%
23	Massachusetts	4,649,000	3,459,193	74.41%	2,556,459	54.99%
24	Michigan	7,072,000	6,677,079	94.42%	3,848,844	54.42%
25	Minnesota	3,422,000	3,067,802	89.65%	2,192,640	64.07%

TIPS

Did You Know?

To find statistical data on the Web, you can do a Google search. You can download U.S. federal statistics in multiple formats from the official FedStats site at www.fedstats.gov/cgi-bin/A2Z.cgi. State and municipal data is also available in great abundance. You can find central access to this material at the federal compendium, FirstGov, which is available at www.firstgov.gov.

Did You Know?

A query definition is a file containing a definition of the data you import into Excel from an external source. The query definition indicates the data source, the rows to include, how rows added to the source are accommodated by the query, and the frequency with which the data is updated. You can view and modify query properties by clicking the Data tab and then clicking Properties in the Connections group.

COPY A WORD TABLE
into Excel

If you create a table or other collection of data structured as rows and columns in Microsoft Word, you can import that information into Excel and take advantage of Excel's many features. Creating a table in Word is often satisfactory; however, sometimes you start creating a table in Word that becomes long and elaborate. At that point, maintaining the information in Excel may make more sense than maintaining it in Word.

In Excel, you can perform calculations on the data, use functions, and apply filters, all of which would be time consuming, if not impossible, in Word. When you copy a table from Word and paste it into an Excel worksheet, you may lose some formatting, and some of the data may transfer as text instead of as numbers. You can correct these problems. For information on converting text to numbers, see Task #26. For information on formatting, see Task #s 68, 69, and 70. After you import the table into Excel, you can proceed to add data to the list by using a form, as explained in Task #36.

❶ In Word, select the table you want to copy.

❷ Click the Home tab.

❸ Click the Copy button.

Word copies the table to the Windows Clipboard.

❹ In Excel, click a cell, making sure there are enough cells below and to the right to accommodate the Word table.

❺ Click the Home tab.

❻ Click Paste.

The table is copied into Excel.

A formatting button appears.

⑦ Click the formatting button.

● The Word formatting is applied by default.

● Click here if you want to match the Excel formatting (○ changes to ◉).

You can click and drag columns to adjust them to fit the imported data.

You can add formats to the data.

TIPS

Did You Know?

You can import data that consists of text separated by commas, tabs, semicolons, or other delimiters. Click the Data tab and then, in the Get External Data group, click the From Text button (📄). The Import Text File dialog box appears. Click your file and then click Import. The Text Import Wizard appears. The wizard steps you through the process of importing your file.

Customize It!

When you transfer data into Excel the formatting button appears. To prevent unwanted Word formatting from accompanying the imported content, click the menu and click Match Destination Formatting (○ changes to ◉). The Paste Options menu remains visible until you begin another Excel task.

IMPORT A TEXT FILE
into Excel

Many software applications have an option you can use to export the application's data to a text file. You can import text files from other applications into Excel by using the Text Import Wizard. You can then use Excel to analyze the data. In fact, after you import data, you can use it in a PivotTable, create charts with it, or manipulate it just as you would any other Excel data.

On the first page of the Data Import Wizard, you can use the Start Import at Row field to specify the row

in your text file with which you want to begin the import. If your data has titles or other information you do not want to import at the top of the file, this feature gives you the ability to skip those rows.

The Text Import Wizard can handle any delimited or fixed-width file. A delimited file uses a comma, semicolon, tab, space, or other character to mark the end of each column. A fixed-width file aligns each column and gives each column a defined width.

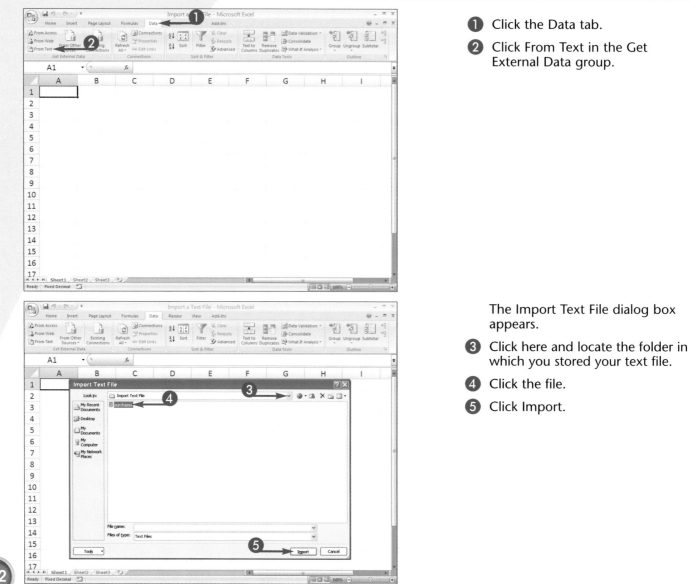

1 Click the Data tab.

2 Click From Text in the Get External Data group.

The Import Text File dialog box appears.

3 Click here and locate the folder in which you stored your text file.

4 Click the file.

5 Click Import.

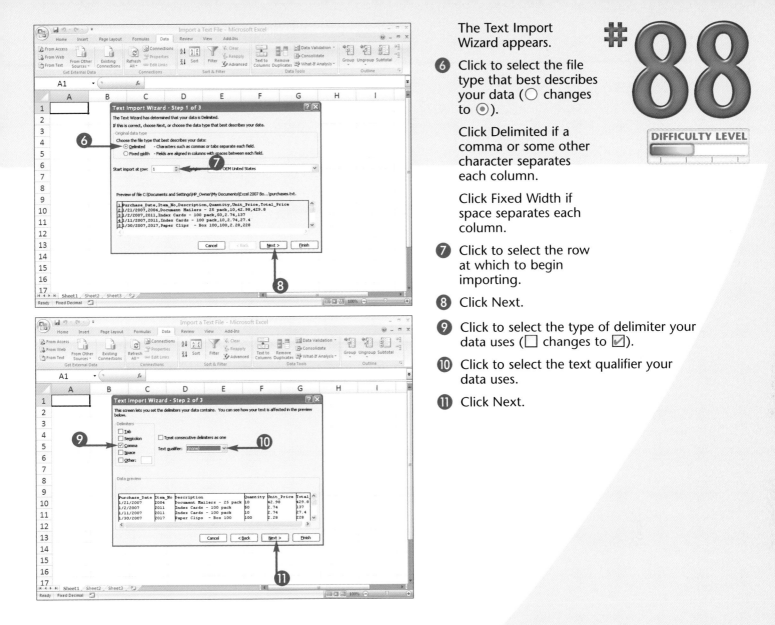

The Text Import Wizard appears.

88

6 Click to select the file type that best describes your data (○ changes to ◉).

Click Delimited if a comma or some other character separates each column.

Click Fixed Width if space separates each column.

7 Click to select the row at which to begin importing.

8 Click Next.

9 Click to select the type of delimiter your data uses (□ changes to ☑).

10 Click to select the text qualifier your data uses.

11 Click Next.

TIPS

Did You Know?

If you are importing a fixed-width file, you tell Excel exactly where each column begins by clicking the location in the Data Preview window. Excel inserts a break line. You can adjust the location of the line or delete the line.

Did You Know

Excel has an option you can use to break individual cells into columns. The feature works a lot like the Text Import Wizard. You select the cells you want to divide, and then you click Text to Columns on the Data tab. The Convert Text to Columns Wizard opens. Use it to divide your cells into columns.

IMPORT A TEXT FILE
into Excel

If you are importing a delimited file, you tell Excel the type of delimiters the file uses. You can specify more than one delimiter. Some delimited file formats surround text data with a text qualifier, such as single or double quotes. The Text Import Wizard has a Text Qualifier field. You can use it to specify whether your data has a text qualifier, and if so, what that qualifier is.

After you define the layout of your data, you must define the data type contained in each column. You

have three options: general, text, and date. General converts numeric data to numbers, dates to dates, and everything else to text. If you have numeric data that is text, use the text option to have Excel convert the data to text. If you have dates, click the date option and specify the format you want to use.

If there is a column you do not want to import, click the Do Not Import Column option.

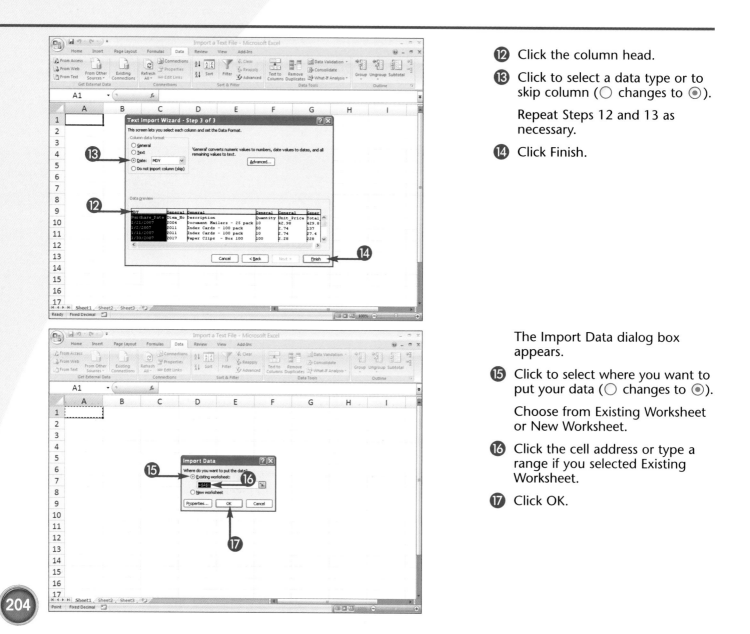

⑫ Click the column head.

⑬ Click to select a data type or to skip column (○ changes to ◉).

Repeat Steps 12 and 13 as necessary.

⑭ Click Finish.

The Import Data dialog box appears.

⑮ Click to select where you want to put your data (○ changes to ◉).

Choose from Existing Worksheet or New Worksheet.

⑯ Click the cell address or type a range if you selected Existing Worksheet.

⑰ Click OK.

Excel imports the data.

You can format and analyze your data.

Did You Know?

Text files created by other software applications may be in one of many popular file formats. You can identify the file format by the file extension. Files with a .csv extension are delimited with commas. Another popular extension is .txt. The exporting program usually delimits .txt files with tabs.

Did You Know?

You can export your Excel worksheet as a text file. Excel provides you with several formats from which to choose, including .prn, .txt, .csv, .dif, and .slk. To export a worksheet as a text file, click the Office button, click Save As, and then click Other Formats. Choose the option you want in the Save as Type field in the Save As dialog box.

IMPORT AN ACCESS DATABASE
into Excel

Many organizations use more than one application to manage data. Excel is an excellent choice for managing, analyzing, and presenting numbers. Databases such as Access help you store, filter, and retrieve data in large quantities and of every type. By importing Access data into Excel, you can apply easy-to-use data analysis techniques to complex Access databases.

Instead of using worksheets, in Access you must organize your information into data tables, each of which stores information about one part of the entity

of interest to you: customers, products, employees, transactions, and so on. To help keep track of these tables in Access, you must create and assign unique identifiers, called keys, to each table or have Access automatically assign keys to each customer, product, employee, transaction, and so on. Access uses the keys to link tables to each other.

Excel simplifies the use of Access data tables. When you import a data table, you can select tables or columns of interest from multiple tables and display the results in a single worksheet.

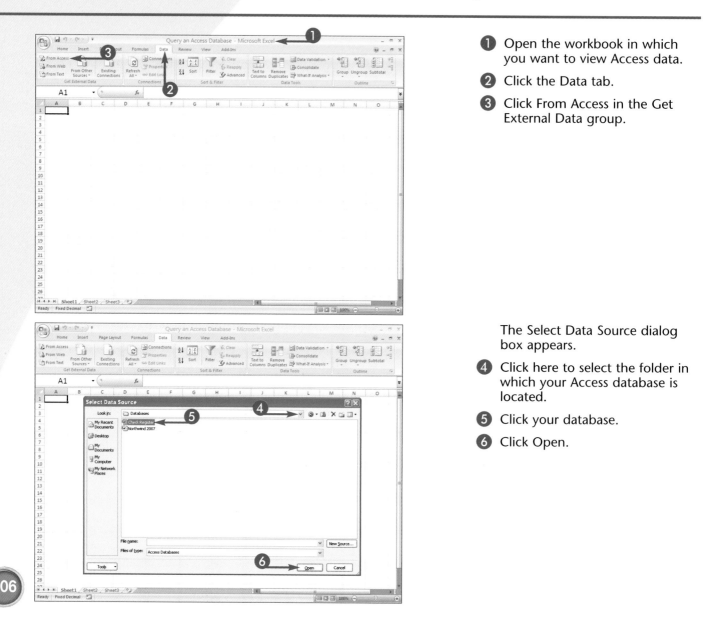

① Open the workbook in which you want to view Access data.

② Click the Data tab.

③ Click From Access in the Get External Data group.

The Select Data Source dialog box appears.

④ Click here to select the folder in which your Access database is located.

⑤ Click your database.

⑥ Click Open.

● The Select Table dialog box appears.

⑦ Click the table you want to open.

⑧ Click OK.

● The Import Data dialog box appears.

⑨ Click to select how you want to view your data (○ changes to ◉).

Choose from Table, PivotTable Report, or PivotChart and PivotTable Report.

⑩ Click to select where you want to put your data (○ changes to ◉).

Choose from Existing Worksheet or New Worksheet.

⑪ Click the cell address or type a range if you selected Existing Worksheet.

⑫ Click OK.

Your data appears in Excel.

Check No	Client ID	Ref No	Check Date	Amount
50234	CL-305	11137	3/1/2007	1015.15
50235	CL-300	11138	3/1/2007	3379.4
50236	CL-300	11139	3/1/2007	605.71
50237	CL-302	11140	3/1/2007	4810.37
50238	CL-323	11141	3/1/2007	4691.22
50239	CL-330	11142	3/1/2007	3143.82
50240	CL-318	11143	3/1/2007	3928.45
50241	CL-300	11144	3/1/2007	1852.42
50242	CL-323	11145	3/1/2007	1817.57
50243	CL-317	11146	3/1/2007	3284.35
50244	CL-329	11147	3/1/2007	3606.71
50245	CL-310	11148	3/1/2007	1996.15
50246	CL-300	11149	3/1/2007	2941.65

TIPS

Did You Know?

The Northwind database is a large database elaborated over many years and distributed with Access on the Office CD. The database includes information about the products, customers, employees, and other attributes of a fictional gourmet food store. To follow along with this task or to experiment with importing and querying a database, you can install the Northwind database.

Did You Know?

You can apply the technique described in this task to any database that has an ODBC (Open Database Connectivity) driver, a standard interface. With Excel, you can import databases such as Oracle or Microsoft SQL Server, and desktop databases such as Visual FoxPro.

Query an
ACCESS DATABASE

The Query Wizard is part of Microsoft Query, a separate application that comes with Microsoft Office. Microsoft Query is an application that makes it easy for you to generate queries in Structured Query Language (SQL), a standard in the corporate world.

The Query Wizard provides a point-and-click interface for importing tables or selected columns into Microsoft Excel. Once you have selected the columns or tables you want, you can filter and sort. The Query Wizard provides 16 filter criteria from which you can choose. In addition, you can create multiple filters by using and and or.

Use or when you want the wizard to select data that meets either condition. For example, ask the wizard to select all dresses that are blue *or* have red buttons. The wizard returns every blue dress and every dress with red buttons. Alternatively, ask the wizard to select all dresses that are blue *and* have red buttons. The and selection criterion is more restrictive. The wizard only returns items that meet both selection criteria: blue dresses with red buttons.

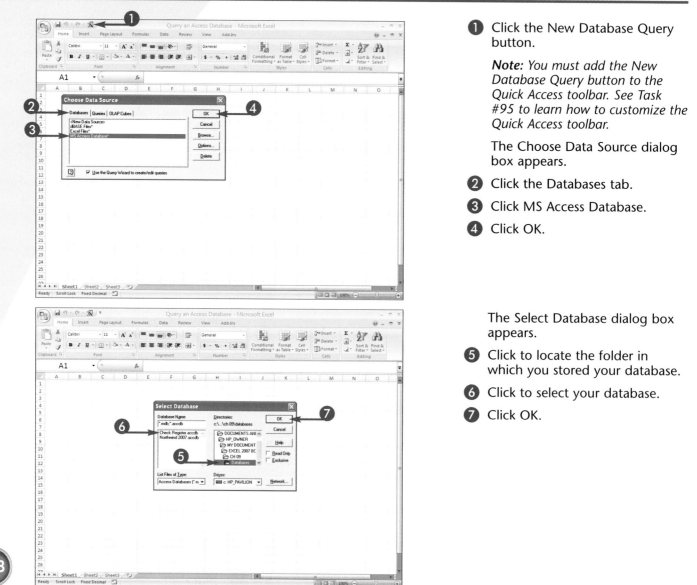

① Click the New Database Query button.

Note: You must add the New Database Query button to the Quick Access toolbar. See Task #95 to learn how to customize the Quick Access toolbar.

The Choose Data Source dialog box appears.

② Click the Databases tab.

③ Click MS Access Database.

④ Click OK.

The Select Database dialog box appears.

⑤ Click to locate the folder in which you stored your database.

⑥ Click to select your database.

⑦ Click OK.

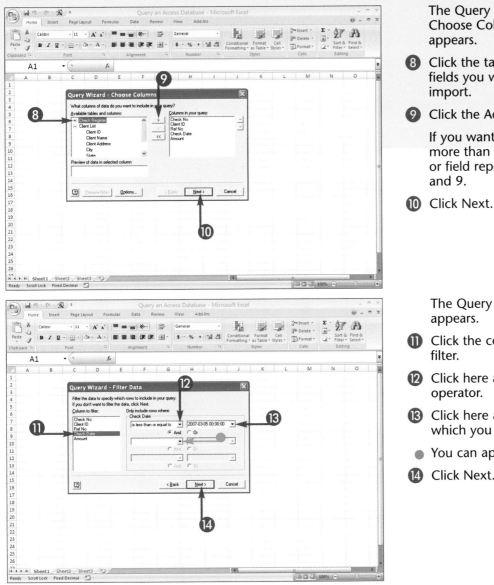

The Query Wizard — Choose Columns page appears.

8 Click the table and/or fields you want to import.

9 Click the Add button.

If you want to open more than one table or field repeat Steps 8 and 9.

10 Click Next.

The Query Wizard — Filter Data page appears.

11 Click the column by which you want to filter.

12 Click here and select a comparison operator.

13 Click here and select the criterion by which you want to filter.

● You can apply additional filters.

14 Click Next.

TIPS

Important!
In this task, you click the New Database Query button (🗔) to access the Choose Data Source dialog box. The task assumes you have installed the New Database Query button on the Quick Access toolbar. See Task #95 to learn how to add commands to the Quick Access toolbar.

Did You Know?
You use the Choose Data Source dialog box to import an Access database. To open the Choose Data Source dialog box, place the New Database Query button on the Quick Access toolbar or click the Data tab, click From Other Sources, and then click From Microsoft Query.

Query an
ACCESS DATABASE

With the Query Wizard, you can also create sorts within sorts. For example, you can alphabetize a list of states, counties, and towns as follows: first in alphabetical order by state, then in alphabetical order by county, and finally in alphabetical order by town.

After importing the data into Excel, you can use Excel's tools to further sort and filter. You can go beyond the wizard and directly manipulate the Access tables from which your query is drawn.

On the final page of the wizard, click View Data or Edit Query in Microsoft Query and then click Finish for a graphical view of the underlying data tables. You can work directly with criteria fields, add tables, and connect tables by shared fields. You can also run and view queries.

When you finish creating your query, you can save your query. Saved queries become available in Excel for viewing, analysis, charting, and so on. To learn how to run a saved query, see Task #91.

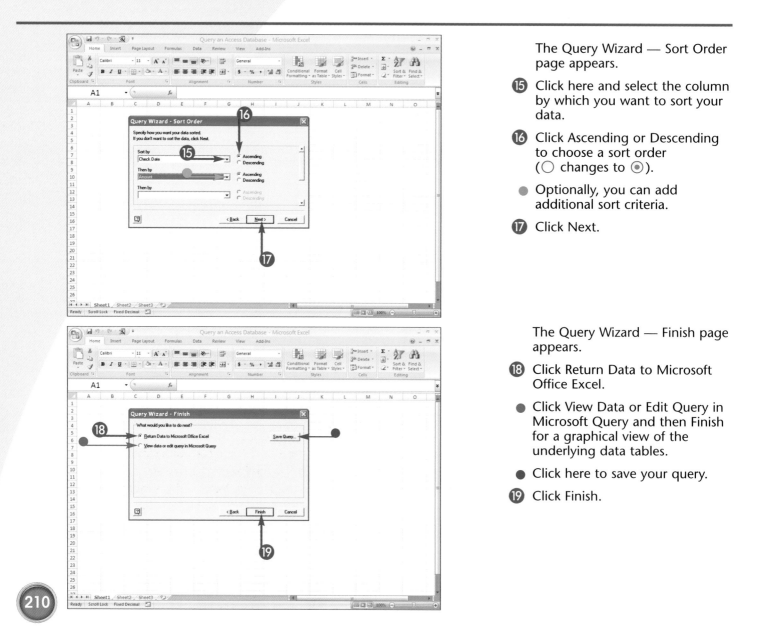

The Query Wizard — Sort Order page appears.

⓯ Click here and select the column by which you want to sort your data.

⓰ Click Ascending or Descending to choose a sort order (○ changes to ◉).

● Optionally, you can add additional sort criteria.

⓱ Click Next.

The Query Wizard — Finish page appears.

⓲ Click Return Data to Microsoft Office Excel.

● Click View Data or Edit Query in Microsoft Query and then Finish for a graphical view of the underlying data tables.

● Click here to save your query.

⓳ Click Finish.

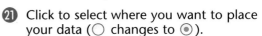

The Import Data dialog box appears.

⓴ Click to select how you want to view your data (○ changes to ⊙).

Choose from Table, PivotTable Report, or PivotChart and PivotTable Report.

㉑ Click to select where you want to place your data (○ changes to ⊙).

Choose from Existing Worksheet or New Worksheet.

㉒ Click the cell address or type the cell range if you selected Existing Worksheet.

㉓ Click OK.

Your Access data appears in Excel.

#90 CONTINUED

	A	B	C	D	E	F
1	Check No	Client ID	Ref No	Check Date	Amount	
2	50247	CL-324	11150	3/1/2007 0:00	231.69	
3	50236	CL-300	11139	3/1/2007 0:00	605.71	
4	50234	CL-305	11137	3/1/2007 0:00	1015.15	
5	50248	CL-329	11151	3/1/2007 0:00	1461.02	
6	50242	CL-323	11145	3/1/2007 0:00	1817.57	
7	50241	CL-300	11144	3/1/2007 0:00	1852.42	
8	50245	CL-310	11148	3/1/2007 0:00	1996.15	
9	50246	CL-300	11149	3/1/2007 0:00	2941.65	
10	50249	CL-315	11152	3/1/2007 0:00	2979.46	
11	50239	CL-330	11142	3/1/2007 0:00	3143.82	
12	50243	CL-317	11146	3/1/2007 0:00	3284.35	
13	50235	CL-300	11138	3/1/2007 0:00	3379.4	
14	50244	CL-329	11147	3/1/2007 0:00	3606.71	
15	50240	CL-318	11143	3/1/2007 0:00	3928.45	
16	50238	CL-323	11141	3/1/2007 0:00	4691.22	
17	50250	CL-308	11153	3/1/2007 0:00	4770.37	
18	50237	CL-302	11140	3/1/2007 0:00	4810.37	
19	50258	CL-322	11161	3/2/2007 0:00	89.83	

TIPS

Did You Know?

Filtering data improves performance when you work with large databases. Using Microsoft Query can speed up performance. If you work with large databases and want to apply numerous filters and sort orders, MS Query is worth learning.

Did You Know?

On the Finish page of the Query Wizard, if you click View Data or Edit Query in Microsoft Query (○ changes to ⊙) and then click Finish, Excel provides a sophisticated interface you can use to edit your query. Click Help on the Microsoft Query menu to learn how to use this function.

Reuse a
SAVED QUERY

Running a query has benefits beyond opening a database in Excel. For large databases, you can use filters to restrict which rows and columns you view. By saving the query, you can quickly return to the queried data, refresh the data, and perform all worksheet operations, such as applying functions, using PivotTables, and creating charts.

Regardless of the data source, queries have a similar format and you can reload them quickly. On the Data tab, you can click Properties to review query properties and change properties as needed.

Refreshing updates the data so you can see any changes made to the data in Access since the last refresh. To break your connection to the Access database, click the Data tab and then click Connections. The Workbook Connections dialog box appears. Click the name of your query and then click Remove.

You can import queries into existing or new worksheets. After you import them, the worksheets look like any other worksheet. Saving changes to the workbook leaves the original query definition untouched, so that you can reuse the query later.

① Open your Excel worksheet.

② Click the Data tab.

③ Click Existing Connections.

The Existing Connections dialog box appears.

④ Click the name of your saved query.

⑤ Click Open.

The Import Data dialog box appears.

⑥ Click to select how you want to view your data (○ changes to ⦿).

Choose from Table, PivotTable, or PivotChart and PivotTable Report.

⑦ Click to select where you want to place your data (○ changes to ⦿).

Choose from Existing Worksheet or New Worksheet.

⑧ Click the cell address or type a range if you selected Existing Worksheet.

⑨ Click OK.

The results of your query appear in your worksheet.

⑩ Click the Data tab.

⑪ Click Refresh All.

Excel refreshes your data.

TIPS

Did You Know?

You can add the Import External Data button (⬚) to the Quick Access toolbar. You can then click the button to open the Select Data Source dialog box. From the Select Data Source dialog box, click the name of a query you saved and then click Open. Excel opens your saved query. See Task #95 to learn how to add items to the Quick Access toolbar.

Did You Know?

You can edit a saved query. Click the Data tab, click From Other Sources, and then click From Microsoft Query. The Choose Data Source dialog box opens. Click the Queries tab, click your query name, and then click Open. Your query is available for you to edit.

Import an Excel worksheet
INTO ACCESS

Excel tables enable you to take advantage of basic database features like sorting and filtering within Excel. By importing worksheets into Microsoft Access, you can better manage growing lists by taking advantage of additional database features. As a relational database, Access offers the benefits of integrated wizard and design tools that enable you to build customized forms, queries, and reports. Another benefit is size. Unlike a workbook, a database is, for practical purposes, limited only by the amount of available disk space.

Before importing a worksheet into Access, you need to format it as a table. Your columns may have headings; however, you should try to eliminate blank columns, rows, and cells. Exported Excel lists should also avoid repeating information. For example, instead of including a customer's name and address in every record of a transaction list, split the worksheet into two lists: one with customer information and the other with transaction information. The two lists become, in Access, two tables linked by a key field.

① Open an Access database.

② Click the External Data tab.

③ Click Excel in the Import group.

The Get External Data — Excel Spreadsheet dialog box appears.

④ Type the path to the file you want to import.

● Alternatively, click the Browse button and locate your file.

⑤ Click OK.

The Import Spreadsheet Wizard appears.

⑥ Click the worksheet you want to import.

⑦ Click Next.

The next page of the Import Spreadsheet Wizard appears.

⑧ Click if your data does not have column headings (☑ changes to ☐).

⑨ Click Next.

The next page of the Import Spreadsheet Wizard appears.

⑩ Click to select a column heading.

⑪ Set the Field options for the column.

⑫ Repeat Steps 10 and 11 for each column.

⑬ Click Next.

TIPS

Did You Know?

You cannot import more than 255 columns into Access because the maximum number of columns an Access table supports is 255.

Did You Know?

When you export, every row in a column should have the same data type. A column with more than one data type can cause errors during the export process. Access looks at a column's first eight rows to determine the column's data type.

Import an Excel worksheet
INTO ACCESS

Each record in an Access database must be unique. A primary key field is a field, such as a record number, that you use to ensure that a record is unique. You can have Access create primary key field values or you can create your own. For example, if no two employees in your company have the same employee number, you can use employee number as a primary key field. You keep Access data in multiple tables. You use key fields to link tables together.

You can import into Access any single page of a workbook or a named range. Use the Import

Spreadsheet Wizard to import Excel data. The wizard enables you to set several field options during the import process. You can change field names and data types or you can choose not to import a field.

You can index a field during the import process. An index speeds up the retrieval of information in Access. You should always index primary key fields. Select the Yes (No Duplicates) Option in the Indexed field. This option ensures that each primary key field entry is unique.

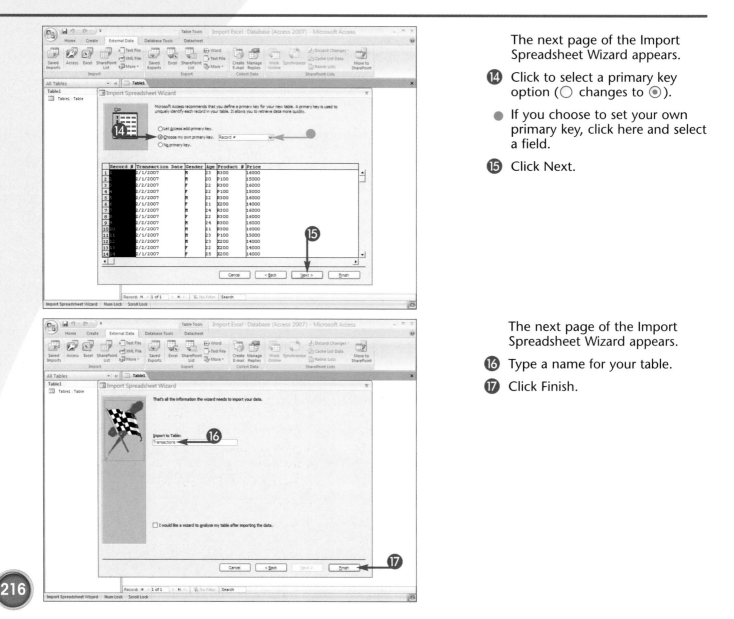

The next page of the Import Spreadsheet Wizard appears.

⑭ Click to select a primary key option (○ changes to ⊙).

● If you choose to set your own primary key, click here and select a field.

⑮ Click Next.

The next page of the Import Spreadsheet Wizard appears.

⑯ Type a name for your table.

⑰ Click Finish.

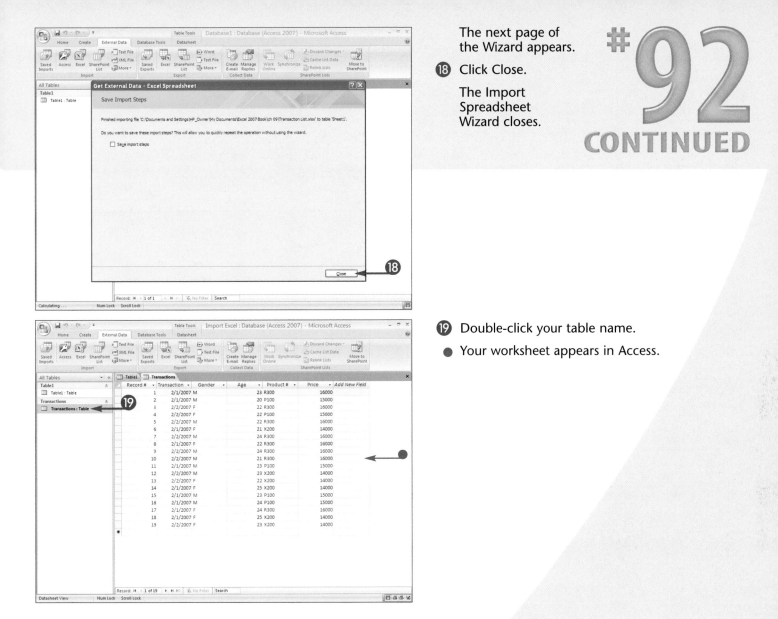

The next page of the Wizard appears.

⑱ Click Close.

The Import Spreadsheet Wizard closes.

92 CONTINUED

⑲ Double-click your table name.

● Your worksheet appears in Access.

TIPS

Did You Know?

You can append Excel data to an existing Access table. On the first page of the Get External Data — Excel Spreadsheet Wizard, click Append a Copy of the Records to the Table (○ changes to ◉) and then select the table to which you want to append.

Did You Know?

On the first page of the Get External Data — Excel Spreadsheet Wizard, you can choose to link your Access data to Excel. If you link your data, any changes you make to the Excel data are reflected in Access. You can use Access to query the data or create reports, but you cannot update your data in Access.

Using Excel with
MAIL MERGE

Office applications have complementary benefits. Microsoft Word, for example, enables you to do just about anything with words, while Excel provides a more structured environment for working primarily with numbers. Word includes a Mail Merge feature with which you can merge information from Excel into Word documents of your own design. Use Mail Merge to create mailing labels, form letters, printed envelopes, directories, and other useful documents.

Using Excel with Mail Merge has three major steps. First, create an Excel list consisting of addresses or other structured data. Second, access the list in Word. Third, use Mail Merge to integrate the list into your Word document.

You can use Mail Merge with letters, name badges, CD labels, notebook tabs, business cards, and more. On the Mailings tab, click Start Mail Merge and select an option. Word automatically formats the output to fit your purpose.

After you import your Excel list into Word, you can use the Edit Recipient List option to edit it.

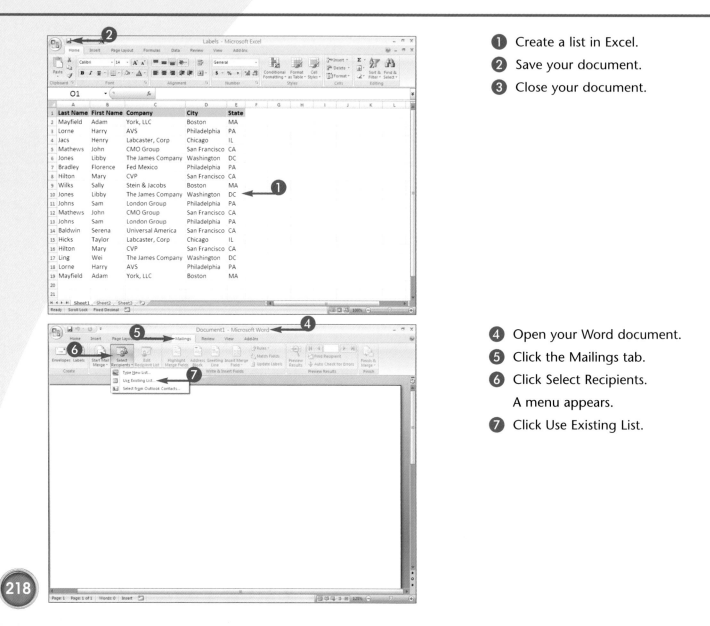

① Create a list in Excel.

② Save your document.

③ Close your document.

④ Open your Word document.

⑤ Click the Mailings tab.

⑥ Click Select Recipients.

A menu appears.

⑦ Click Use Existing List.

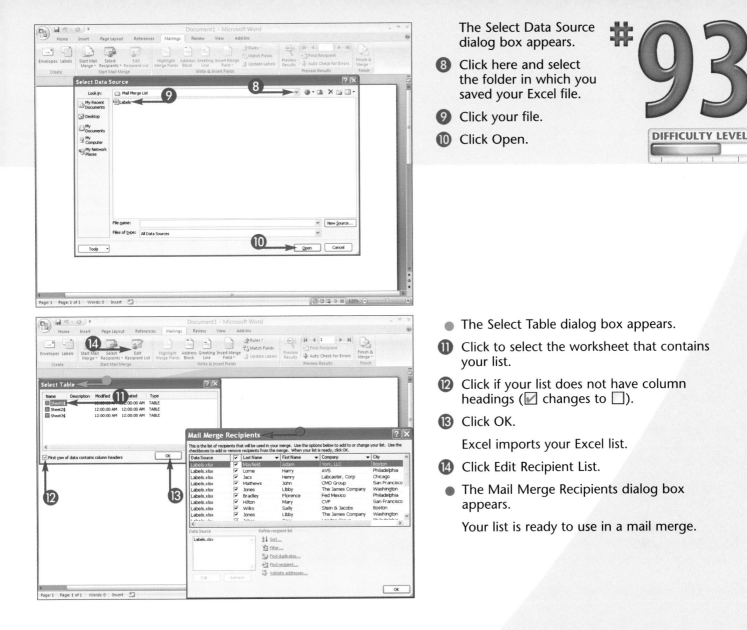

The Select Data Source dialog box appears.

⑧ Click here and select the folder in which you saved your Excel file.

⑨ Click your file.

⑩ Click Open.

● The Select Table dialog box appears.

⑪ Click to select the worksheet that contains your list.

⑫ Click if your list does not have column headings (☑ changes to ☐).

⑬ Click OK.

Excel imports your Excel list.

⑭ Click Edit Recipient List.

● The Mail Merge Recipients dialog box appears.

Your list is ready to use in a mail merge.

TIPS

Did You Know?

When creating an Excel list for mail-merge purposes, begin by identifying your data needs. For name badges, for example, you might not need address information, but you might need a new column called Affiliation. For shipping labels, you might need a customer ID number in addition to address information. For multiple tasks, you can use existing lists as templates to create new ones.

Did You Know?

The Mail Merge Recipients dialog box displays all the data in your list. You can use it to select, sort, and filter your list before you perform your mail merge. You can also use it to find duplicates in your list or to find a particular recipient.

Customize Excel

Excel has a large number of integrated features you can customize and adapt to suit your purposes. This chapter introduces a few important ways in which you can customize Excel.

One simple way is to install additional features, called add-ins. This chapter shows you how to install the add-ins included with Excel and how to find add-ins available from third-party developers.

You also learn to tailor Excel by placing items on the Quick Access toolbar. Items on the Quick Access toolbar are independent of the tabs in the Ribbon and you can access them with a single click. You can add many options that are not available in the Ribbon to Excel via the Quick Access toolbar.

When working with large worksheets, you can open multiple windows to view different parts of a worksheet at the same time. This chapter teaches you how. You also learn to create custom views. If you filter data, hide columns or rows, or create special print settings, you can save your changes in a custom view and recall them when you need them. Another task shows you how to create custom number formats for use in a workbook.

The task on macros introduces an enormous topic, which more than any other task enables you to extend and customize Excel. After you learn how to create a macro, you learn how to assign a macro to a button and how to add the button to the Quick Access toolbar.

Add features by
INSTALLING ADD-INS

Installing add-ins gives you additional Excel features not available in the Ribbon by default. An *add-in* is software that adds one or more features to Excel. Bundled add-in software is included with Excel but not automatically installed when you install Excel. Bundled Excel add-ins include the Lookup and Conditional Sum Wizards, both of which simplify complex functions. The Euro Currency Tools add-in enables you to calculate exchange rates between the Euro and other currencies. Task #s 56 and 66 introduce two of the statistical add-ins in the Analysis Toolpak.

You install the bundled add-ins by using the Excel Options dialog box. Once installed, the add-in is available right away.

In addition, you can take advantage of third-party add-ins. This type of software adds functionality in support of advanced work in chemistry, risk analysis, modeling, project management, statistics, and other fields. Third-party add-ins usually have their own installation and usage procedures. Consult the developer of these programs for documentation.

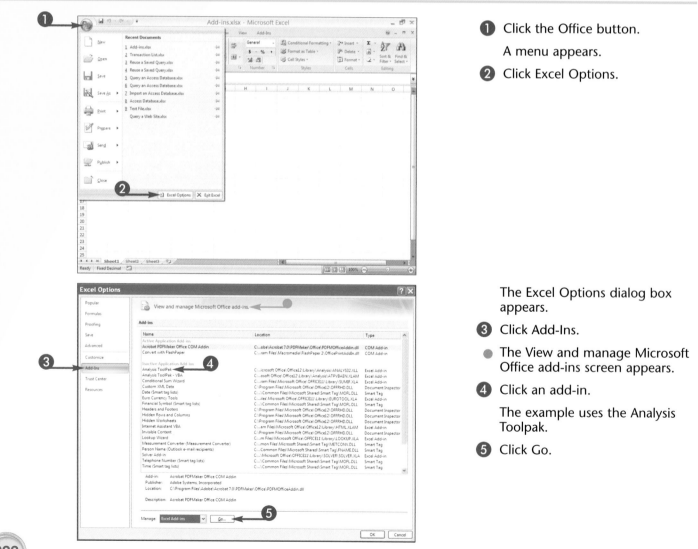

① Click the Office button.

  A menu appears.

② Click Excel Options.

The Excel Options dialog box appears.

③ Click Add-Ins.

● The View and manage Microsoft Office add-ins screen appears.

④ Click an add-in.

  The example uses the Analysis Toolpak.

⑤ Click Go.

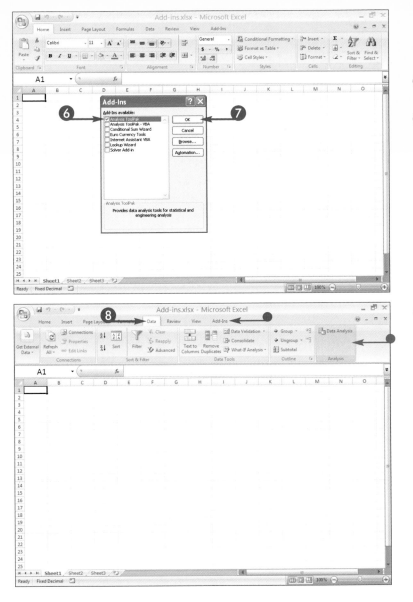

The Add-Ins dialog box appears and provides access to several options.

⑥ Click to select an add-in (☐ changes to ☑).

⑦ Click OK.

DIFFICULTY LEVEL

⑧ Click the Data tab.

● Excel places the Data Analysis Toolpak on the Data tab.

● Excel places many other add-ins on the Add-Ins tab.

TIPS

Remove It!
Removing an add-in is easy. Click the Office button, click Excel Options, click Add-ins, click the add-in you want to remove, and then click Go. The Add-Ins dialog box appears. Click to deselect the add-in you want to remove (☑ changes to ☐) and then click OK. Excel removes the add-in.

Did You Know?
To learn about special-purpose Excel add-ins in your field, you can perform a Google search by going to www.google.com. Your search terms should include Excel, the field of knowledge — for example, chemistry — and other information you might have, such as vendor name. Third-party vendors are responsible for supporting their own products.

Customize the
QUICK ACCESS TOOLBAR

You can add features you frequently use to the Excel Quick Access toolbar. The Quick Access toolbar enables you to access commands with a single click. Right-clicking a Ribbon command provides you with a way to add commands in the Ribbon to the Quick Access toolbar easily.

You can also add features that are not in the Ribbon to the Quick Access toolbar by accessing the Customize Quick Access Toolbar screen and clicking the commands you want to add. Excel divides the

commands into categories to make it easier for you to find the command you want. You can specify whether the command should appear on the toolbar of all Excel workbooks or only on the Quick Access toolbar in the workbook you specify. By default, the button will appear in all workbooks. Task #s 8, 20, 36, 77, and 90 demonstrate features you must add to the Quick Access toolbar before you can use them. The Quick Access toolbar can appear above or below the Ribbon.

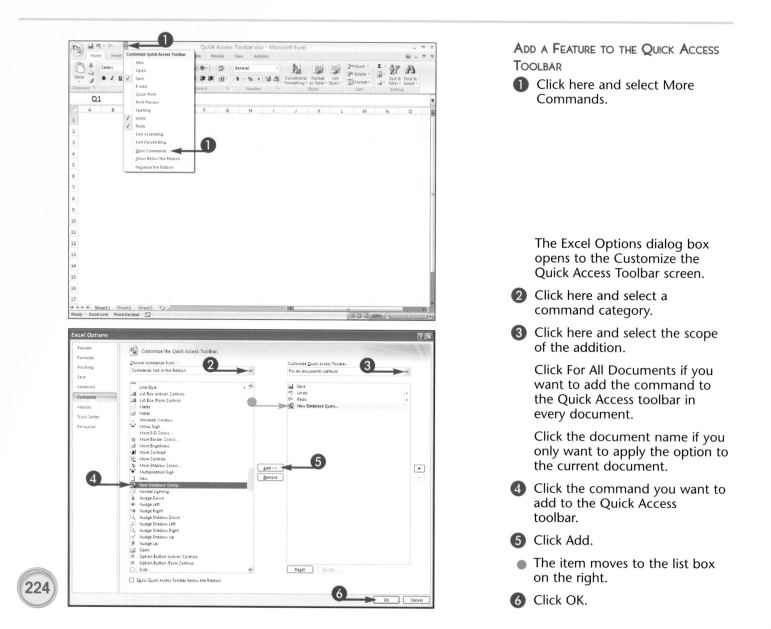

ADD A FEATURE TO THE QUICK ACCESS TOOLBAR

① Click here and select More Commands.

The Excel Options dialog box opens to the Customize the Quick Access Toolbar screen.

② Click here and select a command category.

③ Click here and select the scope of the addition.

Click For All Documents if you want to add the command to the Quick Access toolbar in every document.

Click the document name if you only want to apply the option to the current document.

④ Click the command you want to add to the Quick Access toolbar.

⑤ Click Add.

● The item moves to the list box on the right.

⑥ Click OK.

- Excel places the option on the Quick Access toolbar.

  Click the option to use it.

  Note: *This example uses New Database Query. See Task #90 to learn more about using the New Database Query button.*

MOVE THE QUICK ACCESS TOOLBAR BELOW THE RIBBON

1 Right-click the added option.

  A menu appears.

2 Click Show Quick Access Toolbar Below the Ribbon.

- Excel places the Quick Access toolbar below the Ribbon.

TIPS

Did You Know?
You should review all of the options listed under Commands Not in the Ribbon. This is particularly true if you have used a previous version of Excel. If certain commands from previous versions are not in the Ribbon, you may find them listed under Commands Not in the Ribbon. For example, in previous versions you could format your documents quickly by using AutoFormat. Excel 2007 uses styles, but you can still access AutoFormat via Commands Not in the Ribbon.

Did You Know?
You can restore the Quick Access toolbar to the default setting by clicking the Reset button in the Customize the Quick Access Toolbar dialog box.

MULTIPLE WINDOWS

DIFFICULTY LEVEL

When a worksheet contains a large amount of data, you cannot see all of it at the same time. Excel enables you to open additional copies of the worksheet, each in its own window, so you can view them simultaneously yet manipulate them independently. You can view the worksheets side by side, stacked, tiled, or cascaded. The zoom settings control how much of a worksheet appears on your screen.

TIP

Did You Know?

If you have a large worksheet and want to view different parts of the worksheet at the same time, you can split the worksheet. Click the View tab and then click the Split button ([image]). Excel splits the worksheet into four parts. To remove a splitter, drag the splitter off the screen or click the Split button again.

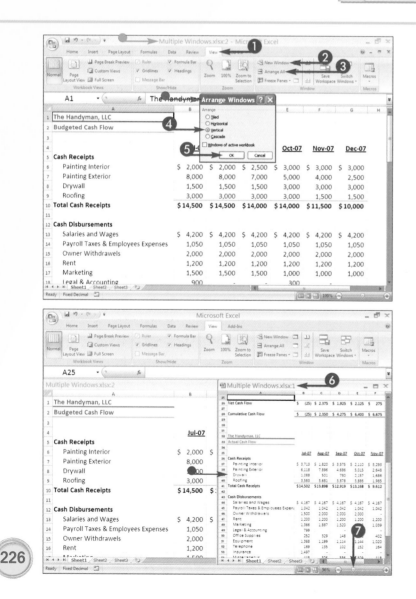

① Click the View tab.

② Click New Window.

● Excel creates a new window.

Note: *Excel opens a copy of your worksheet in a new window. The copy may be directly on top of the old window so you may not be able to discern that it is there.*

③ Click Arrange All.

● The Arrange Windows dialog box appears.

④ Click an option (○ changes to ⊙).

Note: *Horizontal places the windows on top of each other. Vertical places the windows side by side. Tiled places the windows in columns and rows. Cascade places the windows on top of each other with the Title bar for each window displayed.*

⑤ Click OK.

Excel displays all open windows.

⑥ Click a window to activate it.

You can navigate around each window independent of the other window.

⑦ Drag to adjust the zoom.

● Excel resizes the contents of the window.

A CUSTOM VIEW

After you create a worksheet, you may want to filter your data, hide columns or rows, or create special print settings. For example, you may want to keep information on every quarter of a year in a single worksheet but be able to present one quarter at a time. You can filter your data, hide columns, set print settings, and save these settings by creating a custom view. You can then recall the view whenever you need it.

TIP

Did You Know?

To hide columns or rows, select the columns or rows you want to hide. Click the Home tab and then click Format in the Cells group. A menu appears. Click Hide and Unhide. Another menu appears. Click to choose from Hide Rows or Hide Columns. When you want to display your columns or rows again, click and drag to select the columns or rows on both sides of the hidden cells; then on the Home tab choose Format, Hide & Unhide, Unhide Columns or Unhide Rows.

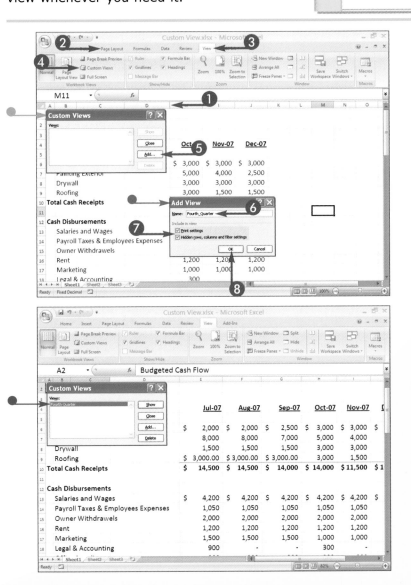

① Hide rows or columns in your worksheet.

Missing letters or numbers indicate hidden columns or rows.

② Set your print settings by using the Page Layout tab.

③ Click the View tab.

④ Click Custom Views.

● The Custom Views dialog box appears.

⑤ Click Add.

● The Add View dialog box appears.

⑥ Type a name for the view.

⑦ Click to include Print settings and/or Hidden rows, columns, and filter settings (☐ changes to ☑).

⑧ Click OK.

● Excel adds the view.

To use the view, open the workbook, click View, Custom Views, click the name of the saved view, and then click Show.

Create a
CUSTOM NUMBER FORMAT

Excel provides many formats for presenting numbers, dates, times, currencies, and other types of information involving numerals. You can use these formats or you can create custom formats for specific purposes. For example, you may want to include the letters SSN before Social Security numbers or include an area code in parentheses before a telephone number.

Creating formats requires you to use number codes. Common codes include 0 or # to stand for any digit. Use 0 if you want Excel to enter a 0 when the user

does not type another number. Use # when you only want the digit typed to appear. To represent a Social Security number, use the code 000-00-0000. For a phone number with area code, type (000) 000-0000. When using one of these examples, type numbers into the cell with the custom format; Excel adds the dashes and parentheses automatically. To code text, simply place the text in quotes: for example, "SSN" 000-00-0000.

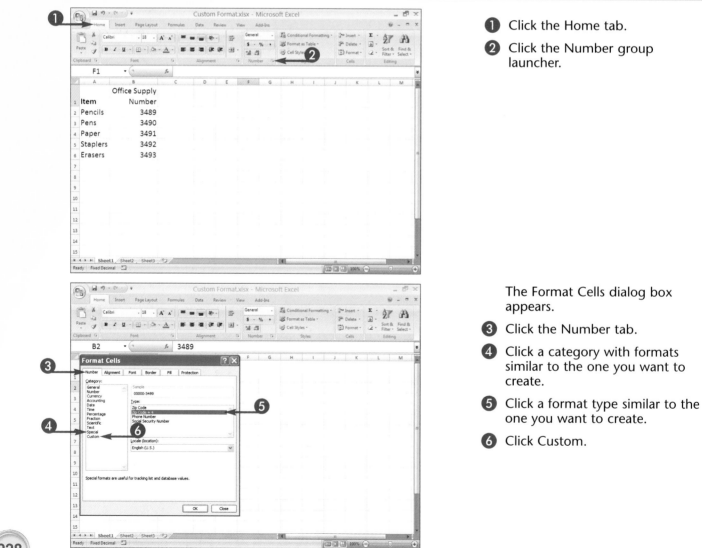

① Click the Home tab.

② Click the Number group launcher.

The Format Cells dialog box appears.

③ Click the Number tab.

④ Click a category with formats similar to the one you want to create.

⑤ Click a format type similar to the one you want to create.

⑥ Click Custom.

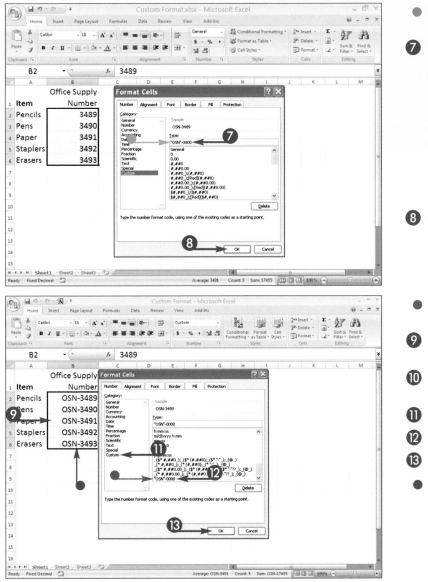

- The Type box appears in the dialog box.

7 Type the appropriate codes to represent your format.

Use a period (.) for a decimal point and a comma (,) to separate thousands.

Note: *See Excel Help for a complete guide to codes.*

8 Click OK.

- Your format now appears at the bottom of the list of Custom format types.

9 To apply the format, select one or more cells.

10 Repeat Steps 1 and 2 to reopen the Format Cells dialog box.

11 Click Custom.

12 Click your custom format.

13 Click OK.

- Excel applies the custom format to the cells you selected.

![TIPS]

Did You Know?

To use a custom format in another workbook, copy a formatted cell from the workbook with the format and paste it into the workbook without the format. The format then becomes available in the Format Cells dialog box.

Caution!

Excel correctly applies custom number formats as long as you type the correct number of digits. For example, for the format ##-##, if you type too many digits, Excel correctly places the two numbers starting from the right but incorrectly formats the excess digits on the left.

Automate your worksheet with
MACROS

A macro enables you to automate a common task, such as entering a series of dates or formatting a column of numbers. You create a macro by recording each step of the task and then assigning all of the steps to a keyboard shortcut. Pressing the assigned keyboard shortcut replays the steps.

You can use the Store macro in field of the Record Macro dialog box to define the scope of your macro. If you choose Personal Macro Workbook, Excel stores your macro in a workbook named Personal.xlsb and

makes your macro available to you whenever you use Excel.

To run a macro, you can use the shortcut you assigned to the macro before you recorded it, or you can choose a button, place it on the Quick Access toolbar, and then click the button to run the macro. To find out how to place a button you can use to run a macro on the Quick Access toolbar, see Task #100.

When you save a workbook that contains a macro you must save it as an Excel Macro-Enabled Workbook.

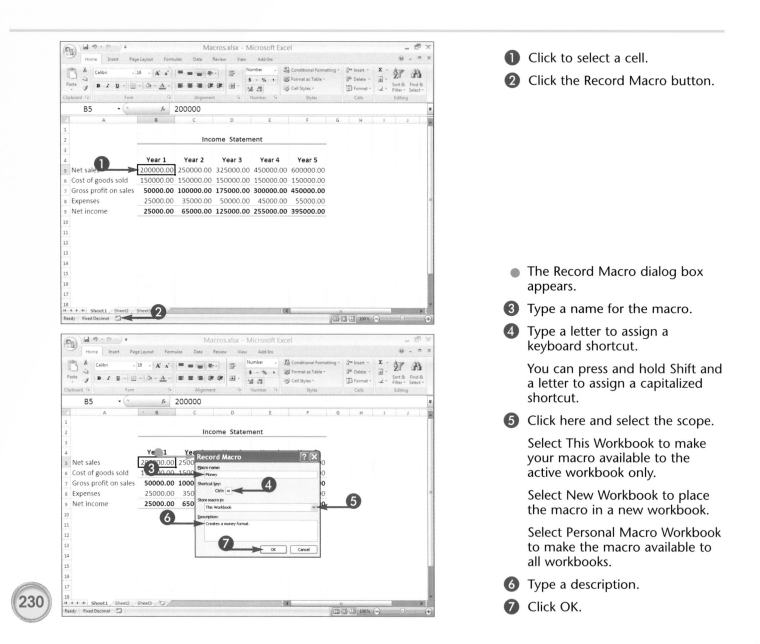

① Click to select a cell.

② Click the Record Macro button.

● The Record Macro dialog box appears.

③ Type a name for the macro.

④ Type a letter to assign a keyboard shortcut.

You can press and hold Shift and a letter to assign a capitalized shortcut.

⑤ Click here and select the scope.

Select This Workbook to make your macro available to the active workbook only.

Select New Workbook to place the macro in a new workbook.

Select Personal Macro Workbook to make the macro available to all workbooks.

⑥ Type a description.

⑦ Click OK.

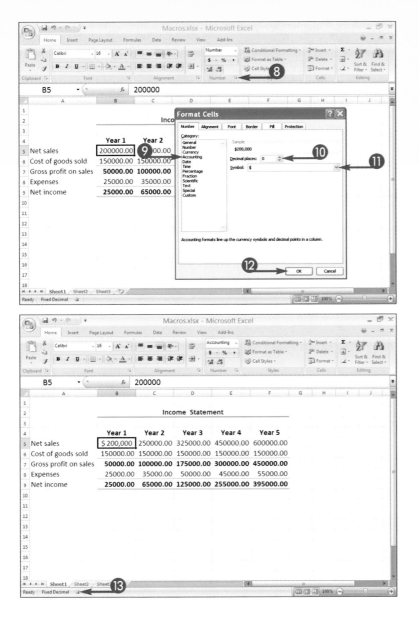

Excel starts recording every keystroke and command.

You can record any set of keystrokes. This example creates a money format.

⑧ Click the Number Group launcher.

⑨ Click a formatting category.

⑩ Type the number of decimal places.

⑪ Click here and select a symbol.

⑫ Click OK.

⑬ Click Stop Recording.

You can now apply the macro anywhere in the workbook by selecting the cells you want to format and typing the keyboard shortcut you chose in Step 4.

TIPS

Did You Know?

By default, you can find the Macro Recording button on the status bar. You decide what options display on the status bar by right-clicking the bar and displaying the Customize Status Bar menu. When working with macros, make sure you select Macro Recording and Macro Playback from the menu.

Did You Know?

Macros are limited in the kinds of tasks they automate. If you have programming experience or aptitude, you can edit and enormously extend Excel macros by using the Visual Basic Editor, available by pressing Alt+F11.

Add a button to
RUN A MACRO

You can create a button to run your macro. For a common task such as applying a format, a button can speed up your work and spare you the annoyance of repeatedly opening a dialog box and making the same selections.

To assign a macro to a button, you must first create the macro, as explained in Task #99. Then you choose a button to represent the macro and move the button to the Quick Access toolbar. Once the button is on the Quick Access toolbar, simply click the button to run the macro.

As an alternative to running your macro with a button, press Alt+F8 to open the Macro dialog box. Click the macro name and then click the Run button. To change the shortcut key, while in the Macro dialog box, click Options. The Macro Options dialog box appears. Type a new shortcut key. You can also use the Macro dialog box to delete your macro by clicking the macro and then clicking the Delete button.

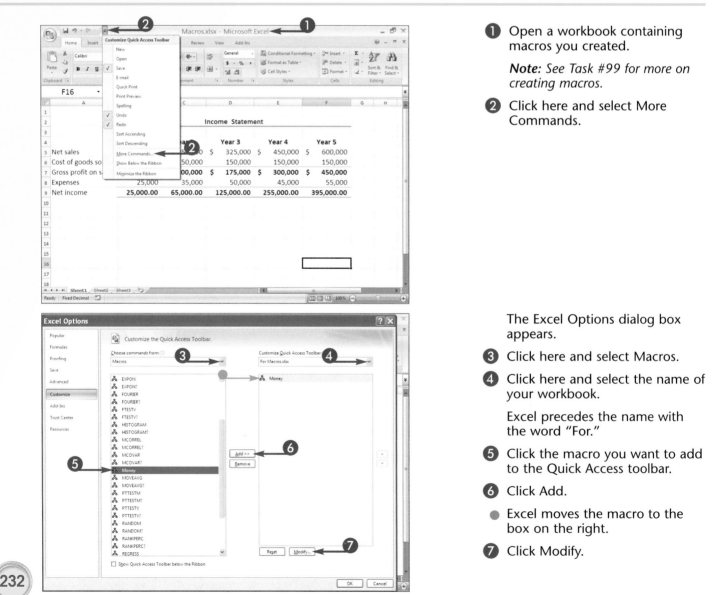

① Open a workbook containing macros you created.

Note: See Task #99 for more on creating macros.

② Click here and select More Commands.

The Excel Options dialog box appears.

③ Click here and select Macros.

④ Click here and select the name of your workbook.

Excel precedes the name with the word "For."

⑤ Click the macro you want to add to the Quick Access toolbar.

⑥ Click Add.

● Excel moves the macro to the box on the right.

⑦ Click Modify.

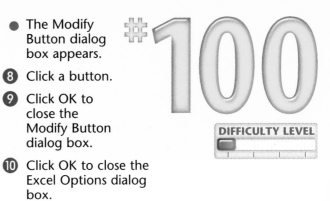

- The Modify Button dialog box appears.

8 Click a button.

9 Click OK to close the Modify Button dialog box.

10 Click OK to close the Excel Options dialog box.

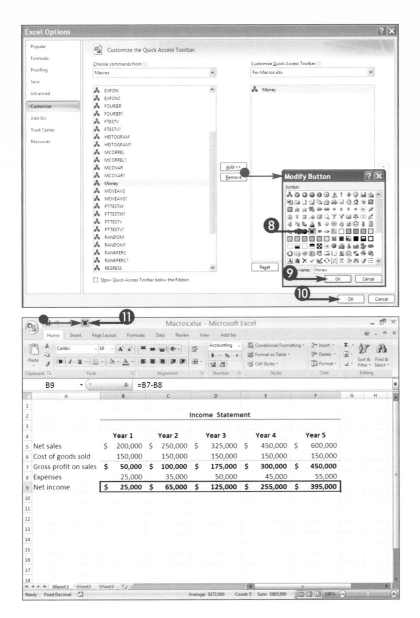

- The button appears on the Quick Access toolbar.

11 Click the button to run the macro.

TIPS

Did You Know?

You can assign a macro to a graphic. Start by placing the graphic in your worksheet. Right-click the graphic and a menu appears. Click Assign Macro. The Assign Macro dialog box appears. Click the macro you want to assign to the graphic and then click OK. Now all you have to do is click the graphic to run the macro.

Did You Know?

The Developer tab contains the tools you can use to create macros. To view the Developer tab, click the Office button, click Excel Options, click Popular, and then click Show Developer tab in the Ribbon. When you return to Excel, you can access the Developer tab.

Index

Symbols and Numbers

(pound signs), error messages, 49, 55
{ } (curly braces), in arrays, 41
3-D charts, 136, 138–139
3-D text, rotating, 168–169

A

Access databases
    appending data to, 217
    editing queries, 210
    editing saved queries, 213
    exporting to, 214–217
    importing from, 206–207
    keys, 206–207, 216–217
    linking to Excel, 217
    maximum table size, 215
    Microsoft Query, 208
    Northwind, 207
    primary keys, 216–217
    Query Wizard, 208–211
    querying, 208–211
    reusing saved queries, 212–213
    saving queries, 210
    SQL (Structured Query Language), 208
Accounting format, 154–155
adding. *See* **creating**
add-ins, 127, 222–223
addition. *See* **calculations; formulas; functions**
Advanced Filter dialog box, 94–95
Align Left button, 161
Align Right button, 161
aligning
    graphics, 172–173
    numbers in cells, 158–159
    text boxes in worksheets, 168–169
    text in cells, 160–161
Allow Users to Edit Ranges dialog box, 181
Analysis Toolpak, 127
analyzing data
    See also Access databases
    See also PivotCharts
    See also PivotTables
    See also statistical functions
    See also tables
    goal seeking, 130–131
    named cells, 129
    scenarios, 128–129
    what-if analysis, 128–129
annotations. *See* **comments; linking Excel to, Word; text boxes**
area charts, 140–141
arithmetic. *See* **calculations; formulas; functions**
arrows, 166–167
ascending versus descending order, 86–87
audio options, 19
AutoFill, 8–9, 20–21
AutoFill Options button, 9, 21

automation
    average calculation, 25
    filling a data series. *See* AutoFill
    formula entry, 25
    macros, 230–233
    number count, 25
    sum of values, 25
AutoSum, 24–25. *See also* **formulas; Function Wizard; functions**
AVERAGE (mean) function, 125
averages
    automatic calculation, 25
    calculating, 45
    in databases, 101
axis labels
    definition, 134
    displaying, 138–139
    rotating, 151
axis values, displaying, 138–139

B

background images, 174–175
backward compatibility, 185
bar charts, 140–141
bevels, text, 168–169
bins, chart, 148–149
blank cells
    skipping when copying, 65
    in tables, 104
blank lines between PivotTable groups, 115
blank rows and columns in PivotTables, 111
bold text, 167
Border button, 159
borders
    cells, 158–159
    photographs, 170–171
Bottom Align button, 161
bottom N values, 39, 93
brightness, photographs, 170–171
Bring to Front option, 173

C

calculated fields, 118–119
calculations
    See also AutoSum
    See also formulas
    See also Function Wizard
    See also functions
    date and time, 48–49, 50–51
    goal seeking, 35
    loans
        calculators, 34–35
        IRR (internal rate of return) function, 36–37
        NPV (net present value) function, 37
        PMT (payment) function, 34–35
    products, 46–47
    square roots, 46–47
    symbols and special characters in, 11

Index

comma delimited (CSV) format, 184
Commands Not in the Ribbon, 225
comments, 16–17, 197. *See also* linking Excel to, Word; text boxes
compact PivotTable form, 114
Compatibility Pack, 185
compatibility with older workbooks, 185
complex filters, 92–93
complex sorts, 88–89
conditional
    formatting, sorting, 90–91
    formulas, 40–41
    highlighting, 72–73
    item counting, 43
    sums, 42–43
conditional formulas (IF) function, 40–41. *See also* COUNTIF; SUMIF
conditional item count (COUNTIF) function, 43. *See also* COUNT; IF
Conditional Sum Wizard, 43
conditional sums (SUMIF) function, 42–43. *See also* SUM
confidence levels, in charts, 147
constants
    creating, 28–29
    in formulas, 30–31
contrast, photographs, 170–171
Copy as Picture feature, 176–177
copy command (Ctrl+C), 65
copying
    cells, 66–67
    data
        to Clipboard, 62–63
        between workbooks, 78–79
        within worksheets, 64–65
    formats, 66–67, 69
    graphics to Clipboard, 65
    image properties, 165
    Paste Special, 64–65
    ranges between worksheets, 63
    ranges within worksheets, 64–65
    skipping blank cells, 65
    sort levels, 89
    styles
        with Format Painter, 69
        between workbooks, 70–71
    values, 66–67
CORREL (correlation) function, 126–127
Correlation tool, 127
correlation versus causation, 126–127
COUNT (count) function, 125. *See also* COUNTIF
COUNTIF (conditional item count) function, 43. *See also* COUNT; IF
counting items
    automatic, 25
    conditionally, 43
    COUNT function, 125
    COUNTIF function, 43
    DCOUNT function, 100–101
    filtered records, 100–101
creating
    charts, 134–135
    comments, 16–17
    headings, PivotTables, 114–115
    PivotCharts, 122–123
    PivotTables, 112–113

styles, 68–69
    validation lists, 4–5
cropping photographs, 170–171
CSV (comma delimited) format, 184
.csv file extension, 205
curly braces ({ }), in arrays, 41
Currency format, 154–155
Custom List dialog box, 20–21
cut command (Ctrl+X), 65

data
    alignment, 158–159, 160–161
    analysis. *See* analyzing data
    entry
        error messages, 6–7
        with forms, 82–83
        restricting. *See* validating data
        rules for, 6–7
        validating. *See* validating data
    labels, in charts, 139
    tables, in charts, 134, 139
    validating. *See* validating data
    values, reusing. *See* constants
data bars, 73, 74–75
data lookup functions, 102–103
Data Validation dialog box, 4–5
database functions, 100–101
databases. *See* Access databases; PivotTables; tables
date and time
    calculations on, 48–49, 50–51
    entering, 51
    entering in series. *See* AutoFill
    formatting, 49, 51, 154–155
    negative values, 49, 51
    prior to January 1, 1900, 50
    as serial values, 48, 49
    sorting, 88
    workdays between two dates, 50–51
DAVERAGE (database averages) function, 101
days of the week, entering in series. *See* AutoFill; date and time
DCOUNT (counting items) function, 100–101
debugging formulas, 56–57
decimal places, setting, 157
Decrease Font Size button, 159
deleting
    chart data, 144–145
    duplicate records, 85
    filters, PivotChart, 123
    headings, PivotTables, 119
    PivotTables, 111
    sort levels, 89
    validation lists, 5
dependents, formulas, 56–57
diagonal color bands, 162–163
dialog boxes. *See specific dialog boxes*
.dif file extension, 205
#DIV/0 (divide by zero) error messages, 55

division. *See* calculations; formulas; functions
drilling down in PivotTables, 120
DSUM (database sums) function, 101
duplicate records, 84–85
dynamic update
    charts, 144
    PivotCharts, 123
    PivotTables, 115, 123

Edit Data Source dialog box, 144–145
editing
    charts, 137
    data, with forms, 83
    database queries, 210
    pictures of worksheets, 176–177
    saved database queries, 213
    tracking edits, 76–77
embedding worksheets, 194–195
error bars, charts, 146–147
error messages
    ##### (pound signs), 49, 55
    data validation, 6–7
    #DIV/0 (divide by zero), 55
    #N/A (value not available), 55
    #VALUE (wrong argument or operand), 55
estimate of error, in charts, 146–147
Evaluate Formula dialog box, 54–55
Excel 2007, backward compatibility, 185
exponential trendlines, 142
exponentiation (POWER) function, 47
exporting data to Access, 214–217
extending a series. *See* AutoFill

Fill Color button, 159
filling a data series. *See* AutoFill
fills, 137, 162–163
filtering. *See also* hiding
    ascending versus descending order, 87
    charting filtered data, 98–99
    complex filters, 92–93
    counting filtered records, 100–101
    duplicate records, 84–85
    lists, 92–93
    by multiple criteria, 94–95
    options for, 87
    PivotCharts, 123
    PivotTables, 112–113
    simple filters, 86–87
    top or bottom N values, 93
Find and Replace dialog box, 14–15
finding
    data, with forms, 83
    functions, 33
    and replacing, formats, 14–15

flowcharts, 166–167
Font Color button, 159
fonts
    base for, 11
    color, sorting, 90–91
    non-English, 11
    nonstandard characters. *See* special characters; symbols
    size, changing, 159, 168–169
    text boxes in worksheets, 168–169
    Unicode, 11
forecasting values, 140–141, 143
foreign letters. *See* special characters; symbols
Format Cells dialog box, 154–155, 158–159
Format Painter, 164–165
formats, worksheets
    Accounting, 154–155
    Align Left button, 161
    Align Right button, 161
    Border button, 159
    Bottom Align button, 161
    cells
        borders, 158–159
        centering text across, 160–161
        clearing formats, 163
        color, 158–159
        data alignment, 158–159, 160–161
        merging, 160–161
        number formats, 158–159
        text orientation, 160–161
        wrapping text, 160–161
    Center button, 160–161
    clearing, 15
    conditional. *See* highlighting
    copying, 66–67, 69. *See also* Format Painter
    Currency, 154–155
    date and time, 49, 51, 154–155
    decimal places, setting, 157
    Decrease Font Size button, 159
    Fill Color button, 159
    fills, 137, 162–163
    finding and replacing, 14–15
    Font Color button, 159
    font size, changing, 159
    General, 154–155
    Increase Font Size button, 159
    Merge and Center button, 160
    Middle Align button, 161
    named collections of. *See* styles
    negative numbers, 154
    Number, 154–155
    number codes, 228–229
    numbers, 154–155, 228–229
    Orientation button, 160
    PivotTables, 116–117
    tables, 106–107
    text boxes, 168–169
    Top Align button, 161
    Wrap Text button, 160
forms, 82–83
formula bar
    expanding/collapsing, 25
    hiding, 175

Index

Index